Depression and Anxiety Solved Naturally

The Science for Relief of Mood Disorders with Dozens of Proven Natural Strategies

By Case Adams, PhD

Depression and Anxiety Solved Naturally: The Science for Relief of Mood Disorders with Dozens of Proven Natural Strategies
Copyright © 2021 Case Adams
LOGICAL BOOKS
Wilmington, Delaware
http://www.logicalbooks.org
All rights reserved.
Written, edited, formatted and printed in the USA

Publishers Cataloging in Publication Data
Adams, Case
Depression and Anxiety Solved Naturally: The Science for Relief of Mood Disorders with Dozens of Proven Natural Strategies
First Edition
1. Medicine. 2. Health.
Bibliography and References; Index
ISBN-13: 978-1-936251-55-1

Other Books by the Author:

ARTHRITIS - THE BOTANICAL SOLUTION: Nature's Answer to Rheumatoid Arthritis, Osteoarthritis, Gout and Other Forms of Arthritis

ASTHMA SOLVED NATURALLY: The Surprising Underlying Causes and Hundreds of Natural Strategies to Beat Asthma

BOOSTING THE IMMUNE SYSTEM: Natural Strategies to Supercharge our Body's Immunity

BREATHING TO HEAL: The Science of Healthy Respiration

ELECTROMAGNETIC HEALTH: Making Sense of the Research and Practical Solutions for Electromagnetic Fields (EMF) and Radio Frequencies (RF)

HAY FEVER AND ALLERGIES: Discovering the Real Culprits and Natural Solutions for Reversing Allergic Rhinitis

HEALING WITH SOUND: The Science of Sound Therapy

HEALTHY SUN: Healing with Sunshine and the Myths about Skin Cancer

HEARTBURN SOLVED: The Real Causes and How to Reverse Acid Reflux and GERD Naturally

HOLISTIC REMEDIES FOR ALZHEIMER'S: Natural Strategies to Avoid or Combat Dementia

MUCOSAL MEMBRANE HEALTH: The Key to Preventing Inflammatory Conditions, Infections, Toxicity and Degeneration

NATURAL CANCER SCIENCE: The Evidence for Diets, Herbs, Superfoods, and Other Natural Strategies that Fight Cancer

NATURAL SLEEP SOLUTIONS FOR INSOMNIA: The Science of Sleep, Dreaming, and Nature's Sleep Remedies

NATURAL SOLUTIONS FOR FOOD ALLERGIES AND FOOD INTOLERANCES: Scientifically Proven Remedies for Food Sensitivities

ORAL PROBIOTICS: Fighting Tooth Decay, Periodontal Disease and Airway Infections Using Nature's Friendly Bacteria

PROBIOTICS: Protection Against Infection

PROBIOTICS SIMPLIFIED: How Nature's Tiny Warriors Keep Us Healthy

PROVING HOMEOPATHY: Why Homeopathy Works, Sometimes

PURE WATER: The Science of Water, Waves, Water Pollution, Water Treatment, Water Therapy and Water Ecology

THE ANCESTORS DIET: Living and Cultured Foods to Extend Life, Prevent Disease and Lose Weight

THE CONSCIOUS ANATOMY: Healing the Real You

THE GLUTEN CURE: Scientifically Proven Natural Solutions to Celiac Disease and Gluten Sensitivities

THE LIVING CLEANSE: Detoxification and Cleansing Using Living Foods and Safe Natural Strategies

THE MEANING OF DREAMS: The Science of Why We Dream, How to Interpret Them and How to Steer Them

THE SCIENCE OF LEAKY GUT SYNDROME: Intestinal Permeability and Digestive Health

TOTAL HARMONIC: The Healing Power of Nature's Elements

YOUR PLAN FOR LIFE: Personal Strategic Planning for Humans

Table of Contents

Introduction

Ultimately, depression and anxiety can stem from an inner emptiness, but imbalances in the brain and nervous system have been shown to lead to mood disorders, including depression.

This means there are both spiritual and biological factors involved in depression. But when it comes to practical life, the biological factors are primary to the spiritual factors.

For example, we find there are people who experience a spiritual emptiness who are not depressed. They may well exert their emptiness into lifestyle factors including setting achievement goals, and these efforts can serve to defray and distract the person from experiencing depression symptoms.

On the other hand, a person who is on a spiritual path may also experience depressive symptoms if their brain and nervous system have imbalances that affect their moods.

This book will discuss some of the spiritually oriented practices that have been shown by research to help reduce anxiety and depressive symptoms. The focus here is on the metabolic elements within our brain and nervous system that can lead to negative moods and emotions. This book documents numerous studies and investigations that have unfolded strategies for improving our moods and even healing negative emotions relating to imbalances in our brains and nervous systems.

But are there really natural strategies that can improve our moods and negative emotions? Are there foods we can eat that can reduce depression? Are there lifestyle changes, herbs, exercises and other things we can do to reduce depression and anxiety symptoms?

The answer, according to documented clinical research, is yes.

How do we know this?

Science.

In this book we provide the clear scientific evidence that shows clinical scientific evidence that there are daily activities, foods, diets, nutrients, herbs, and lifestyle practices that have been shown to reduce symptoms of depression and anxiety.

According to the research, many of these also produce a wide range of other benefits, including better cognitive health, better memory, a stronger heart and other health benefits.

Who could refuse such a host of benefits? Possibly only the most stubborn of us – those who would prefer to endanger their mental health along with the health of our planet in order to continue the status quo.

Yes, life is full of choices.

It is important to realize that this book is not a treatment for depression, anxiety or any other mood disorder. Rather, this text provides a research source for those who want to investigate and understand natural approaches to these conditions.

The first chapter of this book discusses the surge of depression in our society and some of the metabolic causes and lifestyle relationships. The second chapter discusses how our increasing misalignment with nature's rhythms relates to the massive increase in depression.

The third chapter discusses how diet can affect our moods and emotions, and changing that diet can help reduce depressive symptoms.

The fourth and fifth chapters discuss the particular probiotics, prebiotics, and specific herbs that have been shown scientifically to reduce depressive symptoms, bipolar disorder and negative moods and emotions that can lead to depression and anxiety.

Finally, the sixth chapter discusses a variety of lifestyle strategies that have also been shown scientifically to reduce depressive symptoms. These include spiritual practices that have proven to decrease anxiety and depression. They might even provide the side effect of assisting us with some of our spiritual evolution.

How to read this book: This book contains numerous scientific studies to support the information provided. Some of this research may become a little tedious for a layperson, though it provides clear evidence and a reference for scientific readers.

Thus, a layperson may want to skim those research sections and read through the introductive and conclusive parts of each section to understand the points being made.

Note also that the research will sometimes document the volumes or dosages given to patients. That may be useful for understanding the context of the information.

Even with all of this awareness of this new scientific approach to depression and anxiety, it is still critical that we visit with our doctor to discuss this information and seek clear medical counsel before embarking on any strategy that has not been specifically recommended by your doctor.

Finally, I should inform you that I am not a psychiatrist or psychologist. My background is in integrative and natural health sciences. That said, this book does reference and quote hundreds of studies performed and overseen by psychiatrists, psychologists and other mental health professionals. I give thanks for all the hard work and dedication these scientists have made to help illuminate natural approaches for these devastating conditions.

Chapter One

What are Depression and Anxiety, Really?

Mood disorders are surging today.

Depression and anxiety disorders affect more than 400 million people every year, and a majority of these cases do not respond to drug treatment. It is one of the greatest causes of disability. By 2030, depression is projected to be the number one cause of disability.

Over 16 percent of adults will have depression at one point in their lives. And over 7 percent of the U.S. population will have a severe depression episode annually.

In the U.S. alone, more than $120 billion is spent on major depressive disorder cases. Most of these treatments come in the form of psychotherapy drugs. And psychotherapy drugs are some of the most addictive and mentally-disruptive treatments of conventional medicine.

Depression and anxiety symptoms can certainly relate to feelings of inner emptiness, but they are exacerbated by imbalances among the nervous system, which include neurotransmitter and even mineral imbalances.

For this reason, there are a number of psychiatric drugs that are used for depression, which alter the nervous system's levels of neurotransmitters and minerals. They don't cure the inner emptiness underlying the condition, but they can mask the symptoms.

According to the National Alliance on Mental Illness, one in five Americans are affected by mental health conditions. They compare it to a virus that is spreading across America.

According to the World Health Organization, approximately one in four people around the world will be affected by a mental health condition at some point in their lives. Yes, a quarter of us might have a mental health issue at some point.

The primary mental health conditions affecting people around the world are:

• Depression – an estimated 300 million people around the world are affected by depression disorders.

- Generalized Anxiety Disorder (GAD) – About 6.8 million or 3.1 percent of the U.S. population sufferings from GAD.
- Panic disorder – about 2.7 percent of the U.S. population suffers from PD.
- Social anxiety disorder – up to 15 million people in the U.S. suffer from social anxiety.
- Bipolar affective disorder – an estimated 60 million people around the world have been diagnosed with bipolar issues.
- Schizophrenia – an estimated 23 million people are affected by some form of schizophrenia.
- Dementia – about 50 million people have been diagnosed around the world with some form of dementia. These include Alzheimer's disease and other forms of dementia.
- Developmental disorders – childhood mental health issues include autism and other disorders that affect infants, toddlers and children of other ages.

On top of these issues there are many other types of mood disorders. Mood disorders can range from premenstrual mood issues to menopausal to anger and relationship-related issues. Mood issues are rampant and most people have them at one time or another in our lives.

Many of these mood-related issues have been incorrectly labeled depression, but for the purpose of this text, we will include them.

In this chapter we will discuss some of these types of mood disorders, some of the relationships between depression and our lifestyles, and some of the metabolic mechanisms of depression.

Depression defined

Most people think that depression is sadness. They are not completely wrong, but depression as a disorder is much more than just sadness.

For example, when a person loses someone who is dear to them, they might feel sad. Is this depression? No.

That type of sadness is completely normal, and healthy. It would actually be quite odd if a person who loses someone close and does not feel sad.

And should this happen, we wouldn't go to the funeral and greet someone who lost a loved one and say something like, sorry you have depression. That would be rude and insensitive.

It would also be inaccurate, because depression is not simply sadness.

Clinically, depression is a persistent mood disorder. It is an all-encompassing condition that creates negative thinking and a loss of interest in pursuit of life. Yes, depression can also produce sadness, but this is typically the type of reflective sadness. It is a sadness that is about our situation or about things that happen to us.

This negative thinking and loss of interest mood in depression is considered clinical depression.

Clinical depression will include feelings of hopelessness, anger, anxiety, frustration, irritability, and feelings of worthlessness. These may be accompanied by guilt, blaming ourselves or others, fixation on our past, restlessness, and agitation.

These feelings can produce a number of symptoms. These include fatigue, weakness, insomnia, disrupted sleep or even over-sleeping. They can also reduce our appetite and cause weight loss. But these feelings can also produce food cravings and abnormal weight gain.

Physical manifestations of clinical depression can include low-back pain, headaches and chronic fatigue.

On the cognitive side, clinical depression can also produce slowed thinking, difficulty concentrating, memory issues, and problems making decisions. It can also cause speaking slowly or moving more slowly.

It can also cause a focus on death, suicidal thoughts, and even possibly attempted suicide. (If you are in the U.S., call the Suicide Prevention Lifeline at 1-800-273-TALK.)

Now that we can understand the critical nature of clinical depression, it is important that if we suspect we or someone near to us has any of the above symptoms, we should contact our doctor immediately.

Bipolar Disorder

Bipolar disorder is the relatively new naming convention for a condition whereby the patient suffers from bouts of depression and mania, often alternating or cyclical. In other words, bouts of high energy can alternate with periods of melancholy, sometimes depression.

This was called manic-depression reaction for some time in the 1950s, before the American Psychiatric Association decided to call the condition an illness: "manic-depressive illness." Later, bipolar disorder became the typical naming convention for a condition that affects many people differently.

A diagnosed case of bipolar disorder is typically symptomized by alternating high-energy (manic) and depressive states. The more frequent the alternation and the more elevated the highs and lows are, the more severe the case. And a manic or depressive state that lasts more than seven days can be diagnosed as Bipolar Disorder I according to the National Institute of Mental Health.

The U.S. had the world's highest rates of bipolar disease, at 4.4% of the population, while in the world as a whole, about 2.4% of the population had bipolar disease. That's a lot of folks.

Meanwhile, India has the lowest rates with 0.1% of the population. Not so much.

A 2010 study from the U.S. National Institutes of Health studied bipolar disease rates among 11 nations around the world. The U.S. had the highest rates compared to the other 10 nations.

Many might say it is an issue of diagnosis – as doctors in the U.S. may be looking out for the symptoms, and the access to healthcare may be better.

These may be true, but scientific research has since revealed there may well be other, more simpler reasons. We'll start diving into this in the next chapter.

Postpartum Depression

Pregnancy and delivering a baby often result in what is called postpartum depression. Sometimes delivery produces a feeling of losing self-control. This may result in feelings of helplessness and confusion.

These feelings in turn can result in symptoms of depression, anxiety and posttraumatic stress disorder according to clinical research.

Depending upon the culture and society, postpartum depression can affect from 5 percent to 40 percent of mothers in the period just after giving birth.

Posttraumatic stress can affect up to 37 percent of mothers after a difficult delivery. Even post delivery anxiety also affects between 5 and 20 percent of mothers.

Postpartum stress and anxiety in mothers can significantly decrease oxytocin levels and subsequently, milk production. Studies have also shown that postpartum depression can lead to lower self-confidence and decreased breast feeding.

Postpartum depression will often naturally subside about 6 months after delivery. But sometimes this condition can continue for much longer.

It is assumed this type of depression relates to the relationship between the mother and the child. But there are a variety of metabolic changes that take place within the mother's body after giving birth and during breastfeeding, if the mother is breastfeeding.

These can often collide with whatever is taking place within the hypothalamus-pituitary-adrenal system and subsequent levels of cortisol, serotonin and dopamine.

But the mother's body must also contend with another neurotransmitter involved: oxytocin.

Premenstrual Dysphoric Disorder

This condition – abbreviated as PMDD – is often described as a severe form of PMS – premenstrual syndrome. It is, however, quite different as we'll discover. PMS is often accompanied by mood issues, including some anxiety or depressed feelings. These feelings are typically temporary, lasting a day or two until the next stage of menstruation occurs. They also typically do not interfere with the woman's social or family life.

Thus PMS is typically cyclical and temporary and mild. However, between 5 and 8 percent of women will experience something quite worse, something that does interfere with their social or family life. This is defined as premenstrual dysphoric disorder (PMDD), which impairs a woman's functioning and often leads them to obtain professional diagnosis and treatment.

Premenstrual syndrome and premenstrual dysphoric disorder or PMDD involve a number of symptoms, which include but are not limited to mood swings, anxiety, stress, panic attacks, fatigue, food cravings, insomnia and others.

These symptoms can also coincide with PMS, but to a much greater and more debilitating degree. PMDD will typically appear in the late luteal phase (about a week prior to menstruation).

In the U.S., PMDD is considered a disease. However, many countries – including some in the EU – have rejected this notion that PMDD is a disease.

PMDD is defined in the U.S. Diagnostic and Statistical Manual of Mental Disorders, 5th Edition (DSM-5) as a type of depressive disorder. The diagnosis describes three criteria as laid out by Stat-Pearls Publishing (Mishra et al. 2021):

Criterion A - At least 5 of the following 11 symptoms (including at least 1 of the first 4 listed) should be present:

- Markedly depressed mood, feelings of hopelessness, or self-deprecating thoughts
- Marked anxiety, tension, feelings of being "keyed up" or "on edge"
- Marked affective lability
- Persistent and marked anger or irritability or increased interpersonal conflicts
- Decreased interest in usual activities (eg, work, school, friends, and hobbies)
- Subjective sense of difficulty in concentrating
- Lethargy, easy fatigability, or marked lack of energy
- Marked change in appetite, overeating, or specific food cravings
- Hypersomnia or insomnia
- A subjective sense of being overwhelmed or out of control
- Other physical symptoms, such as breast tenderness or swelling, headaches, joint or muscle pain, a sensation of bloating, or weight gain.

Criterion B - symptoms severe enough to interfere significantly with social, occupational, sexual, or scholastic functioning.

Criterion C - symptoms discretely related to the menstrual cycle and must not merely represent an exacerbation of the symptoms of another disorder, such as major depressive disorder, panic disorder, dysthymic disorder, or a personality disorder (although the symptoms may be superimposed on those of these disorders).

Criterion D - criteria A, B, and C confirmed by prospective daily ratings during at least 2 consecutive symptomatic menstrual cycles. The diagnosis may be made provisionally before this confirmation.

Is this about estrogen?

This brings up the proposal submitted a few decades ago that the depression and anxiety sometimes experienced by women in menopause or perimenopause may be related to anxiety and depression. Some have taken that to mean that the reduction of estrogen production during this time in a woman's life may relate to these mood disorders.

The problem is that this hypothesis has been proven wrong. A 2004 study from the Department of Psychiatry at Taiwan's Chang Gung Memorial Hospital (Hsiao et al.) studied 43 women with PMDD. They tested their levels of anxiety (using the Hamilton Anxiety Scale-A) and depression (Hamilton Anxiety Scale-D).

At the same time, they were tested for estrogen or progesterone concentrations in their bloodstream. The research found no correlation between estrogen or progesterone with PMDD.

With regard to menopause, the evidence is also weak for a relationship with estrogen. One study from the School of Medicine at the estrogen or progesterone concentrations (Gleason et al. 2015) followed 693 women for up to four years after they were given hormone replacement in the form of equine-produced estrogen.

The research found that after four years, the estrogen replacement group did have a slight improvement of their anxiety and depression. But the improvement levels were "small to medium" and it did not occur in those given estradiol transdermal patches.

Therefore, the evidence is fairly weak that estrogen hormone in itself is relevant to PMDD or anxiety and depression in menopausal women.

However, a study from Sweden (Eriksson *et al.* 2006) indicated that a reduction in serotonin availability appears to be related to increased occurrence of premenstrual syndrome and PMDD.

This finding has led to the widespread prescribing of selective serotonin reuptake inhibitors (SSRIs) by conventional medicine for premenstrual syndrome and PMDD.

Seasonal Affective Disorder (SAD)

SAD is considered a mood disorder that often coincides with depression. Sometimes SAD appears to produce depression, and sometimes depression seems to produce SAD.

About ninety percent of humans in modern society now work indoors. One hundred years ago, this statistic was reversed. At least ninety percent if not more, of humans lived and worked outside or in locations where natural light was directly present.

There are many warnings present in the medical literature to stay away from the sun. But decades ago the National Institutes of Mental Health in Bethesda, Maryland made the following statement in a 1988 report (Skwerer *et al.*) on seasonal affective disorder:

> *"Along with food, air and water, sunlight is the most important survival factor in human life."*

Millions of people are diagnosed with seasonal affective disorder (or SAD) every year. Some estimate a good 25 million Americans are afflicted with some form of the disorder – at least the milder yet more pervasive winter blues version of SAD.

According to Norman Rosenthal, M.D., who led the above study and has published many scientific papers on seasonal affective disorder and the necessity of sunlight to mental health, about 6% of Americans had SAD and 14% had winter blues. Today it is estimated that 10 to 20 million people have severe SAD and another 10 to 20 percent of the population have a mild version of SAD.

For some, a move from the southern latitudes to the northern latitudes precipitates the disorder. For some, depression seems to be associated. In nearly all cases, a lack of sunlight is present.

As the fall and winter descend upon those in northern or southern latitudes, sunlight hours decrease and melatonin levels should increase along with levels of dopamine and GABA. These three biochemicals work together to not only sedate and relax our bodies so we are more prepared to sleep and spend less time outside: They also work to boost our moods at the same time. Dopamine and GABA are both mood-boosters that balance the increase in melatonin to relax us during the winter months.

However, poor diets, a lack of exercise, increased stress and a lack of natural light all disrupt the production and release of these mood biochemicals. Stress alone can boost cortisol and adrenaline, which make us more irritable and less relaxed. Stress and a poor diet, together with a reduction of light and exercise, toss our body cycles out the window.

We are now subject to a wicked combination of stress chemicals and imbalanced hormones. The result is the millions of SAD cases throughout our modern society.

SAD becomes a vicious cycle. As our stressload increases and our sunlight decreases, our hormones and other biochemicals go out of whack. Most people will try to resolve the issue with more activity indoors, most of which increases our stressload. As stressload increases, SAD symptoms increase.

In the converse, an increasing amount of research is indicating that a lack of sunshine during the day combined with the lack of complete darkness during the night – as our environment has become increasingly lit up at night – reduces melatonin availability.

In a study done by the Heschong Mahone Group (1999), students learning within environments with the most natural sunlight tested better and exhibited faster rates of learning. Another study supporting this was conducted earlier by Anderson *et al.* (1991).

University of Alabama researchers studied 16,800 adults over the age of 45. Higher levels of sunlight exposure increased cognitive function. The benefit was even greater among depressed or near-depressed adults (Kent *et al.* 2009).

It should be noted that vitamin D supplementation is not necessarily the solution to SAD and winter blues. Natural light is the significant issue in mood disorders, as we'll discuss in depth in the next chapter. This was confirmed in the large study showing that SAD prevalence is less in Iceland – where there is less vitamin D production yet people go outdoors more in the winter – than on the East Coast of the U.S

While vitamin D will certainly help ones health when they cannot get enough vitamin-D-producing sun, even northern sun provides many more benefits that can be put into a pill. These include, as we have discussed, the sun's thermal benefits, natural light benefits, color benefits and biomagnetic benefits. These stimulate the production of important mood hormones including serotonin, dopamine, GABA and melatonin – and melatonin reduce the body's stressload as we'll discuss in depth.

Anxiety Disorders

There are a variety of clinical anxiety disorders. These range from generalized anxiety disorder (GAD) – worrying about everyday possibilities – to specific anxieties about particular issues. Let's review some of the more prevalent forms of anxiety outside of GAD:

Panic attacks: Episodes of intense fear, anxiety or terror. These can result from certain triggers or occur seemingly random. Panic attack symptoms will include shortness of breath, pounding heart, chest pain, and heart palpitations.

Post-traumatic stress disorder (PTSD): A traumatic event may cause a person to have a variety of long-term anxiety related issues. These can range from flashbacks, terrors, nightmares, night sweats and other ongoing responses.

Anxiety phobias: There are a number of anxiety phobias. These include fear of crowds or public places (agoraphobia), phobias of spiders (arachnophobia), fear of heights (acrophobia) and others.

Social anxiety disorder: This may also be accompanied by agoraphobia, but can be distinct. Social anxieties may range from anxiety of public speaking to anxiety about attending parties or other social gatherings. This may also include family gatherings as well.

Substance anxiety disorder: Taking certain drugs or drinking alcohol may cause anxiety in some people.

Separation anxiety disorder: This type of anxiety can result from a childhood experience of separation that continues into adulthood.

Selective mutism: Anxiety related to speaking during some situations may cause problems communicating in some situations.

Medical anxiety: Anxiety related to going to the doctor or receiving medical treatment may be the result of something that occurred in the past, or it may be a fear of side effects or sickness.

There are many other types of anxiety, depending upon the situation and type of response that we have in that situation. Most often the type of anxiety we may face is more of the generalized anxiety, where concerns about money, family, work, and survival in general cause us to be anxious. Natural disasters or other possible unlikely scenarios may also cause someone to be anxious.

Depending upon the type of anxiety, some of these may be responses to something that happened in our past. Indeed, an anxiety based on a past event may not be a form of anxiety disorder. It may be something that is resolved by experiencing the situation without that particular event taking place.

But continuous anxiety about something without a rational cause may also be related to our body and brain's physical responses. This means examining the body's mood chemistry, as we will discuss.

The Growing Use of Antidepressants

Antidepressants are typically prescribed for both anxiety disorders and depression. This is because they alter moods by changing the production and removal of neurotransmitters from our nervous system. We will discuss the mechanisms shortly.

The number of people taking antidepressants has skyrocketed. In a 2020 study published by the U.S. Centers for Disease Control, 13.2 percent of adults are using antidepressant medications. Among women the number is higher, at nearly 18 percent.

A study from Harvard University (Kantor *et al.* 2015) found that prescriptions for antidepressants nearly doubled between 1999 and 2012. The study found that 13 percent of all Americans were prescribed antidepressants in 2012, compared to 6.8 percent in 1999. Most of these are being prescribed to middle-aged people.

The research also found that antidepressant use increases with age, and was highest in women over 60 years of age.

This study also found that 7.2 percent of adults in the U.S. experienced a major episode of depression in 2018.

Drugs for anxiety and depression

A number of other drugs are prescribed for depression and anxiety by doctors in Western medicine. Certainly, drugs that modulate neurotransmitters can reduce symptoms related to nervous responses. But modulating nervous responses often comes at a cost. These include addiction, withdrawal issues and side effects as we'll discuss.

Here is a more complete list of the various drugs that are prescribed for depression and anxiety (Federal Drug Administration, 2021):
- Anafranil (clomipramine)
- Asendin (amoxapine)
- Aventyl (nortriptyline)
- Celexa (citalopram hydrobromide)
- Cymbalta (duloxetine)
- Desyrel (trazodone HCl)
- Elavil (amitriptyline)
- Effexor (venlafaxine HCl)
- Emsam (selegiline)
- Etrafon (perphenazine/amitriptyline)
- fluvoxamine maleate
- Lexapro (escitalopram hydrobromide)
- Limbitrol (chlordiazepoxide/amitriptyline)
- Ludiomil (maprotiline)
- Marplan (isocarboxazid)
- Nardil (phenelzine sulfate)
- nefazodone HCl
- Norpramin (desipramine HCl)
- Pamelor (nortriptyline)
- Parnate (tranylcypromine sulfate)
- Paxil (paroxetine HCl)
- Pexeva (paroxetine mesylate)
- Prozac (fluoxetine HCl)
- Remeron (mirtazapine)
- Sarafem (fluoxetine HCl)

- Seroquel (quetiapine)
- Sinequan (doxepin)
- Surmontil (trimipramine)
- Symbyax (olanzapine/fluoxetine)
- Tofranil (imipramine)
- Tofranil-PM (imipramine pamoate)
- Triavil (perphenazine/amitriptyline)
- Vivactil (protriptyline)
- Wellbutrin (bupropion HCl)
- Zoloft (sertraline HCl)
- Zyban (bupropion HCl)

Antidepressant/antianxiety drug mechanisms

A number of these drugs are called selective serotonin reuptake inhibitors (SSRIs). They work by blocking the removal of serotonin from the system, allowing serotonin to remain in the nervous system for longer. Here is a list of some other types of antidepressants:

Azapirones – partially 5-HT receptor agonists – meaning they bind with 5-HT receptors but not fully.

Melatonin receptor agonists – bind to and activate melatonin receptors

Monoamine oxidase inhibitors (MAOIs) – block the release of monoamine oxidase.

Mu-opioid receptor agonists – activates the receptor typically activated by morphine, which produces analgesia and sedation.

NMDA receptor antagonists – block the action of the N-Methyl-D-aspartate (a neurotransmitter) receptor.

Norepinephrine reuptake inhibitors (NRIs) – block the removal of norepinephrine, keeping more epinephrine and norepinephrine in the nervous system.

Norepinephrine–dopamine reuptake inhibitors (NDRIs) – block the removal of norepinephrine and dopamine, leaving more of these neurotransmitters in the nervous system.

Serotonin antagonist and reuptake inhibitors (SARIs) – block the binding of serotonin with receptors and block removal of serotonin from the nervous system.

Serotonin modulator and stimulators (SMSs) – change the action of serotonin receptors and otherwise boost serotonin in the nervous system.

Serotonin–norepinephrine reuptake inhibitors (SNRIs) – block the removal of both serotonin and norepinephrine, leaving more in the system.

Tricyclic antidepressants (TCAs) – block the removal of serotonin and norepinephrine (similar to SNRIs), leaving more of these two neurotransmitters in the nervous system.

Tetracyclic antidepressants (TeCAs) – block the serotonin 5-HT receptors and block the removal of norepinephrine, leaving more of these in the nervous system.

5-HT receptor agonists – bind to and activate serotonin receptors.

Some antidepressant drugs combine some of these effects. We'll discuss neurotransmitters in more depth a little later.

Side effects

Artificially blocking neurotransmitter receptors or blocking their transport mechanisms that remove them when not needed can create a number of negative side effects.

Besides the potential of addiction from antidepressants as we'll discuss, side effects of these antidepressants can include, among others:

- blurred vision
- changes in appetite
- constipation
- diarrhea
- difficulty urinating
- dizziness
- drowsiness
- dry mouth
- erectile dysfunction
- headaches
- increased sweating
- insomnia
- liver damage
- loss of appetite

- nausea
- nervousness
- restlessness
- ringing in the ears
- sore throat
- tremors (shaking)
- trouble with balance
- upset stomach
- weakness
- weight loss or gain

Some antidepressants can also interfere with speech, driving and other coordination-related activities. For this reason, driving while under the influence of antidepressants can be problematic.

Often, doctors will end up prescribing additional medications to combat these side effects. This can lead to a cascading prescription plan. This is one of the reasons we find many adults taking multiple prescriptions: To manage the side effects of antidepressant medications.

Even with all these side effects, antidepressants are one of the most prescribed medications in the world of conventional medicine.

Addiction and withdrawal

One of the less-discussed risks of antidepressant use is the potential of addiction and subsequent withdrawal effects should the drug be discontinued.

In a study from the UK's University of East London and the University of Auckland in New Zealand (Read *et al.* 2018) 1,829 people who were prescribed antidepressants were surveyed. Of these 44 percent had been taking the drugs for more than three years and were still taking them.

A full 27 percent of the patients reported being addicted to the antidepressants. And 55 percent reported withdrawal symptoms when stopping the drug.

Traditional medicine approaches

One of the shortcomings of conventional medicine's ability to treat depression is the proposal that depression is only a biological condition. Such a proposal ignores the spirit – the personality within the physical body. Adding to the biological needs of the physical body, the needs of the spirit relate to love and the connection with our spiritual needs.

Contrasting this, traditional medicine recognizes three elements as critical to overall health: *Body, mind and spirit.*

The disregard of the spirit – the person within, and its connection with the Supreme Spirit – leads to the desolate theory that chemicals that modulate the nervous system can alone fix anxiety and depression.

Practices and therapies for mental and spiritual well-being are typically offered by traditional healers concurrent to clinical therapies. These include, as we'll discuss, meditation, yoga, tai chi and other therapies.

Traditional treatments for depression and anxiety can include herbs to reduce anxiety and mood-related responses. These can modulate hormone production and neurotransmitter content just as drugs do. The difference is that they typically come with few negative side effects. Many come with positive side effects, however.

The reason for this is that herbs and foods will contain more than just one active constituent as most drugs do. They will often have tens if not hundreds of active constituents. These will help to buffer and balance the effects of those medicinal compounds in the foods or herbs, moderating their potential negative side effects.

This complexity of natural foods and herbs will also have lasting effects on the brain and body's metabolism. This often occurs as a result of subtle yet lasting changes in the body's genetic structure.

Yes, foods and herbs can change the body's genes.

And addiction to natural whole foods and medicinal herbs is rare, with a few exceptions of narcotic herbs – which would not be considered medicinal herbs anyway.

Natural food and medicinal herb recommendations are often accompanied by lifestyle changes, which also can have lasting effects upon the body and brain.

This is where alternative and complementary therapies can affect not just the physical body but the spirit within and its connection to the Almighty.

Exercises that encourage contemplation and meditation have proven successful for treating depression and anxiety because they address the condition of the spirit. Contemplation and meditative exercise foster a person looking deeper. This promotes a spiritual solution for feelings of emptiness and loneliness. We will discuss these in depth later on.

Neuroinflammation and the HPA Axis

Science is increasingly finding that many cognitive disorders such as Alzheimer's and other forms of dementia related to inflammation among brain tissues. Furthermore, many classic mental disorders such as schizophrenia and depression and other mood disorders may also be connected to brain inflammation according to the science.

To this we can quote a statement from scientists at from the French government's scientific investigative body, INSERM (Troubat *et al.* 2021):

> *"Some recent clinical and preclinical evidence suggests that neuroinflammation is a key factor that interacts with the three neurobiological correlates of major depressive disorder: depletion of brain serotonin, dysregulation of the hypothalamus-pituitary-adrenal (HPA) axis and alteration of the continuous production of adult-generated neurons in the dentate gyrus of the hippocampus."*

To unpack this statement a bit, the doctors are stating that depression and anxiety is related to neuroinflammation and neuroinflammation can produce some of the metabolic patterns of depression: That is, a reduction in the hormone serotonin, malfunction within the adrenal system that produces hormones, and the brain's production of a type of brain cell that is often seen in cases of depression.

Consider for a moment, a study by doctors from the School of Medicine at Australia's Deakin University (Berk et al. 2013). The researchers write:

"We now know that depression is associated with a chronic, low-grade inflammatory response and activation of cell-mediated immunity, as well as activation of the compensatory anti-inflammatory reflex system. It is similarly accompanied by increased oxidative and nitrosative stress (O&NS), which contribute to neuroprogression in the disorder. The obvious question this poses is 'what is the source of this chronic low-grade inflammation?'"

In their review of the research, the researchers go on to point out that the depression appears to be associated with systemic inflammation – producing neuroinflammation. The researchers point out that inflammation precursors to depression include poor diet, lack of exercise, smoking, obesity, altered intestinal permeability (leaky gut), atopy, sleep and even dental caries.

Before we dig more into the topic of neuroinflammation, it is important to understand the process of the hypothalamus-pituitary-adrenal (HPA) axis:

What is the HPA axis?

Depression is significantly related to a malfunction that takes place in the hypothalamic-pituitary-adrenal (HPA) axis. The process begins when the HPA is stimulated by negative feedback. This can take place in the form of stress, fatigue, or events in life that create loss or sadness.

This stimulation of HPA in turn stimulates an increase in what is called corticotropin-releasing factor (CRF). CRF is secreted in the hypothalamus.

This CRF over-production in turn stimulates the production of adrenocorticotropin hormone (ACTH) from the pituitary gland.

When ACTH is released into the body, it connects with adreno-cortical cells, which stimulates the production of cortisol from the adrenal glands. Sometimes this is accompanied by the enlargement of the adrenal glands as they release cortisol into the blood.

Cortisol has a number of effects within the body once released. These include increased blood pressure and blood glucose. Research (such as O'Connor et al. 2009) has also found that those with greater cortisol availability in the morning just after waking will tend to have more positive moods.

But the feedback loop of excessive cortisol also serves to create more negative effects for the hypothalamus and pituitary gland. This also serves to impair the immune system.

This metabolic effect of excess cortisol and a continual feedback to the HPA axis produces another issue: It disrupts the chemistry of the neurotransmitter fluid.

The neurotransmitter fluid lies between each nerve cell. The electrical energy that travels throughout the body through the nervous system is transmitted between nerve cells (neurons) through the neurotransmitter fluid.

This produces the landscape for the negative moods and emotions that are common in depression.

What are neurotransmitters?

When the neurotransmitter fluid is changed, our moods and emotional responses are also changed. For better or worse.

Nerve cells – also called dendrites – do not actually touch. They are not connected in the physical sense. Rather, between them exists a space called the synapse. The synapse contains a special chemistry called the neurotransmitter fluid. The neurotransmitter fluid provides the medium for the waveform pulses traveling between neurons.

Through this chemistry, nerve impulses are transformed, moving information from one neuron to another. This enables a broadcasting of information through various nerve channels around the body.

The tiny sea of neurotransmitter fluid contains various biochemical components, most of which are ionic in nature. These ions combine with the protein neurotransmitters to create a system of electromagnetic nervous responses throughout our brain and tissue systems.

Each neuron can range in synapse count. Some might have several thousand while others have significantly less. Through these synapses, each neuron may be firing up to 100,000 electromagnetic pulse inputs into this fluid at one time.

Depending upon its particular makeup at the time, the fluid will provide a combination of excitatory potential and inhibitory potential. This balance serves to escort or conduct information from one nerve to another, while at the same time dampening or filtering these nerve waves to prevent overload and over-stimulation.

This process might well be compared to the process of transistors and resistors we see in integrated circuits. Neurotransmitters are tremendous semiconductors. Their delicate ionic balance precisely buffer and conduct waveform communications within neurotransmitter fluids.

The major neurotransmitters that relate to depression and anxiety include:

Dopamine is critical to our moods and muscle activity. Good dopamine levels contribute to a positive attitude and help fight feelings of depression and anxiety. Dopamine is typically deficient in Parkinson's disease patients and depressed patients.

Serotonin is also called 5-hydroxytryptamine (5-HT). It is a monoamine neurotransmitter that helps produce healthy moods and the ability to relax. When serotonin levels are low, we can experience greater levels of pain and anxiety. Serotonin levels also help us get good sleep.

GABA stands for gamma-aminobutyric acid. GABA is a necessary neurotransmitter for being able to relax and sleep. It is also helpful for reducing stress. GABA is also pain-relieving. GABA is typically synthesized from glutamic acid in the body. Many people do not produce enough of this, however. Especially during times of stress.

Acetylcholine neurotransmitter helps balance our moods and physical activity. This includes better balance, a calm nerve-muscle response and a calmer state of brain activity.

Depending upon the situation, there are some neurotransmitters that are not that good for us if their levels are too high within our neurotransmitter fluid. These include histamine and glutamate. Histamine, for example, is linked to higher levels of stress and tension within the muscles. Histamine can also stimulate skin hives and allergic responses, such as anaphylactic responses.

Neurotransmitters and moods

Two examples of neurotransmitters are acetylcholine and adrenaline (or epinephrine). These two messenger substances conduct and/or magnify specific wave frequencies, which reflect either programmed (autonomic) intention or conscious intention.

Acetylcholine will modulate an instruction to muscle fibers to contract, while adrenaline will modulate instructions that perpetuate the 'fight or flight' response: Causing a quickening of heart rate and blood flow, immediate motor muscle response, visual acuity, and so on.

Each of these biochemicals conducts particular types of waveforms. They will affect the neurotransmitter fluid, but they also interact with waveforms outside the confines of the fluid. For example, acetylcholine also stimulates skeletal muscle cells directly.

This means the intentional response and programming to protect the body in specific ways is being conducted through these messenger molecules-and they are effectively translating that information into physical response.

The chemistry of this neurotransmitter fluid directly relates to our moods, our thinking patterns and our reaction time. The chemistry of the neurotransmitter fluid is most directly affected by our diet.

This can be evidenced clearly by observing someone during a night of heavy drinking. Alcohol changes the chemical composition of the neurotransmitter fluid, resulting in a change in mood, reaction time, balance, and cognitive awareness.

What are microglia?

Research has been revealing that many mental disorders are produced by this neuroinflammation process, involving the microglia cells of the brain.

The microglia are immune cells categorized as macrophages, but they are focused upon the health of the central nervous system — particularly the brain and spine. Microglia roam the neurons of these areas in search for toxins, intruders and possible infections.

Particularly at issue in cognitive issues such as dementia and Alzheimer's disease is the build up of amyloid plaque among brain cells. The microglia are the immune cells that prevent and clean up plaque build up among brain cells.

When the microglia populations are damaged or otherwise altered, the brain and CNS becomes increasingly susceptible to mental disorders such as dementia, schizophrenia, depression, anxiety and mental fatigue.

Neuroinflammation and microglia

Neuroinflammation is the result of damage among brain cells. Healthy microglia populations are focused upon preventing inflammation among neurons, in turn preventing damage to brain cells.

However, when brain cells are damaged, microglia work harder to repair the damage by producing a variety of inflammatory factors. The damage to neurons, evidenced by these inflammatory factors, hamper the brain's function.

Like other types of macrophages, the microglia are formed within the bone marrow. Once they migrate to the brain, they differentiate into particular responsibilities and different regions. Some microglia are focused on infections, others are focused upon toxins or damaged cells. Others stimulate the repair of brain tissues.

Plaque and neuroinflammation

The build-up of plaque among brain cells – connected to dementia – will stimulate the microglia to try to remove the damage.

Damage from oxidative stress and glycation byproducts have been linked to this build up of plaque among brain cells.

This was also discussed in the 2021 INSERM research noted above:

> *"Further recent data indicate that primary microglial activation may also result from a direct impact of chronic stress on vascular function."*

Research by Dr. Akira Monji and associates back in 2012 connected mental disorders such as schizophrenia, depressive states and cognitive issues to these increases in microglia inflammatory factors such as nitric oxide and cytokines. Again, this may not be a causal relationship. But it shows a correlation that must be examined further.

This is similar to the correlation that has been made between Alzheimer's and Abeta plaque. As I discuss in my book on this topic, this correlation misses the essential causal relationships between our diets, lifestyles and other factors that produce the metabolic factors in Alzheimer's disease.

Back to the microglia. When microglia have rapidly expanded in the face of damage to brain cells, they produce a number of inflammatory responses. Dr. Monji's research has shown that the brain tissues of schizophrenia, depression and dementia patients have increased levels of these microglia inflammatory factors.

The research found that one of the central mechanisms of psychiatric drugs is that they reduce levels of these inflammatory factors – temporarily.

Like most pharmaceuticals, this temporary reduction of inflammatory factors does little to prevent or reduce the cause of the inflammation.

Furthermore, by blocking inflammatory factors, the drugs can actually interfere with the repair of the damage that is taking place by the microglia immune cells. This is often the scenario for drugs that are focused upon the symptoms rather than the causes of a condition.

What causes neuroinflammation?

The cause of neuroinflammation, as shown in numerous dementia studies, relates to oxidative damage. Oxidation is produced through an imbalance between toxins that form oxidative radicals and those antioxidants that neutralize those radicals.

When the system is not balanced, oxidation takes place, not only among tissues among the cardiovascular system, but also among brain tissues.

This of course is why recent research, such as a French and Finnish INSERM study (Singh-Manoux *et al.* 2012) linked cognitive decline to increased obesity, diabetes and heart disease.

The study, led by Dr. Mika Kivimaki and associates from INSERM, with support from the U.S. National Institutes of Medicine, studied 6,401 adults between 39 and 63 years old. They found that people who were obese and suffered from metabolic disorder (cardiovascular disease and/or diabetes) had more than a 22% greater cognitive decline than those who were of normal weight with no metabolic disorder.

This study has been confirmed by others that have related cognitive decline to cardiovascular disease, sedentary lifestyles, obesity and increased levels of toxins.

These issues have all been connected to higher levels of inflammation in the body.

The bridge to these relationships has been provided by the Japanese research, finding that neuroinflammation is one of the key factors affecting mental disorders of many types. Brain shrinkage is also linked to inflammation.

Antioxidants and neuroinflammation

Since oxidative stress is directly related to neuroinflammation, it is somewhat logical that antioxidants should be able to help reduce neuroinflammation.

We will discuss a myriad of research showing this to be the case in the diet section of this book.

In the meantime, we can cite numerous studies have shown that antioxidants neutralize oxidative radicals that produce inflammation. The very term "antioxidant" is founded upon research showing that particular phytochemicals directly neutralize the oxidative effects of radicals formed by toxins.

This is supported by the research. For example, in a large French study (Kesse-Gyuot *et al.* 2012) researchers found that a healthy diet with greater antioxidant intake was associated with reduced risk of cognitive decline after the researchers removed factors relating to exercise, alcohol intake, calories, gender, age, education and obesity.

This is of course despite the fact that other research has found that smoking and lack of exercise both increase the rate of cognitive decline, as illustrated in a study by some of the same INSERM researchers (Sabia *et al.* 2012) that linked obesity and cognitive decline.

What this all means is that mental disorders like depression and anxiety are no longer conditions that necessarily fall within the abstract domain of behavioral psychology and psychiatry, where treatments such as lobotomy, electric shock and psychotropic drugs have produced a myriad of adverse mental and physical effects.

Rather, the research is conclusive: Depression, anxiety and many other mental disorders are at least partially produced by poor diets and poor lifestyles, and thus are to a great degree preventable.

This research also brings mental disorders within the realm of natural health and nutrition. What is now known is that a person with a healthy diet containing plenty of antioxidants, together with an active lifestyle, has a significantly reduced risk of having depression or anxiety.

The Role of Stress and Fatigue

Researchers have recently discovered that when we are stressed there is a greater risk of depression. Burn-out syndrome can result in a higher level of stress. And burn-out syndrome can also result in fatigue.

Fatigue and stress often go hand in hand and the combination makes us ripe for feelings of depression.

Stress-induced depression is often diagnosed as asthenic syndrome or psychoneurosis.

Because the sympathetic nervous system regulates the release of adrenalin and cortisol, there are a number of negative side effects of an overly stressed condition.

The issue is called the 'fight or flight' response. While short-term sympathetic responses are not unhealthy, things can get unhealthy when the response is long-term or frequent. When the body is activated in a sympathetic nervous system response, the body goes into overdrive, often at the expense of many metabolic functions.

This of course includes the heart and cardiovascular system because adrenalin and cortisol increase heart rate and narrow the blood vessels. But these also decrease the ability of the digestive system to do its job. The mucosal membranes of these linings shut down and the production of acids and enzymes are interfered with.

When a person's body goes into this overdrive state for too much of the day, there can be a long-term effect: Stress and fatigue, sometimes leading to depression.

Human and animal studies have shown that when we are faced with more stress, the response is to respond with greater fatigue. Research has illustrated that fatigue and stress often relates to cellular energy sensors, which can reduce levels of serotonin as oxygen levels are reduced.

This is why many psychiatric drugs that are used for depression alter the nervous system's levels of neurotransmitters and minerals. They don't necessarily change the body's metabolism for the long term, but they can mask the symptoms.

Family Stressors

The relationship between stress in the family and depression is well documented in the scientific research. We will assume that most readers recognize this relationship, either from the science or from practical experience.

It may not be as well known that family stress can also shorten telomeres. This may not create a causal relationship, but it makes for a distinct correlation between a history of family stress and depression.

A study published in the *Proceedings of the National Academy of Sciences* from Princeton University and the University of Michigan (Mitchell *et al.* 2014) analyzed 40 African American boys who were aged nine as part of the Fragile Families and Child Wellbeing Study.

Half of the children were raised in families that had more instability, less family structure – such as breakups between parents – and were subjected to more severe punishment. Most were also from low-income families. These were identified as 'disadvantaged' children with 'harsh environments.'

The other 20 children were from "advantaged" environments – which means they had more stable families with better parenting quality – meaning not subjected to harsh punishments and many other stress factors. The families of these children were identified as being 'nurturing environments.'

How depression can affect our future

Telomeres are at the end of each chromosome, and each time a cell divides, the telomeres become shorter. Because our life span is connected to how many times our cells can divide, shorter telomeres mean fewer cell division and a shorter life expectancy.

However, research over the past two decades has also found that other factors outside of cellular division shorten telomere length. These include toxins, diet and other factors. Now we find a child's family environment will help determine telomere length.

Telomere length has been linked with a greater risk of early mortality. This means dying sooner. According to scientific research, children who have stressful and unstable family environments will have reduced telomere length.

A study from the The Netherlands' Vrije University Medical Center (Verhoeven *et al.* 2013) found that depression produced shorter telomere length as well. This study tested 1,095 adults diagnosed with major depression, 802 patients in remission from depression, and 510 healthy control volunteers.

This study found that the longer and more severe the depression, the shorter the telomere length. Those with severe depression lasting longer than four years showed the shortest telomere lengths.

Even those with a past depression, even after recovery, had shorter telomere lengths compared to the healthy controls with no depression history.

Another study from Vrije University (Révész *et al.* 2014) confirmed that increased stress will also reduce telomere length. The researchers followed 2,936 adults as part of the Netherlands Study of Depression and Anxiety.

The research found those with higher markers of physiological stress – such as interleukin-6 (IL6), c-reactive protein (CRP), tumor necrosis factor-alpha (TNFa), and cortisol factors – had decreased telomere length.

The researchers calculated that those in the highest quartile (highest 25%) of these stress markers had lower telomere lengths that corresponded to a lifespan reduction (and faster aging) of about ten years.

The research from Princeton discussed above discovered that boys in 'disadvantaged' and 'harsh' family environments had an average of 19% shorter telomere length compared with children from the 'advantaged' and 'nurturing' family environments.

But when family stability was separated from the other factors, it was found that those boys with multiple changes in family structure – such as multiple partners, divorce or moving between parents - had a 40% reduced telomere length compared to the boys with more stable families.

Shorter telomere length was also associated with less household income and single mothers. And having a mother who graduated from high school resulted in an average of 32% longer telomere length.

The bottom line is that we may think that depression can affect our life for years to come. It is a disorder that should be reckoned with immediately.

Chronic Fatigue and Depression

According to the Centers of Disease Control, at least one million Americans have chronic fatigue syndrome (CFS). And CFS is linked to depression in many cases.

But since CFS is often not diagnosed, we know the actual number is significantly higher.

The typical diagnostic criteria for chronic fatigue syndrome is six months or more of chronic fatigue. But many CFS patients also report a number of other symptoms, which include muscle pain, fevers, sore throats, headaches, sleep problems and others.

Most physicians are stymied for treatments for chronic fatigue syndrome. Some consider the condition to be purely psychological so they end up prescribing psychotropic medications or narcotic drugs.

When the person is seen as simply a biological machine, then treating something like chronic fatigue syndrome with pharmaceuticals will often have limited success.

Traditional medicine sees chronic fatigue quite differently. An understanding of the deeper elements of the person – notably the mind-body-spirit connection - is something that traditional medicines have utilized for centuries to treat billions of people.

For example, Traditional Chinese Medicine sees chronic fatigue syndrome as definitely related to depression on a deeper level. The translation of the definition of the condition most closely resembles the word "melancholia" – which relates to a connection with the Chi – the current of life that runs through the body from the spirit within.

Allergies

New research has discovered that allergies can slow brain function, as well as cause lethargy and a loss of energy. The research, led by allergy specialist Talal Nsouli, M.D., an associate professor at Georgetown University, studied 98 patients who suffer from seasonal and environmental allergies.

The study found that 82% experienced extreme fatigue and chronic lethargy, and following treatment, most found increased energy levels.

Dr. Nsouli also found that irritability, depression and symptoms that appear like attention deficit disorder also appear with allergies. High levels of histamine appear to be the cause of the reduced brain function.

Chronic fatigue and asthma have been linked in other research. Research from the Medical Faculty of the University of Maastricht (Kremer *et al.* 2002), for example, found that among 26 patients, psychological well-being was affected by those with allergies.

Pain Drugs

Research has concluded that opioid drugs increase the incidence of depression and anxiety. This was proven in a Veterans Administration study of 355 pain patients.

The study, published in the Journal of the International Association for the Study of Pain (Scherrer *et al.* 2015) followed patients with low-back pain for two years.

The patients had been prescribed varying doses of opioid drugs for pain. The doses were rated by their morphine-equivalent dose.

The researchers found that higher doses resulted in a doubling of depression incidence.

Natural alternatives to pain killer medications include herbs such as meadowsweet, ginger, willow bark, California poppy and others. Contrasting the effects of pharmaceutical opioids, California poppy has been traditionally used for nerve pain as well as for depressive symptoms.

Air Pollution

The relationship between oxidative stress and neuroinflammation relates to some of the relationships we have found between diet and depression as we'll discuss later. The air we breathe can directly relate to the levels of oxidative stress our bodies are dealing with. The worse the pollution in our air, the more oxidative stress our bodies will have as a result.

Duke University researchers (Reuben *et al.* 2021) followed 2,232 children who were twins through adulthood. They were from England and Wales. They focused on particulates in the air that are less than 2.5 micrometers (PM).

They found that exposure to these PM2.5 air pollutants during childhood resulted in a greater risk of mental illness by age 18 years old. The worse the exposure the greater the incidence of depression in the children later on.

Smoking

Yes, most of us now know that first-hand, second-hand and even third-hand smoking is unhealthy. If we don't, we need to dig out from the hole we've been hiding in.

But how many of us have connected smoking – which would necessarily include first-, second-, and third-hand smoking – with stress and anxiety? How about depression?

Research from Virginia Commonwealth University and multiple Chinese university and hospital research institutions (He et al 2014) determined that smoking is associated with greater severity of symptoms among the depressed.

The researchers tested 6,120 Chinese women between 30 and 60 years old who had been diagnosed with severe depression. They collected patient data from 53 hospitals throughout China.

Of these 6,120 depression cases, nearly four percent were current smokers and two percent formerly smoked, while nearly six percent were lifetime smokers. Smoking rates are generally lower in China than in the U.S. Research has found Chinese smokers may be less than three percent of the population.

Most of the patients who smoked – over 60 percent – took up smoking prior to their onset of depression.

The researchers found that lifetime smokers reported more stressful life events, had higher levels of neuroticism, more thoughts of suicide and had more panic attacks and phobias compared to non-smokers.

While the researchers could not associate smoking with a greater risk of depression, they suggested the study data illustrates that smoking and depression may have common underlying factors.

Other studies have confirmed the link between smoking and depression. A study from the Henry Ford Health System (Breslau *et al.* 2004) studied 4,414 people between 15 and 54 years old, and found that those with four or more depressive disorders were more than twice as likely to have nicotine dependence and were 50% more likely to smoke daily.

A review from Norway's University of Bergen (Tjora *et al.* 2014) followed 924 kids from ages 13 to 30 years old. They found that early adolescent smoking predicts early adolescent depression and vice versa.

They also found that both smoking and depression tended to continue into adulthood.

What is the mechanism?

Researchers have suggested these findings point to the fact that smoking not only produces the oxidative stress that affects the release of serotonin. It also alters the body's production of dopamine – another hormone/neurotransmitter necessary for brain and nerve cell function. The enzyme monoamine oxidase – also called MAO – is also altered by smoking.

MAO is needed to breakdown and therefore regulate other neurotransmitter/hormones such as serotonin, melatonin and adrenaline. In other words, smoking interferes with the regulation of these important mood-related biochemicals.

This is also why Tai chi has been shown to reduce depression.

As we discuss here, secondhand smoke and even third-hand smoking can have similar effects as smoking directly.

Secondhand smoking means a non-smoker is inhaling the tobacco smoke, while third-hand smoke means the residues of smoking – on furniture and other materials – can also have health consequences.

Light

Our environment is involved in different mood disorders. Take SAD for example. For decades it has been assumed that seasonal affective disorder (SAD) relates only to the amount of light.

Not completely true.

For example, this does not explain the lower levels of SAD among many northern climate cultures such as Eskimos as compared to lower latitude dwellers. SAD, as most know is considered a debilitating disorder causing depression, anxiety, fatigue, and lethargy, there are curious exceptions.

A study from Iceland's National University Hospital (Maqnusson and Stefansson 1993), found that Icelanders experience lower SAD prevalence than do people on the east coast of the United States.

In another study from Turku University's Central Hospital (Saarijarvi *et al.* 1999), the prevalence of SAD was higher among women and younger ages, but notably also more prevalent among those with a higher body mass index.

There is still a strong relationship between SAD and levels of light exposure. This is substantiated by lots of research showing SAD prevalence is higher in areas with more rain and less outdoors weather.

This correlation doesn't necessarily mean light exposure is the only cause for SAD. The characteristics of the above studies are also consistent with people who are less likely to go outdoors at any time of day. For example, many other studies indicate lower rates of SAD among those who exercise outdoors, day or night.

With that in mind, let's discuss how our hormone and neurotransmitter production is connected to our body's cycles, the earth's cycles, and light.

Chapter Two

Depressing our Natural Rhythms

When light enters our eyes, it stimulates cells in our retina. This information is then communicated through our optic nerves to the hypothalamus and pituitary gland. This communication of light then stimulates the release of hormones and neurotransmitters that regulate and balance our moods.

This means that our moods and emotions are directly related to the kinds and timing of light that our eyes are exposed to.

This chapter delves into this little-discussed element of depression and anxiety that may well be the major reason for the significant increase in depression and anxiety among so many young people. The modern era has introduced something that our bodies and minds have not been exposed to throughout our evolution: Smartphones, tablets and computers.

This statement may conjure up the effects of social media on young minds as they grapple with likes and followers. But this is actually not the flashing red light at the root of this connection between our screens and depression.

The issue is the physiological affect of staring at a screen lit with backlights imposing wavelengths of unnatural light directly into our eyes. These are wavelengths of light that disrupt our hypothalamus-pituitary-adrenal (HPA) axis.

Remember from the previous chapter that the disruption of the HPA axis is at the root of most types of clinical depression. This is because these screen lights change our body's release of the various hormones and neurotransmitters that directly affect our moods and energy levels.

Our neurotransmitters bathe between our nerve cells and shade our emotional and mood responses as we go through our daily lives. Remember too that most antidepressants, as discussed in the last chapter, work by trying to adjust our body's neurotransmitters.

This is backed by scientific research.

Doctors from the United Kingdom's University of Exeter (O'Loughlin *et al.* 2021) studied data on 451,025 people. They found that those who maintain their natural body clock related to sleep and time waking had a lower incidence of depression and anxiety.

The researchers also used genetic data to determine the natural body clock ("early riser" or "night owl"). The research also discovered that those who were out of sync from their natural body clock were more likely to experience depression and anxiety and reduced wellbeing.

With this in mind, let's take a closer look at this connection between our body's clock rhythms and our moods.

Light and Moods

Just as the relationship between light and neurotransmitters provides a clear link to mood disorders, the effect light therapy on depression provides an undeniable link. That is because studies have shown that light therapy directly affects our moods and depression.

Research from the University of Maryland's School of Medicine (Reeves *et al.* 2012) studied depressed patients. They were split into two groups. One group was given an hour of bright light therapy. The other (control) group was given an hour of dim light therapy as a placebo.

The reason the control group was given dim light is that dim light doesn't have enough power to invoke the same hormonal changes that bright light does.

The researchers found that the patients given bright light therapy had reductions in their depression scores ranging from 120% to 130%, using two different depression-testing systems.

A number of other studies have found similar findings on depressed patients. This particular study is significant because it applied a placebo test against the light therapy system - something many other light therapy studies have not done.

Indoor light ranges from 60 lux at low lamp level to 200 lux on average. The brightest indoor lighting – think flood lights – might produce up to 1,000 lux.

Light levels of over this 1,000 lux typically require some sort of daylight. For example, 1,000 lux is about typically available in the twilight period – just after sunset or just before sunrise.

Studies show that the typical American only gets about 100 lux per day on average, experiencing only quick bursts of any higher lux, and then barely over 1,000 lux.

This means that most people today are getting substantially deficient amounts of natural light.

Shift workers

Research on shift workers has also confirmed the role that light plays on our moods. These studies have found that shift workers that work at night and sleep during the day typically have significantly higher levels of mood disorders.

Research has also found that for shift workers, light above the 1,000 lux level for three hours will re-establish sleep cycles and positive moods within 48 hours.

By comparison, other techniques shift workers use, such as coffee and alarm clocks can take up to eight days to re-establish one's sleep cycle.

That said, levels of over 4,000 lux are needed for most endocrine-stimulating functions. Going outside into the sunlight is required to achieve these levels.

Those who get outside and connect with the nature's combination of waves – visible light, ultraviolet light, geomagnetic sun pulses, the earth's magnetic pulses and fresh air – are less likely to experience the depression, fatigue and other symptoms experienced by those who do not get outside into nature.

In a 2009 study (Virk *et al.*) researchers tested 15 depressed patients who were diagnosed with seasonal affective disorder. They administered different lengths of 10,000 lux of white cool fluorescent light for 20 minutes, 40 minutes and 60 minutes and compared the depression scores with the depression scores of the patients prior to treatment.

The researchers found that 40 minutes of the light therapy significantly improved moods among the patients, and reduced their depressed states. The improvement was greater than the 20 minutes of therapy. But surprisingly, the 60 minutes of light therapy did not result in significantly better improvement of depression than either the 20 or the 40 minutes of therapy.

Depression levels in the latter study were measured using the 24-item NIMH scale, a standardized measurement of depression symptoms. The level of seasonal affective disorder depression was gauged using the SIGH-SAD scale (Structured Interview Guide for the Hamilton Depression Rating Scale). They also used Wilcoxon Signed Rank testing. Other studies have used the Profile of Mood States-Depression-Dejection subscale and the Beck Depression Inventory II.

The researchers used a 10,000 lux light box made by Sunbox for the bright light therapy. The patients starred at the center of the light box to receive their therapy.

These findings are consistent with other studies, most that utilized both synthetic light, but some that used natural light. In one, McGill University researchers (aan het Rot *et al.* 2008) found that natural bright light significantly reduced acute tryptophan depletion-related depressed moods.

Research led by Dr. Martin Feelisch, Professor of Experimental Medicine and Integrative Biology at the University of Southampton found that UVA rays have numerous benefits including modulating moods.

The researchers tested 24 people. They gave the subjects a series of 20-minute exposure tests. These included sunlamps with just UVA exposure and the sunlamps with all UV rays blocked.

The researchers found that the 20-minute UVA suntanning sessions significantly lowered their blood pressure. But they also found that an important compound in the bloodstream was raised with UVA exposure: Nitric oxide.

In other research, nitric oxide has proved to help blood vessel health in many ways. It helps blood vessel flexibility, and helps widen the blood vessels.

Nitric oxide also helps stimulate the production of serotonin. Serotonin is an important compound for brain health. It also helps prevent mood disorders, including depression.

This is one reason why sunshine exposure helps reduce seasonal affective disorder.

The researchers eliminated the possibility of these effects being caused by the heat of the lamps. When the sunlamps' UV rays were blocked, there were no such effects.

The researchers also tested levels of vitamin D in the subjects and found there was no rise in vitamin D. So the reduction in blood pressure had nothing to do with vitamin D levels.

Still other studies have shown that bright light increases cognition, improves sleep and has a myriad of other benefits. For this reason, going outdoors strengthens immunity. And playing outside reduces ADHD risk in children.

For those who assume this connection between sunlight exposure and depression can be replaced through vitamin D supplementation: A number of studies correlated this due to the fact that vitamin D levels are typically higher in regions where there is better weather and more people get outside.

But science has since de-coupled the relationship between vitamin D supplementation and depression. Reviews of research trying to connect D supplements with reducing depression have found a lack of definitive evidence.

The connection has also been studied carefully since. For example, a study from medical schools in The Netherlands (de Koning et al. 2019) studied vitamin D supplementation and depression using 155 people with depression. Vitamin D3 supplementation had no effect on depression symptoms compared to the placebo group. Other studies have concluded this lack of evidence.

This leaves the depression connection to sunlight itself. While the production of vitamin D in the body can certainly aid in the production of better hormones and neurotransmitters, the association between vitamin D and depression itself is left to exposure to sunlight, which as we are discussing, directly modulates the body's secretion of mood neurotransmitters.

This direct association between sunlight exposure and moods has been proven in the research over and over for the past three decades.

Nighttime Light Pollution

Being exposed to high levels of artificial outdoor light at night contributes to insomnia and greater use of sleeping pills. This is the conclusion of research from South Korea's Seoul National University College of Medicine (Min and Min 2018). The researchers analyzed health records of 52,027 people without diagnosed sleep disorders.

They found that their sleeping pill use correlated with their residential location relative to artificial outdoor light intensity.

The brighter the outdoor lighting, the more likely were sleep issues and the greater and more frequent use of sleeping pills. Other research that has shown that late night artificial nighttime lights disrupts circadian rhythms, increasing the risk of mood disorders.

This relationship between sleep and nighttime light also connects the dots between sleep and depression. When a person is not sleeping due to issues relating to light, this means their HPA axis has been disrupted.

If the HPA axis is disrupted, the body not produce enough melatonin to relax and go to sleep. That actually compounds the problem because melatonin release and reduction helps time the release of the body's other neurotransmitters.

On top of that, the disruption of the HPA axis due to a lack of sunlight reduces the bodies production and timed release of dopamine, serotonin, acetylcholine, GABA and other hormones and neurotransmitters leads to negative moods and emotions.

This is because the release of these hormones and neurotransmitters are directly linked to the pineal gland, which responds to the light that enters the eyes and stimulates the release of mood hormones and neurotransmitters from the pituitary gland.

Smartphone, computer and tablet use and our body rhythms

Researchers from Brigham and Women's Hospital in Boston, Massachusetts (Chang *et al.* 2015) determined that tablets and laptops that emit significant blue ray radiation disturbs sleep in ways not previously known or understood. The study was published in the *Proceedings of the National Academy of Sciences*.

The scientists tested twelve volunteers for two weeks. They were split into two groups. During five straight nights of the first week, six of the volunteers read ebooks of their choosing on an iPad® device four hours prior to going to bed. The other six read from a printed book of their choosing during the same time.

Some read the printed book during their first week while others read from the tablet in order to randomize the order of their reading.

During the second week, those who read from the tablet during the first week read a printed book while those who read from the printed books the first week read from the tablet during the second week.

The research found several effects in those who read from the computer tablet:

• Those reading the tablet took longer to get to sleep
• Those reading the tablet secreted less melatonin
• Those reading the tablet were less sleepy the next evening
• Those reading the tablet had delayed circadian rhythms
• Those reading the tablet had significantly less REM-stage sleep

As I illustrate the science in my book, *"Natural Sleep Solutions,"* our circadian rhythm is significantly tied to the quality of our sleep. In this study, those who read the tablet at night were found to have their circadian rhythms delayed by an hour or more.

Melatonin and blue light

The researchers also connected the study's results with the amount of blue light that we are exposed to when looking at computer screens. This blue light specifically effects our body's melatonin levels.

Melatonin is a hormone that promotes healthy sleep. As lights are dimmed in the evening, our body begins to produce more melatonin and decreases the production of cortisol. Melatonin allows our body to relax and sleep.

In the morning, our body will begin producing more cortisol and less melatonin. This stimulates our body's energy levels and helps wake us up.

This illustrates how important it is to have the proper levels of melatonin at night as we go to sleep. Many insomnia cases are accompanied by decreased levels of melatonin as we go to bed.

The bottom line is that our melatonin/cortisol cycles are critical for healthy sleep, and healthy moods.

While the potential disturbance of our melatonin/cortisol cycles are minimized during the day by the surrounding light, blue light at night has a specific effect on our melatonin levels.

The Brigham researchers measured the blue light of various other computer devices, including laptops, LED monitors, cell phones and other electronic devices. They all emitted similar levels of blue light.

Neuroscientist Dr. Anne-Marie Chang, one of the study authors of the study, confirmed these relationships:

> *"We found the body's natural circadian rhythms were inter-rupted by the short-wavelength enriched light, otherwise known as blue light, from these electronic devices."*

The reality that blue light exposure decreases melatonin levels has been confirmed by the research. For example, a study from Thomas Jefferson University (Brainard *et al.* 2015) studied 24 volunteers who were tested while undergoing three different tests with light.

They were exposed to different lamps with different spectra in each test. With greater exposures of the short-wavelengths of 400 to 500 nanometers, the volunteers' levels of melatonin were decreased.

Light pollution

This lends to the notion that too much of certain kinds of light during the evening would be compared to polluting the body. Light pollution not only creates a short-term issue with sleep loss and quality, but also has a long-term effect over time.

To this end, leading sleep researcher Dr. Charles Czeisler added:

> *"In the past 50 years, there has been a decline in average sleep duration and quality. Since more people are choosing electronic devices for reading, communication and entertain-ment, particularly children and adolescents who already experience significant sleep loss, epidemiological research evaluating the long-term consequences of these devices on health and safety is urgently needed."*

Bipolar disorder and circadian rhythms

Bipolar disorder is also connected to light pollution according to the research.

In a study from France's INSERM (Geoffroy *et al.* 2013), researchers studied 25 people with bipolar disorder and 28 healthy people. The subjects underwent sleep studies and actigraphy – the monitoring of sleep and activity cycles.

The researchers also analyzed the patients for the existence of a particular genetic sequence called the ASMT variant, which appears linked with a lack of melatonin production.

The researchers found that those with bipolar disorder tended to have dramatically different circadian cycles with respect to waking and sleeping patterns.

This confirms previous research that has found bipolar disorder related to a disorganized circadian cycle as it relates to the body's normal response to light.

The acetylserotonin O-methyltransferase (or ASMT) gene is involved in this process, as it oversees to production of two enzymes need to produce melatonin in the body.

Because this gene is related to light exposure, it is apparent that bipolar disorder may be a byproduct of a lack of regulated sun exposure, either on the part of the subject or their parents.

This reality is backed up by numerous studies linking bipolar disorder with dysfunctional sleep cycles. This was confirmed in another INSERM (Boudebesse *et al.* 2012) review of research. When the circadian rhythms are off, melatonin production is altered. And significant alteration over time has an epigenetic effect upon certain alleles.

This also ties in with part of the reason Americans have such dramatically high rates of bipolar disorder. Americans spend much of their lives indoors, as opposed to other countries that work out of doors and spend more time out of doors.

The rise of the screens

Smartphones are sure convenient. But the more we use them, the more they can disturb our sleep. And we need sleep to stay healthy.

This is not good news for the surge of smartphone users. About 85 percent of Americans now use a smartphone according to Statista research in 2020.

This kind of broad use led researchers from the University of California at San Francisco (Christensen *et al.* 2016) to study the effects of smartphone use on sleep.

The scientists tested 653 adults for one year - between 2014 and 2015. The subjects each downloaded a special application that measured their screen time and frequency. The application operated in the background. Every 30 days it would compile their screen use frequency, which was collected by the researchers. Those who had no screen time during the month were excluded from the results.

The participants were located throughout the United States, with a variety of occupations, ages and economic status.

The researchers calculated their results in 30-day windows. They found that people use their smartphones an average of 38.4 hours during a 30-day window. This netted out to an average of an hour and a half per day. Their daily use ranged from 53 minutes to 2 hours and 12 minutes.

Those with more screen time turned out to be younger. Females tended to have higher screen times, as did blacks, Hispanics and non-smokers. More screen-time was not associated with income or physical activity. Neither was it related to higher BMI – like more television watching is. Obviously, people can stay active with their smartphones.

Another interesting statistic found in the study: Searching for medical information was the most common use for their smart-phones.

Regardless, those who used their smartphones more also had significantly lower sleep quality. They also had shorter sleep duration, less sleep efficiency and longer sleep onset latency (getting to bed later).

Poor sleep and more screen time occurred among those who didn't use their smartphones at bedtime. But the more the people used their smartphones at bedtime, the worse their sleep was.

We discussed research on how bedtime computer and tablet use is linked to poor sleep earlier.

Remember that this occurs from the over-exposure to blue light, which ranges from 380 to 500 nanometers in wavelength. As mentioned, computers, televisions, tablets and smartphones all emit lots of blue light.

Too much blue light affects our body's circadian rhythms, along with our body's production of melatonin. And because a reduction of melatonin supply has been linked to cancer, we can say that too much screen time can increase our cancer risk.

So does the sun's rays as it collides with our atmosphere. In fact, blue light is what creates the blueness of the sky. But the sun's rays also produce a number of other healthier wavelengths. These include UVB – which causes our bodies to produce the healthiest form of vitamin D.

Is smartphone and computer use worse than television?

This effect is also similar for television use. A study from Harvard tested 8,317 children from 138 elementary schools. They tested sleep levels against television use and video game use.

The researchers found that both television use and video game use at night significantly reduced sleep duration among the children.

This is consistent with the fact that most of today's televisions and computers utilize back-lit screens and thus emit similar levels of blue light.

Which screens are better?

The solution? Using our screens judiciously. We're not just speaking of sleep here. These are electromagnetic devices that emit radiation after all. I discuss numerous strategies to combat the ill effects of EMFs in my book on the subject, *"Electromagnetic Health."*

But certainly, screens are now an unavoidable part of our lives. So which screens are best and how should we use them?

Plasma screens, LED (light emitting diode) and LCD (liquid crystal display) screens work differently, but we are still left staring directly at beams of light that produce lots of blue light. Let's review these along with some alternatives:

Plasma screens

Most smartphones and computers use LCD technology, but newer computers and televisions can also be plasma screens. They tend to be more expensive however, and their size is typically limited by cost.

In a plasma screen, we are staring at tiny electronic lamps the size of pixels that are switched on or off. On-state pixels are thus tiny florescent lamps that shine into your eyes. When we are staring at a plasma screen, we are staring into numerous lights – just as we might stare at an array of fluorescent lights. Yes, we are staring into millions of tiny lights when we stare at our computer or phone screens. A larger plasma screen can have more than 6 million light cells.

LCD screens

In an LCD smartphone, computer or flatscreen TV, we are staring at liquid crystals that are polarizing beams of light. The light beams come from behind the screens. These are basically like fluorescent lights shining into our eyes. These beams of light are also called back lights. This why these devices are referred to as back-lit screens. As the light hits the liquid crystals, they will polarize the light into either a red, green or blue colors. Or the liquid crystal can block the light to create black.

The liquid crystals are each connected to a transistor, which modulates the polarity as the light shines through it.

LED screens

Most LED TVs are also liquid crystal displays, but their back lights are LED lights instead of fluorescent. Their LED lights are also typically placed behind and around the liquid crystals. These allow for a flatter TV and possibly lower energy use. The plus is that you aren't staring right into fluorescent lights in an LED TV. So there may be a slight reduction in blue light in LED screens compared to LCDs, but since both are backlit, they are both significant blue light emitters.

OLED screens

The newest organic LED screens (OLEDs) are different. These are not backlit. Instead of backlighting, these use individual OLED subpixels, which will display light through electron transfer through organic (carbon) based materials. The result is about a third less blue light than produced by LCD televisions. One test by LGD showed 3.1 times more blue light is emitted from LCD screens compared to OLED screens.

Projectors

Another potential option, especially for nighttime use, is to use a projector. A projector will emit blue light just as a television will. But this light is reflected onto a wall, so it is not shining directly into the retina. The back lighting is being disbursed onto the wall rather than directly into your eyes.

This technique is also used to look at solar eclipses and other solar images. The harmful rays of the sun are being projected onto a secondary and not into the eyes. This removes their backlight effect.

Background light

For screens other than projectors, we can also employ our own background lighting. A mix of natural light in the room will help to prevent our eyes from fixating upon only the light coming out of our screens. In other words, looking at a computer screen in the dark is not such a good idea. Remember that the sun also produces blue light, but because there is a mix of spectra coming from the sun, the blue light portion is not as prominent. This is why natural light is the best fit for our eyes.

Blue light blockers

There are now several commercially available tools to reduce our blue light exposure at night, or even through the daytime if we are on our computers all day.

One tool is a pair of blue light blocking glasses. These are relatively inexpensive. They can look like sunglasses or like reading glasses.

Another tool is an app or software that reduces the blue light exposure of the screen. There are now apps available for cell phones and tablets. I haven't come across an app like this for a PC but I have seen screens that overlay over PC screen that block blue light. These types of strategies may especially be helpful if we find that we have to answer an email or text late at night on occasion.

Sleep and Mood

Yes, blue light at night can disrupt our HPA axis as we've been discussing. But sleep also has its own links to depression.

The connection between insomnia and depression is revealed through a number of means. Numerous studies have shown that depressed patients improve with better quality sleep.

The mechanisms relate to several key neurotransmitters and hormones.

The first association between sleep and depression is dopamine and serotonin. These two neurotransmitter/hormones affect moods and the perception of well-being. They also affect sleep quality. When a person is low on either dopamine or serotonin or both, the risk for depression increases. Serotonin is particularly associated with both anxiety and depression.

Serotonin levels and dopamine levels decrease with increased sleep debt. Sleep debt is the build up of lost sleep over a period of days, weeks, months or even years. Sleep research has shown that those with heavy sleep debt will also have low levels of both dopamine and serotonin.

Selective serotonin reuptake inhibitors (SSRIs) are typically prescribed for depression and anxiety, but they are also often prescribed for insomnia. As we discussed earlier, SSRIs work by blocking the infusion of serotonin by nerve cells. This effectively leaves more serotonin available in the bloodstream. This readily-available serotonin in the blood provides an artificial means for increasing relaxation. For this reason, SSRIs are one of the most popular drugs for depression, anxiety and sleeplessness.

An example of dopamine's impact on sleepiness is Parkinson's disease, which is characterized by low levels of dopamine and increased rates of depression. In one study of bright light therapy (Willis and Turner 2007) and Parkinson's patients, the light therapy increased dopamine levels, which elevated their mood and increased their sleep quality.

Depression and insomnia also have a common connection in that they both require effective GABA (Gamma-aminobutyric acid) receptor modulation. Changes in light are accompanied by the inhibitory neurotransmitter, GABA.

For this reason, non-benzodiazepine hypnotics interact with the GABA receptor complex and modulate the GABA-BZ receptor chloride channel. This stimulates the sedative effects of these drugs. This also helps produce some of their side effects as well.

Melatonin of course, is the hormone that drives sleep, and our body's production of melatonin precedes increased sleepiness. The neurotransmitter-hormones melatonin and serotonin are both stimulated by changes in light availability.

Research shows that one can increase serotonin, dopamine and melatonin levels, as well as stimulate a healthy modulation of the GABA receptor with plenty of sunshine and a strenuous workout early in the day. Each of these has been associated with better quality sleep and a reduction in depression. A healthy diet and good sleeping hygiene are also essential.

Numerous studies have put most of the pieces together. A lack of sleep can produce depressed symptoms. And depression can be difficult to differentiate from insomnia. Here is a sampling of some of the conclusions of this research:

> *"It can be difficult to distinguish between primary sleep complaints and those associated with psychiatric disorders. Insomnia is often a symptom of underlying anxiety, depression, or panic disorder. A survey of office-based physicians showed that 30% of patients diagnosed with insomnia were also diagnosed with depression. Another study found that approximately 40% of patients presenting to sleep specialists have a psychiatric disorder." (Garma 2003)*

A 2015 study (Zhai *et al.*) reviewed the research linking sleep duration and depression. The researchers pooled results from 25,271 people for short sleepers and 23,663 for long sleepers.

The study results found that those getting too little sleep had a 31 percent greater risk of depression. And those who got too much sleep had a 42 percent increased risk of depression.

The researchers concluded:

> *"This meta-analysis indicates that short and long sleep duration was significantly associated with increased risk of depression in adults."*

When we sleep, our body recovers from muscle aches and injuries. But the mind also recovers from stresses and performance anxieties. These have been found in multiple studies that have shown that moods improve with better sleep.

When we sleep the neurons within our hippocampus and amygdala are refreshed. Our cells are also healed and our immune system cleans up invaders. Our gut bacteria also goes into high gear while we sleep.

The need for REM-stage sleep

What is REM-stage sleep? This is the sleep phase where the body and brain does much of its recovery. It is a cycle characterized by rapid eye movement (hence REM) and a period of dreaming. In addition, the body's skeletal muscles are practically paralyzed.

But something else happens when we enter REM-stage sleep. The release of serotonin, histamine and a number of other normal waking neurotransmitters is blocked, and other waking neurotransmitters such as GABA are significantly decreased. Meanwhile the body's production of acetylcholine is increased, and this provides a feedback loop that blocks the release of the other monoamine neurotransmitters.

REM-stage sleep has been shown to be a necessary part of our sleep cycle. Those with less REM-stage sleep have been shown to have higher rates of depression, Alzheimer's, mood disorders and others. Health dangers of reduced REM-sleep include heart disease, diabetes and obesity. Less REM-stage sleep has been linked with earlier death as well.

This doesn't count daytime sleepiness, which is a health and safety risk. Should we fall asleep driving or at work, that can be very dangerous.

A study of 5,888 men and women from the University of Pittsburgh (Newman *et al.* 2000) found that daytime sleepiness - the result of a lack of REM-stage sleep and a reason to nap during the day - doubled the risk of dying from cardiovascular disease in women and increased it by 40% in men.

This entire relationship - REM-stage sleep and early death - was confirmed in an international multi-center study that tested 636 people - half of whom had a sleep disorder called idiopathic REM sleep behavior disorder.

The researchers found that those with the REM-stage sleep disorder had over double the risk of having a heart attack, *significantly more depression* and depression medications than those without the disorder.

The bottom line is that we don't just need sleep every night - as if sleep is just one long continuous thing. We need a certain amount of REM-stage sleep every night, and if we don't get enough of it, there will be negative health consequences.

This means that having an afternoon nap in itself is not a problem. What is the problem is the lack of REM-stage sleep that occurred the night before. This is added to the fact that a person taking an afternoon nap will also be less likely to catch up on that REM-stage sleep loss the next night.

They will likely repeat the cycle again the next night and day.

How much should we sleep?

One study reports that almost a third of U.S. adults get less than six hours sleep a night on average. The data was based upon a National Health Interview Survey (NHIS) sponsored by the Centers of Disease Control. The report showed that 40.6 million adult workers reported getting an average of less than six hours.

The National Sleep Foundation recommends that adults sleep between 7 and 9 hours.

The study also found that short sleep varied significantly by occupation. Those who work in the manufacturing industry reported the least sleep among occupations, with 34% reporting less than six hours. Night shift workers reported even less, with 44% getting less than 6 hours a night.

Night shift workers in the transportation industry had the least amount of sleep of night shift workers, with almost 70% reporting less than six hours a night.

Health care night shift workers were close behind, with 52% getting less than six hours a night.

Getting too little sleep is rampant, and insomnia is also at epidemic levels. One out of ten Americans suffer from chronic insomnia according to the CDC.

Insomnia is linked to suicides among teens according to other research. Depression, Parkinson's and dementia are linked to a lack of sleep.

Conventional doctors prescribe numerous pharmaceuticals to promote sleep. But research has found that most sleep medications can be addictive if used for a long duration.

Many sleep medicines also cause daytime drowsiness, as well as depression as we discuss in this book. Natural sleep remedies are popular because they are provide relaxation and extended sleep without the side effects found in many pharmaceuticals.

Night Owls vs. Morning Persons

Staying up late and sleeping in can be fun, and the internet is producing more night owls around the world. Yet multiple studies have showed that night owls tend to suffer more heart disease, eat poor diets, and suffer more from depression and bipolar disorder. Night owls also tend to die sooner according to the research.

To some degree, these outcomes may be linked, as we'll discover in this article. But it is important to know that most of the findings were separated from the effects of inadequate sleep. But inadequate sleep does indeed have a compounding effect as well.

Definitely, staying up late and sleeping in also relates to our daylight hours and our circadian rhythms. This circadian rhythm aspect is reflected by researchers referring to the dichotomy of evening or morning persons as "chronotypes." Let's discuss this further after reviewing some of the research findings on the subject.

'Evening persons' and wellness

A study from the Northwestern University School of Medicine and the UK's University of Surrey (Knutson and von Schantz 2018) surveyed 433,268 people to determine whether they were morning persons or evening persons (AKA 'night owls').

The research found that 27 percent of the people were identified as 'definite morning type' persons, while 35 percent were 'moderate morning types.' The study found that 28 percent were 'moderate evening types' and 9 percent were 'definite evening types.' These four chronotypes allowed the researchers to compare the study participants.

The researchers followed the participants for six-and-a-half years. They recorded instances of psychological illness, heart disease, diabetes and death (mortality) among the population during the six-plus years.

The researchers compared all the chronotypes, but the 'definite morning' versus the 'definite evening' types were closely analyzed.

The researchers found those who were definite evening types had a 94 percent increased incidence of psychological disease compared to definite morning types. Evening persons also had a 30 percent higher incidence of diabetes.

The evening types also suffered 23 percent more from gastrointestinal issues. They also had 25 percent more neurological conditions and 22 percent more respiratory conditions.

Furthermore, the night owls - definite evening types - had a 10 percent greater incidence of death during the period compared to the definite morning types.

Night owls suffer more depression

The above study is consistent with another study that focused on chronotype and depression from the University of Warsaw. The researchers studied university students and found that morning-type persons suffered from significantly less depression compared to the evening type students.

There were three elements of the depressive symptoms established by this study. They included somatic depression, interpersonal relationships and positivism. The researchers found that morning type students suffered less depression of all three aspects. Morning types had greater positivism and better interpersonal relationships. They also had less incidence of somatic depression compared to night owls.

Bipolar disorder and our rhythms

A number of studies have focused on the relationship between morning or evening types and bipolar disorder. The research has been illuminating, to say the least.

A number of studies have found a relationship between being a night owl and bipolar disorder. A 2017 review of research from Brazil's Federal do Ceará University found 42 studies that investigated bipolar disease and circadian rhythm and/or chronotype. The researchers stated:

"In conclusion, disruption in circadian rhythm and evening-ness are common in bipolar disorder."

"Eveningness" is a research term relating to being a night owl. But this doesn't mean that every person with bipolar disorder is a night owl.

For example, in a study from McGill University's Department of Psychiatry (Kanagarajan *et al.* 2018), researchers investigated bipolar disease and chronotype. They studied 53 patients diagnosed with bipolar disorder, and found that 24 percent were definite evening persons. As suggested by the UK study, the general population tends to be in the range of 9 percent night owls.

But there may be some other form of circadian rhythm disruption in bipolar disorder as found in the review.

In this regard, a study from the Portugal's Porto Medical School (Melo *et al.* 2017) reviewed research related to circadian rhythms and bipolar disorder. They found that a number of studies found bipolar disorder related to altered melatonin levels, cortisol rhythms, sleep disruption and body temperature.

Chronotype also linked to heart disease

A study from the University of Pennsylvania and the University of Delaware (Patterson *et al.* 2018) examined data from 439,933 people from the United Kingdom. This study compared sleep duration as well as chronotypes.

The researchers classified 'definite morning person' or 'definite evening persons' as well as 'somewhat' morning or evening types.

They also categorized the subjects into one of three groups: 'Short' sleepers (less than or equal to 6 hours a night); 'adequate' (7-8 hours); or 'long' (more than 9 hours a night).

This means the researchers could relate both the sleep duration and the evening types to heart disease risk factors.

The researchers found that night owls (definite evening types) tended to smoke more, have less physical activity and more sedentary behavior. They also tended to be more overweight or obese and had lower fruit and vegetable consumption. They also had a greater risk of cardiovascular disease – likely related to most of the above factors.

But when compared with sleep duration, it turned out that the long-sleepers had worse scores in all of these areas with the exception of tobacco use, where the short-sleeper night owls had the greatest rates of smoking – followed closely by the long-sleeper night owls.

In other words, being a night owl in itself lends to greater heart disease risks, but being a night owl and sleeping in is worse for our health.

The researchers wrote:

> "... results from this study have shown that long-sleep duration interacted with evening preference to emerge as the sleep combination that had the highest, or next to the highest, prevalence and odds (as compared to adequate sleepers with morning preference) for all five cardiovascular risk factors examined (tobacco use, physical inactivity, high sedentary behavior, obesity/overweight and eating less than 5 daily servings of fruit and vegetables). Whereas adequate sleep duration with a morning, or somewhat morning, preference was associated with the lowest prevalence and odds for all risk factors, except fruit and vegetable intake (where short-sleep and morning preference had the lowest prevalence and odds)."

Morning exercise and sleep

A study presented at the 58th Annual Meeting of the American College of Sports Medicine found that early morning exercise increases sleep quality.

Chronic sleep shortage has been linked to Parkinson's, dementia, cognition problems, depression, asthma, diabetes, obesity, high blood pressure and others.

The study, done by researchers from Appalachian State University and led by Scott Collier, PhD, FACSM, assistant professor, found that exercising at 7 a.m. resulted in deeper sleep and more REM sleep cycles, than exercising at 1 p.m. or 7 p.m.

Nine adults were studied, including six men and three women.

The participants worked out for thirty minutes on a treadmill at the appointed times, changing occasionally to clarify test results.

The 7 a.m. exercise routine produced 75 percent more deep sleep and 20 percent more sleep cycles.

Other research has found that many people do not get adequate sleep quality or quantity. The Centers for Disease Control and Prevention has characterized lack of sleep quality and quantity an epidemic. This is especial true and worrisome for adolescents, who stay up late to text with friends or interact with the computer.

Are you a morning type person or a night owl?

For those who sometimes stay up late, this is a more complicated question. It isn't related directly to staying up late. It is also related to when we get up in the morning.

Dr. Susan Krauss Whitbourne gives us the following self-test to determine whether we are a definite night owl, a morning person, or somewhere in between:

1. Considering only your "feeling best" rhythm, at what time would you wake up if you were entirely free to plan your day? 5:00-6:30 a.m. [5 points] 6:30-7:45 a.m. [4 points] 7:45-9:45 a.m. [3 points] 9:45-11:00 a.m. [2 points] 11:00 a.m.-12:00 (noon) [1 point]

2. During the first half hour after waking in the morning, how tired do you feel? Very tired [1 points] Fairly tired [2 points] Fairly refreshed [3 points] Very refreshed [4 points]

3. At what time in the evening do you feel tired and in need of sleep? 8:00-9:00 p.m. [5 points] 9:00-10:15 p.m. [4 points] 10:15 p.m.-12:30 a.m. [3 points] 12:30-1:45 a.m. [2 points] 1:45-3:00 a.m. [1 point]

4. At what time of day do you think that you reach your "feeling best" peak? 5–8 AM (05–08 h) [5 points] 8–10 AM (08–10 h) [4 points] 10 AM–5 PM (10–17 h) [3 points] 5–10 PM (17–22 h) [2 points] 10 PM–5 AM (22–05 h) [1 point]

5. Which one of these types do you consider yourself to be? Definitely a morning type. [6 points] Rather more a morning type than an evening type. [4 points] Rather more an evening type than an morning type. [2 points] Definitely an evening type. [0 points]

Now score yourself

Just add up the points from above, and this is the key to show what chronotype you most likely are: 22-25 Definitely Morning (DM) 18-21 Moderately Morning (MM) 12-17 Neither (N) 8- 11 Moderately Evening (ME) 4-7 Definitely Evening (DE)

The "neither" type above is considered the standard circadian profile according to other research. This is considered as someone who goes to bed between 11 pm and midnight and wakes up between 7 am and 8 am. This also means getting somewhere between 7 and 8 hours of sleep – which is in the adequate zone.

This is linked to a 2012 study (Thun *et al.* see references below) that inventoried the seven types among a population of 166 people.

A healthy circadian cycle

You might be wondering why the time you go to sleep and the time you wake up are important. The issue is how much daylight we are experiencing, because daylight affects our circadian rhythms.

Yes, the preponderance of research identifies relationships surrounding the amount of natural sunlight – or daylight – we get every day. How much sunlight/daylight we receive relates directly to our moods, our activities and subsequently, our health.

It is not an accident that the University of Pennsylvania research above links our chronotype with activities that increase our disease risk – even mortality. In other words, those who don't have adequate sunlight tend to eat more unhealthy foods and tend to have more sedentary activity. And these relate directly to disease.

Yes, these explain how the night owl – who tends to wake up later and thus experience less sun – will tend to have a greater risk of diabetes, heart disease and depression.

Bipolar disorder may be the canary in the coal mine for night owls, because bipolar is also related directly in the research to circadian disruption such as melatonin, cortisol and body temperature cycles.

This is also related to depression symptoms, as confirmed by a 2017 Russian study that tested seasonal affective disorder (SAD) in depression using the winter and summer seasons.

These cycles, as other research has showed, are also linked to our behavior and what we eat. Those whose cycles are better adjusted – by experiencing adequate daylight time each day – will naturally have better health behavior as a result.

This has been illustrated by a number of studies, many of which have been done on shift-workers. The takeaway here is that a lack of daylight hours disrupts our circadian cycle, which in turn leads to poor health consequences such as the ones mentioned above.

Can we adjust our chronotype?

For those who are night owls or evening types, the ability to change this seems impossible. But yes, it can be done. It is simply a matter of adjusting our circadian phases with the use of sunlight.

As I discussed in detail in my book on insomnia, we can easily adjust our circadian rhythm phases with a staged use of sunlight.

Hint: The process is similar to the process of adjusting our circadian rhythm phases after a dose of long-distance airline travel. See the book for more the precise method.

Once we have adjusted our circadian rhythm, there some discipline will be required. This meaning cycling down our activities towards that optimal bedtime and sleep time. But at least our circadian rhythms will cooperate.

This doesn't necessarily mean that all of us have to go to sleep between 11 pm and midnight. As I also show in my book on insomnia, we don't all have the same optimal sleep duration. Some of us naturally sleep more or less than others. So finding the optimal bedtime is worked out by figuring out our optimal sleep duration and then doing the math to find our bedtime and wake time that gives us adequate sunlight.

Then again, these relationships also have a lot to do with how much time we spend outside. The more time we spend outside -- especially in the daytime -- the more normal our body's natural rhythms will be.

But then we have to also control our blue light exposure at night. This means cutting back on the use of smartphones, tablets and computers as the evening goes on. And employing a projector or television that emits less blue light as discussed.

What about Light Therapy Treatment?

As we began this chapter mentioning, light therapy has been proven scientifically to reduce depression and anxiety symptoms.

Illustrating the dramatic effects of light therapy on depression, we can cite a study from the Departments of Psychiatry from the medical schools of Columbia University, Carnegie Mellon, Northwestern University, University of Pittsburgh, and the New York State Psychiatric Institute (Sit et al. 2017).

The researchers tested people with depression with bipolar disorder. They were given either 7,000 lux bright white light or a 50 lux dim red light as a placebo. The light therapy was given during the midday.

The patients were tested before and after treatment with the Hamilton Depression Scale With Atypical Depression Supplement (SIGH-ADS), the Mania Rating Scale, and the Pittsburgh Sleep Quality Index.

After between four to six weeks of treatment, the researchers found that of the light-treated group, there was a 68 percent remission rate. The light-treated group had average depression scores of 9.2 compared to 14.9 among the placebo group. This was not a group of SAD patients. They had depression and bipolar disorder.

The researchers concluded:

> "The data from this study provide robust evidence that supports the efficacy of midday bright light therapy for bipolar depression."

But should we not have sun available, there are also prescriptive uses of UV lamps. Care must be taken, however, because some UV lamps have been shown in numerous studies to be carcinogenic.

To cement the success of light therapy, doctors from the American Academy of Neurology reported in 2020 that depression can be countered with light therapy.

The researchers tested 35 people with depression after a concussion with a tabletop light device or a placebo light device. They found that receiving blue light therapy improved symptoms by an average of 22 percent. The placebo group's depression worsened by 4 percent in comparison.

A 2020 review (Tao et al.) of 23 randomized controlled studies that included 1,120 depressed patients found that light therapy was more effective that many other treatments. The researchers stated:

> "The meta-analysis demonstrated the light therapy was significantly more effective than comparative treatments."

They also documented that it was clinically useful:

"Light therapy has a statistically significant mild to moderate treatment effect in reducing depressive symptoms, can be used as a clinical therapy in treating non-seasonal depression."

We have discussed how light can affect our moods, increasing bouts of depression and anxiety.

Light therapy can be done simply by going outside and spending a few hours outside. This can be done rain or shine, heat or cold, regardless of the latitude. Anywhere there is daylight, we can receive light therapy.

That said, the sunnier it is when we go outside the better.

It should be noted that light therapy is effectively duplicating what nature already provides when we go outside during the midday in most places during most seasons. Yes, there are places in the world that are dark during much of the daytime during the winter months. And a stormy day may not render as much light.

But for most of us, light therapy is available to us for free by simply going outside for 30 minutes to an hour each day during the midday.

Depending upon the latitude, the brightest sunlight will have over 100,000 lux around midday on a sunny day. Even a shady spot under a tree on a sunny day at midday can have as much as 20,000 lux. A cloudy day will still have about 2,000 lux at midday, though this will be less with storm clouds.

Chapter Three

Diet and Moods

As we consider the dramatic increase of mood disorders in modern society, it is increasingly becoming evident that our diets are a significant cause for this mental health crisis. Research has confirmed that switching to a diet that encourages our body to support our body rhythms and help produce the neurotransmitters that significantly reduce the risk of depression, anxiety and fatigue.

Our moods, related to the release of neurotransmitters like serotonin and dopamine, are directly related to our nutrition according to the research. Let's take a look at some of this research.

Plant-based Nutrition

Multiple studies have confirmed that eating more fruits and vegetables increase positive moods and reduce the incidence and symptoms of depression and anxiety.

Studies have shown that most people consume pitifully small amounts of fruits and vegetables daily. In one large study from Australia for example, researchers found that nearly 30 percent of people only consume fruit between one and three times a week, and about 20 percent only consume vegetables one to three times a week.

Furthermore, less than half of the population will consume any fruit or vegetables on a daily basis.

This is not anecdotal. There are some large population studies proving that fruits and vegetables significantly decrease the incidence of depression symptoms and negative moods. Let's discuss some of the larger studies, along with the supporting evidence.

University of Toronto researchers (Davison *et al.* 2019) investigated depression and nutrition. They analyzed data from the Canadian Longitudinal Study on Aging that followed more than 27,000 people.

The research found that those who ate less fruits and vegetables had significantly more incidence of depression. And conversely, those who ate more fiber-rich fruits and vegetables had significantly less incidence of depression.

This study also found that hypertension, chocolates, snacks and smoking were linked to a higher risk of depression among the Canadians.

Similarly, the same researchers (Davison *et al.* 2020) also investigated anxiety with this same study group of Canadians. This study showed that less fruit and vegetable consumption and greater pastry consumption were linked with greater incidence of anxiety among the large population of middle-aged folks.

This study also linked smoking and other nutritional components with higher incidence of anxiety.

In a multi-center study, researchers from the Physicians Committee for Responsible Medicine in Washington D.C. (Agarwal *et al.* 2014) tested 292 men and women.

The subjects each had a body mass index equal to or more than 25 kg/m2 – a marker for being overweight – or had a previous diagnosis of having type 2 diabetes. A total of 211 people completed the study and completed all the final analyses and examinations.

The research was conducted at ten different corporate sites of GEICO, a major health insurance provider and insurer of U.S. government employees. The subjects were employees of GEICO – which stands for Government Employee Insurance Co.

The researchers tested the patients for fatigue, depression, emotional well-being, anxiety and other parameters utilizing the Short Form-36 questionnaire (SF-36). This is a report of the general well-being and health status of the person, based on the Medical Outcome Study – called the RAND-36.

The questionnaire contains eight sections, which score the patients' level of vitality, physical condition, pain levels, perceptions of health, physical and emotional role functions, their social role function and mental health and well-being.

This is a standardized test that has been in use for nearly two decades.

The researchers utilized before and after scores, following the diet intervention that lasted 18 weeks – about four and a half months.

Half of the group went to a plant-based diet, while the other half made no diet changes – continuing whatever current diet they had, Weekly consultations and cafeteria options were available to the test subjects.

The plant-based diet group was asked to focus their diet on whole grains such as oats and whole wheat breads, vegetables in all forms, nuts and cooked legumes and fruits. They did not restrict the diet with regard to calories or fullness.

Both groups were advised not to alter any other part of their lifestyle, including more or less exercise.

The researchers also utilized 24-hour diet recalls to study the nutrient intake of the subjects.

The researchers used T-testing and Chi-square (X2) testing to control variables and quantify the results.

At the end of the period, the patients' scores in the following areas were significantly higher than at the beginning of the study:

- overall work impairment because of health depression
- anxiety
- fatigue
- emotional well-being
- daily functioning because of physical health
- general health
- impairment because of health
- non-work-related activity impairment because of health

Each of these parameters had higher scores with confidence levels ranging from 98% to 99%.

For example, after the 18 weeks, those who ate more plant-based foods scored an average of 62.9 on the fatigue measure of the SF-36, while the control diet group scored an average of 45.9. For depression the averages were 81.8 versus 74.6 respectively.

For anxiety, the average scores were 72.6 versus 64.9. Fatigue had the highest score difference in scores at 17.1 (62.94 minus 45.88), followed by physical role limitations at 14.4, general health at 12.9 and social functioning at 10.1 (score difference between the two groups).

The researchers concluded that the *"dietary intervention improves depression, anxiety, and productivity"* in their paper.

Researchers from the UK's University of Leeds and University of York (Ocean *et al.* 2019) analyzed and followed about 50,000 people in the United Kingdom over a period of 8 years (from 2009 to 2017).

The researchers questioned each person about the amount of fruits and vegetables they ate a day. They also conducted annual visits along with either a survey or home interview to determine the mental well-being and extent of any psychiatric disorders among the volunteers.

The researchers amassed weekly vegetable and fruit consumption reporting and compared this with moods and psychiatric profiles of the subjects. They scaled a mental well-being rating for each along with a life satisfaction rating for each subject.

The data concluded that well-being and life satisfaction levels were dramatically higher among those who ate more fruits and vegetables.

Those who ate fruits every day had more than three times the life satisfaction levels than those who ate fruits from one to three days each week. Those who ate vegetables every day had over 70 percent higher levels of life satisfaction compared to those who ate veggies one to three days a week.

As for mental well-being, those who ate fruit every day had over double the levels of mental well-being scores compared to eating fruits for between one and three days. And eating vegetables daily resulted in about triple the scores of mental well-being compared to those who ate vegetables for between one and three days.

The researchers also found that increasing fruit and vegetable consumption significantly boosted moods and life satisfaction levels among those studied. For example, increasing vegetable consumption from never to four to six times a week boosted moods and life satisfaction to levels seen in getting married.

They also found that increasing the frequency of fruit and vegetable consumption significantly had a life satisfaction equivalent of an unemployed person finding a job.

They found that those that eat more of these foods have better moods and a better psychological state. Just eating one extra portion of fruits and vegetables a day has a positive effect equivalent to around eight extra days of walking a month for at least 10 minutes at a time according to their analysis.

This mood-boosting effect of fruits and veggies was particularly strong for women. It also worked with different types of diets. But when dietary changes were combined with exercise, even greater improvements resulted.

A study from the University of Manchester (Firth *et al.* 2019) led by Dr. Joseph Firth analyzed 16 studies that totaled 45,826 volunteers. The researchers found that improving one's diet and the nutritional quality of the diet with respect to more fruits and vegetables significantly decreased symptoms of depression. Diets with more nutrition also boosted mental well-being.

The research also established that a general boost in dietary quality – rather than special diets – can benefit the person in terms of moods and depression, according to Dr. Firth:

> *"The similar effects from any type of dietary improvement suggests that highly-specific or specialized diets are unnecessary for the average individual."*

Study co-author Dr Brendon Stubbs, who also teaches at the King's College London, concluded the results by stating:

> *"Our data add to the growing evidence to support lifestyle interventions as an important approach to tackle low mood and depression."*

The study also found that benefits of diet improvement affected women in a more broad way compared to men. This is consistent with other research finding that a woman's body tends to be more sensitive to nutrients and supplements, and drug side-effects are often greater in women.

A diet for mental well-being

We've discussed the relationship between our moods and our mental well-being in general. Our diet can significantly affect this.

A 2019 cognitive health study from Germany's Charite' University (Gehlich *et al.* 2019) tested 22,635 adults from 11 countries around Europe. The study began in 2011 and all participants were tested for their diets. They were also tested for short- and long-term memory, depression, quality of life, mobility and other criteria indicating their general physical and mental well-being.

The researchers found that those who ate more fruits and vegetables had significantly better cognitive and mental health.

The scientists concluded:

> *"Frequent consumption of fruits and vegetables is associated with improved health outcomes, including cognitive and mental health."*

In a diet study from Harvard University (Yuan *et al.* 2019) researchers analyzed 20 years of diet data on 28,000 male health professionals. The men had completed diet questionnaires every four years regarding what they were eating. The study began when the men were 51 years old on average. Within the last four years of the end of the study, they were tested on their thinking and memory skills.

Those who ate the most fruits and vegetables in the years before the thinking questions had the best thinking and memory skills.

The researchers also found that those who ate six or more servings a day of vegetables had a 34 percent less likelihood of developing poor thinking and memory during the 20 years compared to those who ate two servings of veggies.

Orange juice was a surprise winner in this study. The researchers found those who drank more orange juice had a 47 percent less chance of developing poor thinking and memory compared to those who drank less than one serving of orange juice per month. This is consistent with other research finding that citrus boosts cognition.

Researchers from the UK's University of Leeds and University of York (Ocean *et al.* 2018) analyzed and followed about 50,000 people in the United Kingdom over a period of 8 years (from 2009 to 2017).

The researchers questioned each person about the amount of fruits and vegetables they ate a day. They also conducted annual visits along with either a survey or home interview to determine the mental well-being and extent of any psychiatric disorders among the volunteers.

The researchers amassed weekly vegetable and fruit consumption reporting and compared this with moods and psychiatric profiles of the subjects. They scaled a mental well-being rating for each along with a life satisfaction rating for each subject.

The data concluded that well-being and life satisfaction levels were dramatically higher among those who ate more fruits and vegetables. Those who ate fruits every day had more than three times the life satisfaction levels than those who ate fruits from one to three days each week. Those who ate vegetables every day had over 70 percent higher levels of life satisfaction compared to those who ate veggies one to three days a week.

As for mental well-being, those who ate fruit every day had over double the levels of mental well-being scores compared to eating fruits for between one and three days. And eating vegetables daily resulted in about triple the scores of mental well-being compared to those who ate vegetables for between one and three days.

The researchers also found that increasing fruit and vegetable consumption significantly boosted moods and life satisfaction levels among those studied. For example, increasing vegetable consumption from never to four to six times a week boosted moods and life satisfaction to levels seen in getting married.

They also found that increasing the frequency of fruit and vegetable consumption significantly had a life satisfaction equivalent of an unemployed person finding a job.

The right diet can help change our moods quickly

A change in the diet doesn't necessarily require eating more fruits and vegetables for many years. Diet changes can also affect young people in a short period of time.

A diet-depression study from Australia's Macquarie University (Francis *et al.* 2019) tested 101 adults between 17 and 35 years old who had symptoms of depression. Using the Australian Guide to Healthy Eating, the researchers had half of the subjects eat a diet consisting of more fruits and vegetables, and other components of the Mediterranean Diet.

After only three weeks, the researchers followed up with the subjects. They found that those who increased their fruit and vegetable consumption had significantly fewer symptoms of depression compared to the control group, maintained their habitual diet.

Previous studies confirm these findings. Scientists from the UK's University of Reading (Lamport *et al.* 2014) reviewed the research on fruits and veggies and cognition. The researchers found that 17 of 19 large population studies found that a steady diet with more fruits, vegetables and juices resulted in better cognitive health among healthy adults.

The research also found three intervention (changing the diet) studies found that fruits and vegetables boost mental well-being. They also found that drinking 100% fruit juices resulted in better cognition.

This and other studies have shown that plant-based foods are alkaline in nature, and thus reduce the formation and damage of free radicals, which can produce a variety of mental and physical disorders as we age.

Plant-based foods neutralize these free radicals because plants produce antioxidants in order to protect themselves from the onslaught of environmental toxins. These antioxidants transfer to us through these foods.

Raw fruits and vegetables

In a study from New Zealand's University of Otago (Brookie *et al.* 2018) researchers found that eating certain raw fruits and vegetables improve our mental health. The research, headed by Dr. Tamlin Conner, tested 422 people who were between 18 and 25 years old living in the United States and New Zealand.

The subjects were given diet surveys and mental health questionnaires to establish their mental health. Symptoms that were tested for include:
- depression symptoms
- anxiety symptoms
- moods (positive and negative)
- life satisfaction

In terms of the moods, positive mood symptoms included being enthusiastic, excited, energetic, joyful, happy, cheerful, pleasant, good, relaxed, calm, content, and/or satisfied. Meanwhile, negative moods included feeling hostility, stress, irritable, angry, anxious, annoyed, nervous, tense, hopeless, unhappy, dejected, and/or sad.

In order to separate other relationships between mental health, the researchers also established the subjects' sleep, body mass index, physical activity, smoking, socio-economic status and alcohol consumption. By separated the subjects' mental health from these potential relationships. This helped the researchers isolate the relationship between diet and mental health.

Dr. Conner and her research team found that the more raw fruits and vegetables the subjects ate, the less mental health issues the subjects had. In particular, they found that greater raw fruit and veggie consumption led to reduced symptoms of depression, more positive moods and greater life satisfaction scores compared to those who ate less fresh fruit and vegetables.

The general result is that those who ate more raw fruits and veggies were found to be "flourishing" as compared to those who ate more processed foods.

The researchers concluded:

> *"Raw fruits and vegetable intake, but not processed fruit and vegetable intake, significantly predicted higher mental health outcomes when controlling for the covariates. Applications include recommending the consumption of raw fruits and vegetables to maximize mental health benefits."*

The only outlier was that those who ate more processed vegetables were found to have less depression symptoms compared to those who ate less vegetables in general. That also illustrates that when raw veggies aren't available, processed ones are better than none.

But it is clear that raw fruits and vegetables are better. As stated by Psychology Doctoral Candidate Kate Brooks, part of the research team in this study:

> *"Our research has highlighted that the consumption of fruit and vegetables in their unmodified state is more strongly associated with better mental health compared to cooked/canned/processed fruit and vegetables."*

Which foods are better?

The researchers also ranked the foods that were most associated with improved mental health. Here is top ten list, ranked:

- Carrots
- Bananas
- Apples
- Dark leafy greens
- Spinach
- Grapefruit
- Lettuce
- Citrus fruits
- Berries
- Cucumber
- Kiwifruit

While cooked foods were not as helpful as raw fruits and vegetables, a few cooked foods got close. These included:
- Asparagus
- Broccoli
- Dark leafy greens
- Sweet potato
- Zucchini
- Onions/leeks
- Eggplant/aubergine

As far as foods that were most associated with poor mental health, these included any processed meals and foods in general. But significant offenders included candy, French fries and soda.

A study from the UK and Australia's University of Queensland (Mujcic and Oswald 2016) found that eating raw fruits and vegetables significantly improved mental health and decreased symptoms of anxiety and depression.

In a study from the Physicians Committee for Responsible Medicine, researchers found that eating a plant-based diet decreased symptoms of depression, anxiety and fatigue, while boosting well-being, general health, daily functioning, and impairment.

Another study from the UK and Aussie researchers (Mujcic and Oswald *et al.* 2019) found that eating more fruits and vegetables also impacts clinical symptoms and diagnosis of depression and anxiety. The researchers stated:

"We show, in Australian data, that an equivalent result may be true for actual clinical diagnosis of depression and anxiety. We conclude that there appears to be accumulating evidence for the psychological power of fruit and vegetables."

There are a few other studies that have shown that our food choices can indeed help reduce depression. A study from the University of Sydney (Gopinath *et al.* 2016) tested 2,334 people over 55 years old and 1,952 people over 60 years old. The researchers found those with the highest vegetable consumption had a 41 percent lower incidence of depression symptoms. They also found a similar correlation between fruit and vegetable consumption and depression.

The scientists also found that those whose diets had more fiber consumption also had lower incidence of depression.

A study from Yonsei University in the Republic of Korea (Gardner *et al.* 2014) found that healthy food choices improved moods.

For this research the scientists conducted four experiments that tested foods and moods. Their research found that healthy foods produced more positive moods compared to "indulgent foods." A few other studies have found similar relationships.

The bottom line of these studies is clear: Eating raw fruits and vegetables improves our moods and reduces the risk of depression and anxiety. Why? The reason relates to the micronutrients - or phytochemicals - that are contained in fruits and vegetables. The word 'phyto' refers to "plant." Researcher Kate Brooks highlighted this in her comments:

"This likely limits the delivery of nutrients that are essential for optimal emotional functioning,"

Research from the Physicians Committee for Responsible Medicine determined that a diet rich in plant-based foods significantly reduces anxiety, depression and fatigue. The research followed 292 men and women with a body mass index of 25 or more and/or a diagnosis of type 2 diabetes. The subjects were divided into two groups. One group was given advice to increase their consumption of plant-based foods and the other group was advised not to change their diet.

After 18 weeks, the researchers found the plant-based diet group had significantly improved scores in anxiety, depression and fatigue. The plant-based diet group also had less work impairment and less sick days at work.

The plant-based diet group had improved cholesterol, reduced diabetes risk and greater weight reductions compared to the beginning of the study and compared to the control group.

The Physicians Committee for Responsible Medicine is a preventive medicine organization with a membership of 10,000 medical doctors.

Phytochemicals and brain health

Fresh foods contain phytochemicals that help the brain. These include polyphenols such as flavonoids, phenolic acids, stilbenes;, carotenoids such as beta-carotene, zeaxanthin and beta-cryptoxanthin; tocopherols and tocotrienols; and many others.

Many of these micronutrients from foods are heat-sensitive. This means when the foods are cooked, many of these micronutrients will be lost. The cooked foods will no longer contain the micronutrient. Or the cooked food will contain significantly less of the compound.

Then of course there are a variety of other nutrients. These include all the vitamins and minerals that we typically see on nutrient panels of our vitamin supplements.

There are a number of good food-source supplements that contain many of these vitamins and minerals. But because many of these are also heat-sensitive, supplements will not contain the same nutrient found in raw foods.

A good example of this is vitamin E. A vitamin supplement will typically contain alpha-tocopherol. But as we've discussed, there are many other forms of vitamin E found in raw foods. These include:
- alpha-tocopherol
- beta-tocopherol
- gamma-tocopherol
- delta-tocopherol
- alpha-tocotrienol
- beta-tocotrienol
- gamma-tocotrienol

• delta-tocotrienol

As shown in the research linked above, these forms of vitamin E have a number of great benefits that alpha-tocopherol alone doesn't have. Many of these forms of vitamin E are heat-sensitive.

And that is only one example. There are literally thousands of different compounds found in raw fruits and vegetables. And many of these are heat sensitive.

The solution is obvious from the research above. For these and other studies, the World Health Organization recommends that we eat between five and eight servings of fresh fruits and vegetables every day. This equate, according to their research, to between 400 grams and 600 grams of raw fruits and vegetables.

If we follow the examples of scientists, and eat at least five servings of raw fruits and vegetables every day, we will have better protection against mental health issues.

Foods that Boost Neurotransmitters

As we've discussed, between each nerve and brain cell sits in a special bath called neurotransmitter fluid. The composition of our neurotransmitter fluid is directly associated with our mood and nervous condition. And neurotransmitters are directly linked to our diet. In fact, certain foods will increase good neurotransmitters, while others will increase levels of neurotransmitters that increase our risk of allergies, stress and cognitive problems.

A study from Italy's Tourette's Syndrome and Movement Disorders Center (Briguglio *et al.* 2018) investigated the effects of diet on neurotransmitters. Some foods, they found, directly supply neurotransmitters.

These include fruits, plant foods, roots, and other plant-based foods. Here are some foods that directly supply neurotransmitters needed for healthy moods and a healthy nervous system:

Dopamine

As discussed earlier, dopamine is critical to moods and muscles, and contribute to a positive attitude. Here are some foods that contain significant amounts of dopamine:

- Banana peels
- Bananas
- Avocados

- Velvet beans

Modest levels:
- Oranges
- Forest apple (*Malus sylvestris*)
- Tomatoes
- Spinach
- Peas
- Common beans
- Aubergine

Serotonin

Serotonin helps us relax and keep our moods positive. A healthy diet of whole carbohydrate foods such as whole potatoes and whole grain pastas help provide the ingredients for serotonin making, including L-tryptophan.

However, some foods will directly supply the body with 5-HT, the body's precursor for serotonin. Here are some foods that supply the body with 5-HT:
- Prata banana (*Musa* sp.)
- Banana peels
- Bananas
- Red pepper (*Capsicum annuum*)
- Hazelnuts
- Pineapples
- Plums
- Passionfruit
- Kiwis
- Velvet beans
- Spinach
- Chinese cabbage
- Wild rice
- Green coffee beans
- Pomegranate
- Strawberries
- Chicory

- Green onion
- Lettuce
- Nettles

GABA

GABA stands for gamma-aminobutyric acid, and necessary to relax and sleep. GABA is typically synthesized from glutamic acid in the body and many do not produce enough of this during times of stress. But some foods will specifically provide or increase GABA levels in the body. Here are some significant sources:

- Spinach
- Potatoes
- Sweet potatoes
- Kale
- Broccoli
- Shiitake mushrooms
- Chestnuts
- Lupin bean sprouts
- Adzuki bean sprouts
- Soybean sprouts
- Pea sprouts
- Common bean sprouts
- Wheat
- Barley
- Oryza rice (white, black, brown and red rices)
- Buckwheat sprouts
- Green tomatoes
- Mistletoe
- Valerian
- St. John's Wort
- Passionflower

Acetylcholine

This neurotransmitter improves our moods and leads to better balance and calm nerve-muscle responses.

Many foods will either directly supply acetylcholine or provide the metabolites to form it. These include:

- Squash
- Spinach
- Peas
- Radishes
- Mung beans
- Common beans
- Bitter orange
- Wild strawberry
- Nettles
- Mistletoe
- Foxglove

Foods that stimulate problematic neurotransmitters

We've also discussed some of the neurotransmitters that are not that good if their levels are too high. This includes histamine and glutamate, which can increase stress and tension within muscles and nerves. Too much histamine is also involved in skin hives and allergic responses, such as anaphylactic responses.

Foods that can directly increase our body's histamine levels include processed meats, wine, sherry, champagne, cheese, beer, ketchup, soybeans and dandelion.

Then there is glutamate. Higher glutamate levels can lead to increased stress and allergic responses. This includes monosodium glutamate. Foods that increase our body's glutamate levels include meats, fish, cheese, soy sauce, cod, salami, caviar, instant coffee, oysters, Parmesan cheese and other processed foods.

This is also why we often notice that people who eat a diet with plenty of plant-based foods tend to be more relaxed, and sharp. And those who eat a diet rich in red meats and alcohol tend to be more stressed and sometimes even more aggressive. This is due to their balance of neurotransmitters.

For example, a study from the University of Copenhagen (Hansen *et al.* 2018) found that the Western Diet, with higher levels of meat and fat, was linked with differences in neurotransmitters, cognition and brain signaling. They also saw higher levels of oxidative stress in the brain. The researchers wrote:

"Western diets, high in fat and energy, are associated with cognitive deficits in humans and animal models."

The bottom line is that a wholesome diet with plenty of fresh plant-based foods will create a balanced neurotransmitter fluid, resulting in reduced depressive moods and less anxiety.

Fiber and Post-traumatic Stress

As discussed earlier, post-traumatic stress disorder (PTSD) will often include bouts of anxiety and depression. Researchers have found that those who consume more fiber have a lower incidence of PTSD.

Plant fiber yields a number of benefits, including cardiovascular health and digestive health. Fiber also helps reduce the risk of breast cancer and reduces the risk of diabetes among children. Surprisingly, it also reduces the harmful effects of second-hand smoking.

What is fiber?

Fiber is often thought of as a supplement, like psyllium husk from a bottle. These forms of fiber, however, actually offer very little fiber compared to the amount of fiber offered by raw fruits and vegetables.

The best known form of edible fiber comes from the cellulose content in plants. But there are other forms of healthy fiber. Fiber can be divided generally into two types: Soluble fiber and insoluble fiber.

Insoluble fiber is called this because it will not dissolve in water. This also makes it difficult for the digestive enzymes in the stomach and upper intestines to break them down.

Insoluble fiber comes in the form of cellulose, wheat bran, and lignans.

Soluble fiber, which can dissolve in water, is often fermented by the gut's probiotics. That is, with some exceptions. Examples of soluble fiber include psyllium, beta-glucans from mushrooms, oats and barley, inulin, oligosaccharides, resistant starch and guar gum.

Many dietary fibers are fermented by probiotics in the gut. By fermented, we mean that our gut's probiotics utilize them as nutrient sources, resulting in probiotic colony (CFU) expansion.

Research connecting fiber and PTSD

In a 2021 study, researchers from the University of Toronto and the University of Hawaii (Davison *et al.*) analyzed the data from 27,211 Canadians. The Canadian Longitudinal Study on Aging (CLSA) study revealed much about the health and lifestyle among those with a broad Western Diet.

The researchers screened that data to investigate those adults who were middle-aged to older who had been diagnosed with post-traumatic stress disorder (PTSD).

Then the researchers investigated these folks with regard to their diets and lifestyles. They screened out the influences relating to various socioeconomics and health.

The researchers found PTSD was higher among those who had lower incomes, those who were widowed or divorced, or separated.

PTSD was also more prevalent among those who were smokers at some point. Also those with multiple chronic health conditions and chronic pain were more likely to have PTSD.

Nutritionally, there was also a definite trend among those with PTSD. PTSD sufferers were more likely to have poor nutrition. They were also ate more pastries and chocolates. PTSD sufferers were also more likely to have more weight in the mid-section.

Furthermore, those who included at least two or three sources of fiber in their daily diet were significantly less likely to have PTSD.

Notably, these nutritional issues are connected, because pastries and chocolates and other foods of lower nutrient quality are also absent of fiber.

Foods with greater fiber not only render better probiotic colonies. They also typically have significant quantities of nutrients because fiber-rich foods are more minimally processed.

When foods are separated from their fibers during processing, those processing practices also tend to exert more heat and light, destroying many of the micronutrients that the body needs to facilitate cognitive functions.

They also help our bowel movements and capture toxins, reducing toxin release in the bloodstream.

The brain is our body's biggest user of glucose and nutrients by far. The brain cells require constant stimulation in the form of nutrition-rich red blood cells.

Diet for PMDD and Menopause

In the first chapter we discussed mood disorders in these two categories - premenstrual dysphoric disorder (PMDD) and menopause. We discussed the evidence showing that anxiety and depression conditions in these two areas were not directly related to the availability of estrogen.

So we must look to other potential solutions. From the evidence, these likely relate to diet, as we have discussed in this chapter. With that, we can find evidence in a clinical study on menopausal women.

This study, from doctors at the medical college at Italy's University of Molise (Davinelli et al. 2017) tested 60 menopausal women who were between 50 and 55 years old. They were divided into two groups. One was given a placebo, while the other group was given 200 milligrams of fermented soy per day.

The women were tested before and after a 12-week supplementation period. Testing included the Menopause Rating Scale (MRS), the Hamilton Rating Scale for Depression (HAM-D) and the Nottingham Health Profile (NHP) to assess their sleep quality.

After 12 weeks of supplementation, the women given the fermented soy showed significantly improvements in a number of menopausal symptoms. They also had significant improvement in the HAM-D testing and reported better sleep quality.

Fermented soy and soy in general – along with a number of other legumes and whole grains – contain significant levels of equol and resveratrol (the 200 milligrams of fermented soy contained 10 milligrams of equol and 25 milligrams of resveratrol). Many fruits also contain resveratrol.

Equol is a type of estrogen converted from daidzein and genistein using our intestinal probiotics. Sources of these percursers of equol include beansprouts, chickpeas, split peas, red kidney beans, French beans, lentils and many other types of beans and peas (Liggins et al. 2000).

These foods are classified as phytoestrogenic foods. Phytoestrogens will attach to estrogen receptors in a milder fashion compared to estrogen replacement therapy.

Since hormone replacement apparently offers only minor benefits for mood disorders in menopausal women, and equol sources apparently offer significant benefits, we can surmise that phytoestrogen foods such as the ones listed above provide a clearer strategy to reduce anxiety and depression symptoms in menopausal women.

Whether these foods can also reduce the mood conditions seen in PMDD or not is yet to be studied to my knowledge. Since there are no side effects for eating these healthy foods, it would seem worth a try.

Vitamin C

Research has confirmed that vitamin C is more than just an antioxidant. It also elevates moods, reduces depressive symptoms, stress and distress, and reduces anxiety.

Researchers from Canada's McGill University (Wang *et al.* 2013) working with the Jewish General Hospital in Montreal, divided 52 elderly patients among acute care medical centers into two groups. They gave each either 500 milligrams of vitamin C or 5,000 IU of vitamin D each day for ten days.

Utilizing the Profile of Mood States-B test and the Distress Thermometer test, the researchers found that after an average of 8.2 days, the vitamin C reduced mood disturbance by 71% and reduced psychological distress by 51%.

Meanwhile, the vitamin D supplementation had no significant mood effects.

In their conclusion the researchers noted that hospital patients often have lower levels of vitamin C, so the researchers hypothesized that vitamin C's effect may be limited to those who are deficient in vitamin C intake.

Vitamin C's effect upon moods has also been found among diabetics. Another study found that the antioxidant can significantly reduce stress and anxiety among type 2 diabetic patients.

The research (Mazloom *et al.* 2013) divided 45 diabetes mellitus patients into three groups. For six weeks, they gave one group 1,000 milligrams per day of vitamin C, and another 400 IU per day of vitamin E. They gave the third group a placebo.

The researchers used a 21-question test called the Depression Anxiety Stress Scale before and after the treatment period.

After the six weeks, those patients taking the vitamin C experienced a significant reduction in anxiety levels. The other two groups experienced no difference in anxiety.

Yes, patients with diabetes mellitus often suffer from anxiety, depression and stress. This was theorized as diabetes producing greater oxidative stress within the cells and tissues, which impacts brain cells and the production of mood neurotransmitters.

Vitamin C and microvascular function

A clue in vitamin C's ability to affect moods may have something to do with its effect upon our metabolism.

Researchers from the University of Wisconsin (Limberg *et al.* 2013) studied 45 obese adults who were in their early thirties. They found that vitamin C infusions increased blood vessel smooth muscle communications among small capillaries and blood vessels.

This indicates that vitamin C increased the body's ability to transport blood through our microvascular system.

And where is microvascular function most critical? Within our brains.

Our brain cells and nervous system are fueled with oxygen and nutrients supplied through some of the body's smallest (micro) blood vessels.

As these vessels lose their flexibility from oxidative damage, our brain cells suffer because they don't get enough nutrients. As other research has found, microvascular damage among the brain can significantly affect moods and anxiety levels – in addition to increasing the likelihood of dementias such as Alzheimer's disease.

Citrus is not the highest source of vitamin C

Most assume citrus is the best place to get our vitamin C. But there are several foods that are better than citrus for vitamin C.

These include guavas at 228 milligrams per 100 grams (about half a cup or so), yellow bell peppers and black currants at over 180 milligrams per 100 grams, red chili peppers at over 140 milligrams per 100 grams, kale at 130 milligrams per 100 grams and gold kiwis at 105 milligrams per 100 grams.

Tomatoes are also a rich source when the water is taken into account. Sun-dried tomatoes contain over 100 milligrams per 100 grams.

In comparison, an orange contains a little over 53 milligrams per 100 grams.

Note that natural vitamin C sources also contain bioflavonoids and minerals that aid in the absorption and utilization of vitamin C.

Conclusion on Diet

This chapter contains a number of helpful hints in terms of which foods to include in our diet. These are primarily foods in the fruits and vegetables category.

This said, what diet is best for mood disorders? This information provides a roadmap for several diets. These include a vegan diet, a vegetarian diet and the Mediterranean diet.

In 2013, Researchers from the University of Athens School of Medicine (Psaltopoulou *et al.* 2013) conducted a review of research that studied the connection between the Med diet and the risk of stroke, depression, cognitive impairment, and Parkinson's disease. They found 22 well-designed studies that followed many thousands of patients.

Their meta-analysis of these studies found that the Mediterranean diet reduced the risk of depression by 32%, reduced the risk of stroke by 29%, and reduced the risk of cognitive impairment by 40%.

For more information on diet, consider the *Ancestor's Diet* by the author.

Chapter Four

Our Probiotics and Our Moods

It seems unbelievable that tiny bacteria that are thought to only occupy our intestines will improve our moods and help fight depression and anxiety. Well, there is more to it than this. As we'll discuss the science, it turns out that probiotics inhabit more than our intestines.

But even those that do inhabit our intestines will also help improve our moods and emotions. This not anecdotal opinion. It has been proven scientifically. Let's take a look at some of the research.

Scientists and doctors from the UK's Brighton and Sussex Medical School analyzed seven studies in a review published in the British Medical Journal (Noonan *et al.* 2020). The studies investigated whether probiotics could reduce depressive symptoms. The research found 11 out of 12 probiotics studied produced "measurable reductions in depression."

Research from the Netherlands' Leiden Institute for Brain and Cognition (Steenbergen *et al.* 2015) found that supplementing probiotic can reduce negative and aggressive thinking. The research followed and tested 40 healthy people over four weeks in a triple-blind study. They were split into two groups, with one group given a daily probiotic supplement containing seven species of probiotics.

The subjects were tested with a questionnaire that measured their cognitive reactivity and depressed moods. The researchers used the Leiden Index of Depression Sensitivity (LEIDS), which measures negative and depressed thinking. After four weeks, the researchers found that the probiotic group had significantly lower scores on the LEIDS test – including on aggression, control, hopelessness, risk aversion and rumination – compared to the placebo group.

> *"The study demonstrated for the first time that a four-week, multispecies probiotic intervention has a positive effect on cognitive reactivity to naturally occurring changes in sad mood in healthy individuals not currently diagnosed with a depressive disorder,"* the researchers concluded.

Researchers have also been investigating the effects of probiotics on brain health. And it appears probiotics can affect our moods and even our thinking habits and our feelings of stress.

Do you have dysbiosis?

Dysbiosis is a state where the body has an imbalance between probiotic populations and pathogenic bacteria populations. In other words, the system is being overrun by the pathogenic bacteria and there are not enough probiotics in place to control their populations.

When the body is lacking probiotics, or is overgrown with pathobiotic populations, there is typically an intestinal infection of some type. The extent of the infection, of course, depends upon the type of pathogenic bacteria present, and their populations in proportion to probiotic populations.

Many disorders can be traced back to dysbiosis. Some are direct and obvious, and some are not so obvious, and often appear as other disorders. In general, most digestive disorders are either caused by or accompanied by a lack of balanced intestinal probiotic populations. There are several types of dysbiosis.

We can usually detect *putrefaction dysbiosis* from the incidence of slow bowel movement. Symptoms of putrefaction dysbiosis include depression, diarrhea, fatigue, memory loss, numbing of hands and feet, sleep disturbances, joint pain and muscle weakness.

Many of these disorders and others are often due directly to the overgrowth of pathobiotics. The bacteria are burdening the blood stream with endotoxin waste products and neurotoxins; infecting cells, joints, nerves, brain tissues and other regions of the body.

Probiotics reduce stress

We have discussed the link between stress and depression. Turns out that probiotics also help our bodies and brains deal with stress.

Researchers from Ireland's University of College Cork (Bravo *et al.* 2011) found that intestinal probiotics reduce stress by reducing corticosterone and altering GABA in the brain.

The study, led by Dr. John Cryan, a professor of anatomy at UCC, studied the probiotic *Bifidobacterium breve* 6330, and its effects upon brain chemistry. Dr. Cryan and co-researchers found that *Bifidobacterium breve* 6330 reduced a component called the brain-derived neurotrophic factor, or BDNF.

The brain-derived neurotrophic factor, or BDNF, is heightened during periods of stress, family separation, and psychological problems. This has been seen among higher levels of corticosterone and digestive difficulties such as irritable gut syndrome (IBS), Crohn's disease and other digestive disorders.

After feeding the probiotic mix to mice, the researchers saw significant reductions in anxiety and stress responses. The research also found that the effect was most notable among the hippocampus – a area of the brain that monitors and regulates stress response in the body.

The implication is that probiotics like *B. breve* are a key link between what has been termed the gut-brain axis. This has prompted many researchers to label the axis the "microbiome-gut-brain axis."

> *"There is increasing evidence revolving around what is now being called the 'microbiome-gut-brain axis,' that suggests there's an interaction between the bacteria in the stomach and intestines, the gut, and the central nervous system," commented Phil Lempert founder of Food Nutrition & Science and CEO of The Lempert Report.*

The ability of probiotics to reduce stress-related digestive issues has been confirmed in clinical human research as well. In 2008, French scientists (Diop *et al.*) gave 64 human volunteers with high levels of stress and incidental gastrointestinal symptoms either a placebo or *L. acidophilus* Rosell-52 and *Bifidobacterium longum* for three weeks. At the end of the three weeks, the stress-related gastrointestinal symptoms of abdominal pain, nausea and vomiting decreased by 49% among the probiotic group.

Probiotics Change Neurotransmitters

Dr. Cryan also led another study (O'Sullivan *et al.* 2011) published in the *Proceedings of the National Academy of Sciences*. In this study, *Lactobacillus rhamnosus* was found to alter GABA expression in the brain in a way that reduced anxiety and depression. The research found that the feeding *L. rhamnosus* to mice increased their levels of GABA among the cortical regions of the brain, while reducing GABA expression in the stress-related hippocampus, amygdala, and prefrontal cortex regions – regions known to be involved in stress response.

GABA, or gamma-aminobutyric acid, has been the subject of considerable research showing that it can regulate nervous responses. While most assume that GABA always inhibits the flow of electrical activity between nerves, it also can increase nerve activity – depending upon when and where it is expressed.

Do probiotics communicate with us?

Who would have thought that the bacteria that dwell not only in our intestines, but in our oral cavity, our sinuses, lungs and elsewhere could have this affect upon our brain's health and even our thinking? The research is now proving these realities.

Case in point is a study published in *Nutritional Neuroscience* (Mohammadi *et al.* 2015). The researchers tested 70 adults who were divided into three groups. The testing lasted six weeks. One group was given 100 grams a day of a probiotic yogurt in addition to a placebo capsule. Another group was given a non-probiotic yogurt plus a multi-species probiotic capsule each day. The third group was given the placebo capsule and the non-probiotic yogurt each day.

Before and after the six weeks of supplementation or not, the 70 workers were tested for mental health and well-being. The General Health Questionnaire measured their feeling of general well-being. And their levels of depression, anxiety and stress were measured using the DASS questionnaire. DASS stands for Depression Anxiety Stress Scales.

The DASS test originated from the University of New South Wales. It measures depression, with includes hopelessness, a lack of self-worth and a lack of interest in life. Anxiety is measured with not only nervousness, but autonomous muscle reactivity. And stress measures ones relaxation states, irritability and impatience.

In addition, blood tests were taken and analyzed for each subject. This was used to test for what is called the hypothalamic-pituitary-adrenal axis. Some consider this a good test for the gut-brain axis. We'll discuss this in a minute.

Both probiotic groups – the group given the probiotic yogurt and the group given the probiotic cap each day – had significant improvement in both well-being and depression, stress and anxiety scores.

Their well-being scores went from 18 to 13.5 in the probiotic yogurt group and from 17 to 9.8 in the probiotic capsule group. (Lower scores in the GHQ show greater sense of well-being). Meanwhile, the placebo group showed no improvement in scores.

In the depression, anxiety and stress testing, the probiotic groups also showed far better improvement over the six weeks. The DASS scores for the probiotic yogurt group went from 23.3 to 13 and the probiotic group went from 18.9 to 9.4 during the six weeks. (A lower score in the DASS test shows reduced levels of depressive symptoms, lower stress and less anxiety). Once again, the placebo yogurt and placebo capsule group showed no change over the six weeks.

While the source of depression often lies within a spiritual context, the brain and its neurochemistry can significantly affect our moods. Neurochemicals such as dopamine and serotonin are significant in this area, because they affect our body's state of relaxation. And this in turn effects how well we can digest – and the general state of our intestinal tract and something called peristalsis.

Another study has illustrated that probiotics can directly affect depressed thinking. A spiraling of negative or depressive thoughts is also called negative thinking.

Researchers from The Netherlands – in a study published in the *Brain, Behavior and Immunity Journal* (Steenbergen *et al.* 2015), studied 40 healthy adults for a month. They gave half the group a probiotic supplement with *Lactobacillus acidophilus, L. salivarius, L. brevis, L. casei, Bifidobacterium bifidum, B. lactis* and *L.actococcus lactis.* The other 20 people were given a placebo for the month.

Afterward the subjects were tested for what is called cognitive reactivity for sad mood. Cognitive reactivity for sad mood is a cognitive behavior term, used in cognitive behavior therapy. When a person has less reactivity to a particular mood, they are more removed from the mood – and in the case of sad mood – in a better state of mind.

The researchers explained that this reduced reactivity was based upon the subjects' reduced levels of depressive or negative thoughts.

Research from Leiden University (Rhee *et al.* 2009) has studied this element of cognitive reactivity to sad moods along with depression. A questionnaire protocol developed at Leiden – called the Leiden Index of Depression Sensitivity (LEIDS) – has been found to help determine to what degree a person's negative thinking leads to an increase in depressed thoughts.

The researchers concluded that probiotics could be a potential treatment for depression:

> *"Probiotics supplementation warrants further research as a potential preventive strategy for depression."*

The link between the brain and the gut has been known for quite some time in medicine- even among the oldest medicine – Ayurveda. Today we trace the mechanism to the fact that between the gut and the brain lies the vagus nerve. Thus the state of our mental well-being will affect our intestinal well-being. But this also works in reverse.

This is typically termed the gut-brain axis. But in this case, we are learning that there is another element of the axis in our gut's microbial health.

Research from Canada's McMaster University (Zhou and Foster 2015 and Foster *et al.* 2013) also focused upon the gut-brain axis. They found evidence linking gastrointestinal conditions such as irritable bowel syndrome to a variety of neurological conditions such as autism and depression.

The link is provided in the reality that microbes signal each other and also signal our nerves and other elements of our body in an attempt to keep everything copasetic. Their survival is certainly linked to ours.

Research from the David Geffen School of Medicine (Ohsie *et al.* 2009) found that within the lining of our intestinal walls contain cells called enterochromaffin cells. These cells allow signals from our gut bacteria to be communicated to our nerve cells. They also allow nerve cell signals to be communicated to our gut bacteria.

We might just consider these cells to be somewhat like little cell phones – allowing communications between our body and our gut bacteria.

Moreover, the researchers found these enterochromaffin cells sent signals directly to and from the vagus nerve. This of course completes the loop between bacteria and our brain.

This is a serious consideration. Research from the California Institute of Technology (Mazmanian *et al.* 2008) tested several types of bacteria with regard to their affects upon gut immunity and gut motility – the ability of the intestines to move our food along.

They found that probiotics such as *B. bifidum* and *L. acidophilus* produce signals that increase gut motility and gut immunity. Meanwhile pathogenic bacteria such as *Escherichia coli* block these processes.

Be serious. Our gut bacteria are communicating with us.

Probiotics Change the Brain

Researchers from UCLA's Geffen School of Medicine (Tillisch *et al.* 2013) have determined that consuming a milk fermented with probiotics changed the brain activity of women.

The UCLA medical researchers divided 36 healthy women into three groups. One group was given a milk fermented with probiotics twice a day. Another group was given a milk without the probiotics. The other group was given no milk product.

Before the study began the women underwent extensive brain MRI studies and brain activity tasking response analyses. Then the women consumed the probiotic or placebo milk for four weeks followed by repeated testing.

Along with the MRI testing, the researchers tested brain responses to emotional faces, as well as during rest. They utilized analyses that tests emotional response.

After the four weeks, those women who drank the probiotic milk had significantly different brain activity changes. Their task-related responses increased, and their activity within the sensory cortex regions changed, which was illustrated during rest periods. Their midbrain connectivity increased, which the researchers concluded probably explained their task-related response increases.

Their altered brain activity also illustrated changes in the brain signaling pathways for emotional responses among the women.

The probiotics in the fermented milk included *Bifidobacterium lactis, Streptococcus thermophilus, Lactobacillus bulgaricus,* and *Lactococcus lac-*

tis. Each of these species has been shown in other clinical studies to improve health among other organs and tissue regions of the body.

Research has also connected the gut's probiotics to the brain via a conduit between the central nervous system and the enteric nervous system. The enteric nervous system is located in the abdominal region around the digestive tract. Many of our neurotransmitters are produced in this region and the neurons relay mind-body responses between the gut and the brain stem.

The researchers concluded:

> *"Four weeks intake of a fermented milk with probiotics by healthy women affected activity of brain regions that control central processing of emotion and sensation."*

The research was led by Dr. Emeran A. Mayer, a UCLA professor of medicine and a specialist in gastroenterology. He is the Director of the Oppenheimer Center for Neurobiology of Stress. Dr. Mayer is well-known for his research in identifying the gut and its probiotic content as "the second brain."

Probiotics can improve our moods and even improve sleep quality. Is this just a gut-brain axis issue or are there bacteria living in our brains?

The assumption of conventional medicine over the past century has been that the brain is basically sterile. Unless it is infected with bacteria or a virus – such as in bacterial or viral meningitis. But is this proven out completely?

Surely, scientists readily find many species of bacteria in dead brains. But the assumption of conventional medicine has been that the brain was exposed to these species after the patient died in those cases.

Confusing the issue, has been increasing research connecting the use of internal probiotic supplements with less anxiety and depression. We also showed how probiotics can improve bipolar disorder. Now we are discovering that certain probiotic species actually improve moods and sleep.

Furthermore, there is documented evidence showing that Alzheimer's disease is readily linked to gum diseases such as gingivitis. This evidence shows that bacteria are leaking into the bloodstream and infecting nerve and brain cells.

How could they do this if the brain was devoid of bacteria? And how can gut probiotics affect the brain so meaningfully from so far away? The assumption of the gut-brain axis – through the vagus nerve – has not truly been put to the test. Yes, there is evidence that the vagus nerve can be affected by bacteria. But how does that occur? Are bacteria talking to nerve cells?

There is certainly room for that either way. Truly, bacteria in the gut may well affect the vagus nerve through the production of certain chemicals that turn on or off nerve responses. But bacteria may also arrive in the brain as well, as we'll discuss.

The problem, of course, is that we don't have the equipment to trace living bacteria within a living body. We might have CT-scans and X-rays, but these do not image bacteria. Unless of course, the bacteria were somehow colored with a radioactive element. But that produces other potential problems.

Before we discuss this issue of brain bacteria in more depth, let's review some research proving that probiotics affect our moods and sleep.

In a 2019 study, researchers from the University of Verona studied 38 healthy people over a four-month period. The researchers randomly divided the patients into two groups. One group was given a 4 billion CFU blend of probiotic bacteria for six weeks. The probiotic species were *Lactobacillus fermentum, L. rhamnosus, L. plantarum, and Bifidobacterium longum.*

The other group was given a placebo supplement.

Before the study began, each of the subjects was assessed for mood behavior, sleep quality and personality issues. They were also assessed for anxiety, depression and anger. Then after three weeks, the subjects were all tested again for the same parameters. Then at the end of the six weeks, and three weeks after stopping the supplement, the subjects were all tested the same, comparing their scores with before the test.

The researchers found that the group taking the probiotics had significant mood improvements. They also had significantly reduced levels of depression, anger and fatigue.

The probiotics group also reported better sleep after taking the probiotics, using several tests, including the Leiden Index of Depression Sensitivity-Revised Test (LEIDS-R), the State Trait Anxiety

Inventory (STAI), the Beck Depression Inventory (BDI), the Profile of Mood State (POM), and the Pittsburgh Sleep Quality Index (PSQI)

The study showed similarly significant results in the other tests, and for the sleep quality, the researchers concluded:

> *"More precisely, the experimental group participants reported that their sleep quality improved after 6 weeks of probiotics intake."*

Are there Bacteria in the Brain?

With regard to moods, anger and depression, just how does this work? Of course, the "gut-brain axis." But what if bacteria also inhabit the brain?

In November of 2018, Dr. Rosalinda Roberts and fellow researchers at the University of Alabama in Birmingham disclosed their research findings that show clear evidence of healthy brains incubating probiotic bacteria.

Dr. Roberts is a professor of Psychiatry and the Director of the Alabama Brain Collection. She and her associate researchers published a study abstract at Neuroscience and discussed her findings during their annual meeting.

The study tested postpartum brain samples (those who recently died). These included both human brains and mice brains. Utilizing special electron microscopes, they found 34 cases where the healthy brains were hosting bacteria. They found substantial quantities of the mostly rod-shaped bacteria in the substantia nigra, hippocampus and prefrontal cortex.

Most probiotics are rod-shaped bacteria.

The scientists also found bacteria in other parts of brain tissues, including the striatum, and within intracellular tissues, dendrites, myelin axons and glial cells. Abundant numbers were found within the blood-brain barrier cells.

The researchers virtually eliminated the potential for contamination and noted that hosted brains did not show any signs of inflammation. This would be the case if the bacteria were damaging the brain.

The researchers reported:

> *"The observation that the location of the bacteria was highly specific and deep within the specimens also argues against contamination. Interestingly, there were no structural signs of inflammation in any of the brains examined. It is presently unclear the route of entry bacteria take to the brain, but the evidence of them in axons and at the blood brain barrier supports previous speculation."*

The previous speculation the researchers are identifying:

> *"It has been proposed that bacteria can enter the brain through the blood brain barrier, and/or via nerves that innervate the gut."*

The bottom line is there is clear evidence that probiotic bacteria can climb into nerve cells. This means there is the potential that bacteria actually travel through the vagus nerve from the gut to the brain and this is evidenced by their finding bacteria within the nerve cells and myelin sheaths.

It is not so weird that our gut probiotics are affecting our moods, sleep, depression and anxiety if there are bacteria living in our nerves and brains. And it isn't odd that Alzheimer's is linked to bad oral bacteria either.

Probiotic supplementation has been shown to improve moods. In a study of 132 people from the University of Wales (Benton *et al.* 2007) those who consumed a probiotic drink for three weeks reported significantly better moods than the placebo group.

Probiotics and Bipolar Disorder

Dr. Faith Dickerson and research associates from Johns Hopkins University School of Medicine studied bipolar disorder at a Sheppard Pratt Health System hospital (Dickerson *et al.* 2018).

The researchers tested 66 bipolar patients who had come into the hospital with a manic episode. The patients were randomized, and half were given probiotics in a capsule for six months. The others were given a placebo during the same time.

The researchers found that about 50% of the placebo patients required hospitalization during the study.

But only a third of that number needed hospitalization in the probiotic group.

In other words, the probiotics significantly helped the bipolar patients, to the point where there were only a third of the hospitalizations.

Those patients who took the probiotics also required less treatment. The placebo group required an average of 8.3 days of hospitalization per stay. Meanwhile, the probiotic group only required an average of 2.8 days of hospitalization.

Those who also suffered from systemic inflammation got a significant benefit from the probiotics according to the research results.

The researchers used two strains of probiotics in the supplement. These were *Bifidobacterium lactis* and *Lactobacillus rhamnosus*.

This is important because not all species and strains will work the same. Both of these two species are found in breast milk. They also have been found to help mind-body issues in other studies.

We have discussed other studies that showed probiotics can significantly help depressive symptoms, as well as anxiety. Several probiotic species produced positive results in these studies, including *Lactobacillus acidophilus, L. salivarius, L. brevis, L. casei, Bifidobacterium bifidum,* and B. *lactis.*

As we can see from the above study, there are common species showing positive results.

Other studies have shown that probiotics can significantly alter brain activity as well as emotional responses.

The absolute finding among these studies is that our gut's probiotics affect our moods and our mental well-being.

It only makes sense for us to consider these findings carefully. Especially when so many in modern society are suffering from mental conditions.

Chapter Five

Herbs for Anxiety and Depression

Herbal medicines have been utilized for thousands of years to modulate our moods. Traditional medicines have employed these medicines and have been passing down their benefits and dosage experience from one generation to the next. This means these herbs have been used by billions of people over that period of time.

This long-term use has created a clear understanding of the safety of herbal medicines. This doesn't mean that herbal medicines don't have any negative side effects – some do.

But if employed at the right dosages in the right situations, most herbal medicines have very few if any harmful side effects. This is because most herbal medicines contain dozens if not hundreds of medicinal constituents. And these various constituents have been combined by nature to provide buffers and moderating elements.

Contrasting this, most pharmaceutical drugs have one medicinal constituent. This will create a number of metabolic changes in the body, some causing harmful side effects. This is despite the fact that most pharmaceutical drugs were originally produced as analogues to compounds found within herbal medicines.

For example, in the 1800s, salicin and salicylic acid were isolated from meadowsweet herb and willow bark herb by chemist Raffaele Piria. These natural anti-inflammatory and pain-relieving compounds were utilized for years. But then an analogue version of salicylic acid was synthesized in the lab in the 1850. Eventually, another analogue, acetylsalicylic acid was created by the Bayer company. This became the base compound for Aspirin.

What was interesting is that the analogue salicylic acid and later Aspirin came with a harmful side effect. They harmed the gastrointestinal lining and increase the risk of gastrointestinal bleeding.

But even more interesting is that meadowsweet and willowbark, from which the salicin was derived, are actually healthy to the stomach in addition to helping relieve pain. For this reason, both of these herbs have been historically employed by herbalists to help relieve ulcer and gastrointestinal bleeding.

How can this be? Because meadowsweet and willowbark also contain numerous other medicinal compounds in addition to the salicin content isolated and analogued by the chemists and turned into one of the first pharmaceutical drugs.

The point is that medicinal herbs are extremely complex – far more complex than our pharmaceutical industries. Nature makes herbs with hundreds of different compounds in such a way that make them gentle and kind to our body – as well as robust in their effects from a medicinal context.

This point about herbal medicines having numerous positive effects on the body is applicable to our discussion of depression. We find that while most of the herbs mentioned in this chapter will create numerous health benefit. But they will also directly affect our neurotransmitters and our moods.

This is not my opinion. Nor is it just the opinion of a bunch of herbalists. As I document in this chapter, numerous studies have conclusively found that these herbs can significantly improve our moods by altering our neurotransmitters and thus helping to correct our HPA axis.

Lavender

Lavender has been shown clinically to reduce depressive moods and soothe anxiety. Both aromatherapy and the consumption of the herb has both been studied. Let's take a look at some of this research.

In a clinical study (Bazrafshan *et al.* 2020) of 60 elderly subjects half were given two grams of lavender in a teabag to use twice morning and night in a tea. The other 30 subjects were given a placebo. The study lasted for two weeks.

The subjects were all given the Beck Depression and Spiel Berger Anxiety Inventory tests before and after the study period.

At the end of the two weeks, the average depression scores went from 17.8 to 16.3. The placebo group's score increased during the period, from 16.3 to 18.3.

Meanwhile depression and anxiety state and trait scores also significantly improved among the lavender group but not the placebo group.

The researchers concluded:

> *"The results of the present study showed that consumption of lavender herbal tea can reduce depression and anxiety scores*

and since it is inexpensive and accessible, it is suggested to be used as a complementary treatment in reducing anxiety and depression."

In a study of postpartum depression, researchers (Kianpour *et al.* 2016) tested 140 women who were admitted to the hospital for birthing.

The researchers randomly divided the women into two groups. One group was given aromatherapy and the other was not given aromatherapy after delivery.

The aromatherapy consisted of three drops of lavender essential oil every eight hours for a period of four weeks.

The researchers tested each mother with the 21-item Depression, Anxiety, and Stress Scale and the Edinburgh stress, anxiety, and depression Scale tests before and after the aromatherapy period.

The researchers found that the stress, anxiety and depression scores for the women at one month and three months after delivery were significantly lower in the aromatherapy group compared to the non-aromatherapy group.

Lavender essential oil can alleviate premenstrual emotional mood changes, say scientists. This confirms other research showing Lavender aromatherapy produces overall calming effects.

Research from Japan's Shitennoji University and Kyoto University (Matsumoto *et al.* 2013) tested 17 women with an average age of 20 years old who experienced premenstrual emotional symptoms in the late luteal phase of their menstrual cycle.

The women were selected from Shitennoji University after the researchers conducted medical questionnaires and medical histories from a larger group of women.

The women were tested during two different monthly cycles.

Their cycle phases were determined by measuring their body temperatures and their levels of estrone and pregnanediol-3-glucuronide – taken from urine samples.

During the first test, half the women inhaled the scent of Lavender essential oil – generally called aromatherapy – for ten minutes. The other half of the women were tested using water as a control.

During the second test, the control group inhaled the Lavender aromatherapy while the other group was tested with the control.

The researchers tested the effects of the aromatherapy using two different measurements. The first was heart rate variability (HRV) measured by electrocardiograph. Other research has established that reduced heart rate variability (HRV) is associated with increased stress and anxiety and related symptoms.

The other measurement used to test their emotional states was the Profile of Mood States index – a standardized test that uses a five-point scale (ranging from "not at all" to "extremely") for 65 different adjectives describing a subject's current state of mind and mood. Examples include "irritability," "fatigue" and so on.

The researchers found from both tests that the groups inhaling the Lavender had increased heart rate variability – indicating improved moods and reduced stress. They also found that the Profile of Mood States test results were significantly better in the Lavender aromatherapy groups compared to the two control groups.

Some of the more significant improvements in the Profile of Mood States test were in the depression, dejection and confusion categories. These three categories are typically lower for premenstrual syndrome sufferers.

The improved symptoms of the Lavender aromatherapy groups continued for up to 35 minutes following the ten-minute aromatherapy.

The researchers surmised that the improvement from Lavender aromatherapy was due to Lavender affecting the women's parasympathetic nervous system:

> *"This study indicates that short-term inhalation of Lavender could alleviate premenstrual emotional symptoms and could, at least in part, contribute to the improvement of parasympathetic nervous system activity."*

Lavender boosts serotonin

Meanwhile, Lavender aromatherapy shows promise as a natural and safe way to boost serotonin levels. Recent research from China's School of Pharmaceutical Sciences indicates that Lavender essential oil aromatherapy elicits the stimulation of both serotonin and dopamine from the brain – both of which can elevate moods and produce calmness.

Confirming this, researchers from Taiwan's Taipei Medical University Hospital (Chien *et al.* 2012) found that Lavender aromatherapy elevated moods and increased sleep quality in a clinical study of 67 women who were aged between 45 and 55 years old.

This study also showed that Lavender increased heart rate variability – another sign of serotonin boosting - among the women.

This is likely also why lavender aromatherapy also reduces depression. We'll discuss aromatherapy methods later on.

The Japanese researchers analyzed their Lavender essential oil and determined the major constituents included about 75% linalyl acetate and linalool, as well as ocimene, caryophyllene, ocimene and lavendulyl acetate.

Lavender (*Lavandula* sp.) aromatherapy has been used for centuries by herbal practitioners for calming anxiety and for mood disorders. There are more than three dozen medicinal varieties of Lavender, and Lavender's recorded use dates back over two thousand years.

St. John's Wort

The pharmaceutical industry is threatened by St. John's Wort. That's because study after study has shown that this natural herb effectively and safely treats depression just as well as antidepressants but without the serious side effects. This is a threat to the pharmaceutical companies because one in four Americans in their 40s and 50s are now taking antidepressants.

As a result of this threat, we find repeated warnings about St. John's Wort, as though it is somehow dangerous. But the reality is, most of the adverse effects purported in these reports are produced when the herb is taken along with pharmaceutical medications.

This isn't to say that St. John's Wort (*Hypericum perforatum*) is free of potential side effects. When it is correctly prescribed and taken, the research clearly proves it is a safe and effective medicinal herb.

Really?

Researchers from the Akasha Center for Integrative Medicine and the Pardee RAND Graduate School (Apaydin *et al.* 2016) investigated the clinical research on St. John's Wort for treating major depressive disorder.

The researchers used two independent reviewer systems to screen and assess clinical studies for bias and quality. The Cochrane Risk of Bias assessment was used to qualify bias and quality.

The researchers found 35 clinical studies that treated depression patients for at least four weeks with St. John's Wort. They were all placebo-controlled and randomized.

In all, the clinical studies treated nearly 7,000 depression patients with St. John's Wort or placebo. The treatments utilized an extract that used 0.3 % hypericin and 1-4 % hyperforin, or a placebo.

The researchers found that compared to placebo, St. John's Wort was effective at treating major depression by an average of 53 percent. The clinical results also found that St. John's Wort's effectiveness closely matched the effectiveness of pharmaceutical antidepressants.

> "The included studies showed the efficacy of St. John's Wort for depression symptoms was comparable to antidepressant medication, with St. John's Wort being neither inferior nor superior."

In terms of remission, St. John's Wort treatments resulted in remission 17 percent more than the use of antidepressants, though the researchers could not qualify this as significant:

> "Patients who received St. John's Wort did not experience remission from depression at statistically significantly lower or higher rates than patients who received antidepressants."

Yet the St. John's Wort treatments resulted in far fewer side effects compared to pharmaceutical antidepressants. The researchers found that the side effects were comparable to the side effects reported by the placebo groups:

> "Adverse events reported in randomized clinical trials were comparable to placebo and fewer compared with antidepressants."

St. John's Wort also resulted in fewer digestive side effects and fewer nervous system side effects compared to pharmaceutical antidepressants:

> *"In the included randomized clinical trials comparing St. John's Wort to standard antidepressant medications, there was evidence that more patients taking antidepressants experienced adverse events. Specifically, St. John's Wort was associated with fewer adverse events in the gastrointestinal and neurologic organ systems."*

The researchers concluded St. John's Wort's total effectiveness:

> *"St. John's Wort monotherapy for mild and moderate depression is superior to placebo in improving depression symptoms and not significantly different from antidepressant medication."*

This is serious stuff. A medicinal herb that costs a fraction of the price of pharmaceuticals works just as well if not better than the pharmaceutical, and more safely.

Depression scores halved

An example of the clinical studies this review included in its meta-analysis is a study from Berlin's Charité Humboldt University (Uebelhack *et al.* 2004). For six weeks, the researchers gave 900 milligrams of Hypericum extract or a placebo to 140 patients diagnosed with moderate depression.

The study found the Hypericum treatment group's Hamilton Depression Scale scores went from an average of 22.8 points all the way down to 11.1 points – halving their levels of depression after only six weeks of treatment.

Not the first major review to find these results

This is not the first major review of clinical research showing that St. John's Wort successfully treats depression.

In another major Cochrane review from Germany's Technical University of Munich (Linde *et al.* 2008) researchers analyzed 29 quality clinical studies that included 5,489 depression patients.

Again, the researchers found that St. John's Wort extracts were between 28 and 87 percent effective, with a similar effectiveness as pharmaceutical antidepressants.

The researchers concluded:

> *"The available evidence suggests that the hypericum extracts tested in the included trials a) are superior to placebo in patients with major depression; b) are similarly effective as standard antidepressants; c) and have fewer side effects than standard antidepressants. The association of country of origin and precision with effects sizes complicates the interpretation."*

As mentioned above, most of St. John's Wort's side effects come when it is combined with pharmaceutical medications of one sort or another.

When St. John's Wort is combined with SSRIs, it can produce serotonin syndrome – which can also be caused by SSRIs and other serotonin medications alone. St. John's Wort can also decrease the effectiveness of some drugs, as it slows their absorption. For example, pharmaceutical contraceptives can become less effective if combined with St. John's Wort.

There is a whole list of medications that St. John's Wort can potentially interfere with.

The key is not to take St. John's Wort when taking other medications of any sort.

How does St. John's Wort work?

Like most herbal medicines, St. John's Wort contains a myriad of medicinal compounds. These work together to buffer each other and create a synergistic healing mechanism.

The central compounds in St. John's Wort are hypericin, hyperforin, pseudohypericin and adhyperforin. These help balance the body's levels of dopamine and serotonin. St. John's Wort also helps balance 5-HT receptors, increasing GABA – which produces a calming effect.

This myriad of effects has caused medical researchers to dub St. John's Wort as a "neuroprotective agent." Its use for all sorts of mood disorders and anxiety is well documented throughout the world.

St. John also contains quercetin, quercitrin, hyperoside, avicularin, rutin, kaempferol, various flavonoids, oligomeric procyanidines and other compounds.

This natural myriad of compounds in St. John's Wort means that it also confers other benefits. Other clinical uses of the herb has included seasonal effective disorder, premenstrual syndrome, menopause, hemorrhoids, skin rashes, wounds and infections. It has been shown to have proven antifungal and antiviral effects. St. John's Wort also reduces inflammation.

It's true that St. John's Wort can cause slight photosensitivity in some people. But this is typically minor and can occur as a result of a number of other medicinal plant extracts. This effect is often mitigated when the whole herb is taken instead of an isolated extract.

The plant is called St. John's Wort because its flower blooms right around the birthday of Saint John the Baptist's birthday of June 25.

Due to St. John Wort's potential ability to interfere with pharmaceuticals, it is suggested that a consult with a doctor is advised before using it (along with any other herb mentioned here).

Kava Kava

Kava's leaves are heart-shaped for a reason. Kava has a long and proven record of medicinal benefits. It's time we set the record straight for this incredible herb.

Clinical research proves it treats anxiety and depression. It also boosts cognition. All this with a record of safety. Let's review the evidence.

What is Kava Kava?

Kava Kava (*Piper methysticum*) is a traditional herb with centuries of use among the islands of the Pacific. These include Fiji, Papua Guinea, Samoa, Solomon Islands and other Micronesia islands. These islanders consume Kava by simply mixing the whole powdered root with water. Often it is served in a coconut shell in a ceremonial social event.

The *Piper methysticum* plant grows in the tropical jungle and lays down an impressive root system. This might be compared to the impressive roots of the ginger or the ginseng plants. Kava's roots are harvested and dried. They are then pulverized into powder. This root powder is typically consumed in whole form, though supplement companies will often produce extracts.

Kava relieves anxiety

A number of human clinical studies have shown that Kava relieves anxiety. In a review of the research from the University of Melbourne, four of six human clinical studies conducted with *Piper methysticum* for anxiety showed that:

> *"The current weight of evidence supports the use of kava in treatment of anxiety with a significant result..."*

A more pervasive review was done by California's Global Neuroscience Initiative Foundation (Lakhan and Vieira 2010). The review analyzed 24 studies of Kava and other herbal medicines for anxiety. The study found substantial evidence that Kava relieved anxiety. It also treated restlessness and insomnia.

The researchers also reviewed animal studies that showed that Kava has anxiolytic effects "but not sedative or mental impairing" effects "which are typical side effects caused by benzodiazepines." *Piper methysticum* extracts have also been seen to bind to GABA and dopamine receptors, as well as opiate receptors.

In one of these studies (Volz and Kieser 1997) 101 adults were given either Kava or a placebo for 25 weeks. The Kava group showed significant improvement in "primary and secondary anxiety symptoms." Primary anxiety relates to long term stress and anxiety (since childhood) while secondary anxiety relates to clinical disorders

Five other randomized controlled clinical trials and one observational study supported these results. They supported *P. methysticum* as a potential "monotherapy" (meaning no other medications give) or for those who were coming off of benzodiazepines.

The researchers noted that Kava's use with St. John's Wort has not been productive.

Kava relieves depression

Other studies have shown Kava has antidepressant effects. A three-week study from The University of Queensland (Sarris *et al.* 2009) gave 60 adults 250 milligrams kavalactones per day or a placebo.

At the end of the three weeks, the *Piper methysticum* group had significantly lower levels of depression compared to the placebo group, using Montgomery-Asberg Depression Rating Scale scores. The researchers concluded:

> *"The aqueous Kava preparation produced significant anxiolytic and antidepressant activity and raised no safety concerns at the dose and duration studied. Kava appears equally effective in cases where anxiety is accompanied by depression. This should encourage further study and consideration of globally reintroducing aqueous rootstock extracts of Kava for the management of anxiety."*

The Kava was also safe. The researchers also stated:

> *"The aqueous extract was found to be safe, with no serious adverse effects and no clinical hepatotoxicity [liver toxicity]."*

Other studies have supported Kava's antidepressant effects.

Researchers from Italy's University Degli Studi in Siena (De Leo *et al.* 2000) tested 40 women who were in menopause for between one and 12 years. The researchers gave the women 100 milligrams of *Piper methysticum* with and without estrogen replacement therapy (HRT).

After three and six months of treatment, the researchers tested the women for levels of moods and anxiety. The research found the *Piper methysticum* treatment helped the menopausal women with their anxiety with and without HRT. They concluded:

> *"The results of this study show that the association of HRT and Kava-Kava extract may represent an excellent therapeutic tool for the treatment of women in stabilized menopause, in particular those suffering from anxiety and depression, given that Kava-Kava therapy accelerates the resolution of psychological symptoms without diminishing the therapeutic*

action of estrogens on organic disease, such as osteoporosis and cardiovascular disease."

Other studies have shown similar effects. A review of research from the University of Illinois Medical School (Geller *et al.* 2007) found that *Piper methysticum* can significantly reduce mood-related anxiety during menopause.

Kava improves cognition

Okay, so Kava relaxes the muscles and the mind. But doesn't it affect cognition the way other antidepressants and anti-anxiety drugs do? Certainly, as some researchers have pointed out a tendency to "sway" when on Kava.

Despite this effect, there is clear evidence that *Piper methysticum* actually has the opposite effect – it can boost cognition and attention.

After a review of 10 clinical studies of Kava, researchers from Australia's Brain Sciences Institute at Melbourne's University of Technology (LaPorte *et al.* 2011) found that Kava significantly helped cognition, and did not impair cognition as some have assumed. Their report showed that some studies showed significant effects:

"One acute study found that kava significantly improved visual attention and working memory processes while another found that kava increased body sway. One chronic study found that kava significantly impaired visual attention during high-cognitive demand."

The researchers also looked into the mechanisms of Kava's be benefits:

"Potential enhanced cognition may be attributed to the ability of kava to inhibit re-uptake of noradrenaline in the pre-frontal cortex, while increased body sway may be due to GABA pathway modulation."

In a study from the University of Melbourne (Sarris *et al.* 2012) compared Kava to oxazepam. Yes, the *Piper methysticum* helped relieve anxiety. But it was also found that *Piper methysticum* did not have the negative side effects upon cognition the way the oxazepam did. They stated:

> "Kava was found to have no negative effect on cognition, whereas a reduction in alertness occurred in the oxazepam [group]."

Is Kava harmful to the liver?

Kava kava's safety was stained a few years ago by a few case reports of liver toxicity. Let's clear this up right away: The evidence shows quite the opposite. It shows that *Piper methysticum* is safe when taken properly, and the risk to the liver is little, if even at all. In fact, as shown in the cancer research, Kava is helpful for liver cells.

This is evidenced by the fact that in late 2015, two German courts lifted the ban on Kava. They found no good evidence to support the supposed risks of Kava.

A study from the University of Münster (Kuchta *et al.* 2015) analyzed and reviewed the reports of risk of Kava. The research concluded the reports were based on cases of mistaken identity and a lack of quality control on the part of those who administered them. The reality is that reports of liver issues were a few case reports, rather than any larger scale study.

Supporting this: In a large review of research from the University of Melbourne (Teschke *et al.* 2013) that included 24 clinical herbal studies, the researchers stated:

> "Of the 435 clinical trial participants taking kava supplements in our review, some at high doses, no liver issues were reported. Therefore, the current review supports the conclusion that liver toxicity is indeed a rare side effect."

The researchers also analyzed the "few" reports of Kava's liver toxicity – the first of which was reported in 1998, well after many studies had been conducted - and stated:

> "serious side effects may have occurred due to poor quality kava."

Furthermore, researchers from Germany's Goethe University of Frankfurt, the University of Melbourne and the Swinburne University of Technology in Australia have suggested that the reports of liver toxicity come not from ingesting Kava per se. Rather, they suggest that the evidence points to supplies of Kava that have become moldy.

They point to the type of liver toxicity that has resulted in the few cases of slight liver toxicity (mostly resulting in increased liver enzymes) actually being caused by fungal contamination of the Kava rather than the Kava roots themselves.

A paper from the University of Sydney's School of Pharmacy (Rowe and Ramzan 2012) also revealed this possibility. While they weren't convinced they did admit that, "background levels of aflatoxin have been detected in kava samples."

The proposal – based on a thorough examination of the cases of Kava-liver issues as well as new research showing a lack of liver toxicity from properly prepared Kava – completely makes sense.

Why? Because for most of the history of the Kava industry, *Piper methysticum* has been harvested and prepared by native populations among Pacific Islands where the plant is indigenous. The roots are often harvested in bulk and then stored in an exposed facility until preparation. As such, the handling and preparation of the dried Kava powder may easily become subjected to mold or any number of other contaminants as the roots are stored awaiting processing.

A lack of manufacturing protocols in *Piper methysticum* production in the past has thus been largely been left to native harvesting groups, because this was the major source of Kava. Market buyers were in no position to begin dictating protocols.

Increasingly, many Kava suppliers harvest and process using international manufacturing standards such as ISO, GMP and others. Because of the restrictions by first world countries now on the importation of raw ingredients, these protocols are now stricter. Still, it often depends upon the particular importer of the product – whether or not they inspect and demand adherence to good manufacturing practices.

Another study (Olsen *et al.* 2012) which analyzed the components of P. methysticum, found there to be no compound in the Kava that should cause liver toxicity. They concluded:

"To date, there remains no indisputable reason for the increased prevalence of kava-induced hepatotoxicity in Western countries."

Other evidence shows that in many of the reports of liver toxicity, alcohol consumption was involved and in some cases, pharmaceuticals that affect the liver were also involved. These of course include acetaminophen and many other over the counter drugs. After a review of most of the Kava liver toxicity cases (a little over 100), the researchers concluded:

"Alcohol is often co-ingested in kava hepatotoxicity cases."

In other words, there is enough evidence – the lack of toxicity among clinical studies, the potential for mold and other contamination of Kava root, and the ingestion of Kava with alcohol and/or other drugs – to make a case that the risk of liver toxicity from pure Kava when there is no alcohol or drugs consumed is minimal. And most of us know that both alcohol and many OTC drugs damage the liver. In fact, there are tens of thousands of liver toxicity cases every year in the U.S. alone.

Kava's constituents

P. methysticum's central anti-anxiety constituents are kavalactones. In fact, this is why most kava is now standardized to kavalactone content. Constituents mentioned above include flavokawains and methysticin. Others include kawain, yangonin, dihydrokavain, desmethoxyyangonin, and dihydromethysticin. These all have different neurological effects, including MAO-B inhibition in the case of desmethoxyyangonin. Kawain's effects are sedative and tranquilizing, as well as anti-convulsant according to the literature.

The bottom line: *Piper methysticum* provides one of the best proven herbal medications to treat anxiety and depression. It also aids cognition and some of its constituents may prevent and even treat different cancers.

How to take Kava

Unless you are in Fiji at a Kava ceremony, you'll be taking Kava in supplement form or in imported root powder form. If you want to take Kava on a longer-term basis, you might consider a few simple measures:

- Choose a reputable brand known for its focus on quality control.
- Choose a product standardized to kavalactones.
- Extracts are best because of their quality control. Non-alcohol liquid extracts are available.
- Take only the amount as recommended by the manufacturer.
- Take a day or two off for every four or five days used.
- Do not consume alcohol or take any medications with Kava.
- Do not consume Kava with other herbal medications.
- Don't drive after you take Kava.
- If you have sensitive skin, consider staying out of the sun after consuming Kava, as it has been known to cause photosensitivity among some sensitive people – as do other herbs such as St. Johns Wort.

Sage

Sage belongs to the Salvia plant family – derived from the Latin word salvere which means, "to heal." To heal, indeed.

Sage (*Salvia officinalis* and *Salvia lavandulaefolia*) is a delicious cooking and culinary herb. But it has also been used for thousands of years for a variety of ailments.

This beautiful plant with its blue flowers grows wild in many continents. This includes North America. But it is native to the Southern Europe and the Mediterranean region.

Sage used for numerous conditions

For thousands of years, sage has been used in Greek and European medicine to treat a myriad of conditions. These range from intestinal problems to lung and airway conditions, heart disease and circulation problems. It has been used to treat inflammatory issues and low immune function. Sage has also been used to treat oral, sinus and lung infections. We have discussed evidence for sage essential oil for tonsillitis.

Traditional uses for sage have also uncovered another benefit: The ability to boost moods and increase memory and cognitive skills. This benefit isn't just after weeks or months of dosing: It also occurs within hours of consuming the sage.

This last benefit of sage has been the subject of intense research over the past decade. With proven results.

Sage's brain benefits

A 2016 review of research from Australia's Murdoch University (Lopresti *et al.*) investigated the evidence for sage's ability to boost brain health and improve moods.

Sage has been tested in a number of laboratory situations, on both cells and animals. Human studies and laboratory research have revealed that sage exhibits several important brain benefits:

• Strong anti-inflammatory. This helps protect the brain against free radical damage and oxidative stress.

• Blocks and repairs damage to brain cells related to the formation of amyloid-beta plaque.

• A potent inhibitor of cholinesterase.

• Helps protect brain cell health by maintaining higher levels of brain-derived neurotrophic factor (BDNF).

• Connects with GABA receptors

• Boosts serotonin and dopamine

The discovery of these benefits have led scientists to test sage using human clinical research.

In a study from the UK's Northumbria University (Tildesley *et al.* 2005) researchers gave 24 volunteers single doses of either sage essential oil or a placebo. The sage was given in either 25 or 50 microliter doses.

The researchers found that the sage essential oil doses resulted in an immediate improved mood along with a cognitive boost for the subjects. They scored higher on mood ratings and cognitive task tests.

The researchers concluded:

> *"Mood was consistently enhanced, with increases in self-rated 'alertness', 'calmness' and 'contentedness' following the 50-*

microl dose and elevated 'calmness' following 25 microliters. These results represent further evidence that Salvia is capable of acute modulation of mood and cognition in healthy young adults."

Remember, depression is a "mood." And enhancing mood means any depressive symptoms are decreased.

Another clinical study (Akhondzadeh *et al.* 2003) tested 42 men and women with mild cognitive impairment. They were given 60 drops of a sage extract or a placebo for four months. After the four months, the study found the daily sage supplementation improved the moods and reduced agitation among the patients.

The clinical term "agitation" in a hospital or treatment environment means a patient whose moods are depressed, and they display frustration and sometimes even aggressive behavior. An agitated person may simply complain of their situation. Or they may be combative. Both of these symptoms are typical of depressed patients.

The patients who were given the sage also scored significantly higher on cognitive testing (ADAS-cog tests).

Researchers from New Zealand's University of Otago tested Alzheimer's patients with sage essential oil for six weeks. The researchers found the sage improved attention spans and reduced neuropsychiatric symptoms among the patients.

Dose and mechanism

Researchers from Australia's Swinburne University in Melbourne (Scholey *et al.* 2008) tested 20 adults who were over 65 years old. With periods in between, they were given different doses of the sage extract. All were tested for memory efficiency and cognitive function.

The researchers found that those who received 333 milligrams of the sage extract benefited the most. Doses that were higher or lower also showed benefit, but not as much as 333 milligrams per day.

The researchers reported:

"Compared with the placebo condition (which exhibited the characteristic performance decline over the day), the 333-mg

dose was associated with significant enhancement of secondary memory performance at all testing times. The same measure benefited to a lesser extent from other doses. There also were significant improvements to accuracy of attention following the 333-mg dose."

University of Northumbria researchers (Kennedy *et al.* 2006) also tested 30 healthy young adults. They gave them two different doses of dried sage leaf (300 milligrams or 600 milligrams) or a placebo. They were given mood assessment testing and cognitive tasking before and after one and four hours after a dose on three separate occasions.

The researchers found that both doses of dried sage leaf significantly boosted moods and reduced anxiety among those tested. They also boosted memory and cognition. The researchers stated:

"Both doses of sage led to improved ratings of mood in the absence of the stressor (that is, in pre-DISS mood scores) postdose, with the lower dose reducing anxiety and the higher dose increasing 'alertness', 'calmness' and 'contentedness' on the Bond-Lader mood scales."

They also found the volunteers had significantly better alertness, and were able to multitask better. Those taking the sage performed significantly better on Defined Intensity Stress Simulator (DISS) testing. DISS tests multitasking under stress. Those given the sage were calmer and more contented after the doses. The 600 mg dose resulted in better improvements.

The ability of sage to inhibit cholinesterase was deemed a strong factor in the results:

"The results confirm previous observations of the cholinesterase inhibiting properties of S. officinalis, and improved mood and cognitive performance following the administration of single doses to healthy young participants."

Medicinal compounds in sage

There are a number of medicinal compounds found in sage. Those more relevant to protecting brain health include:

• Phenolic acids such as rosmarinic acid, salvianolic acids, sage-coumarin, caffeic acid, lithospermic acid, sagerinic acid and yun-naneic acids.

• Flavonoids such as quercetin, kaempferol, luteolin, apigenin and hispidulin,

• Terpenoids such as carnosol, thujone, camphor, cineole, hu-mulene, caryophyllene, viridiflorol and carnosic acid.

• Polysaccharides such as pectin and arabinogalactans These are all medicinal compounds.

One compound to keep in mind is thujone. This can have both-ersome effects in too high a dose, as it can inhibit the GABA-A receptor. The Committee on Herbal Medicinal Products/European Medicines Agency (HMPC/EMA) has recommended a safe maxi-mum limit of 6 milligrams of thujone per day. Different sage varie-ties can have different thujone levels, but for the most part, thujone is a fractional component.

The research cited above proves that sage not only boosts moods, memory and cognitive function over the long-term. It will also have effects within hours of taking it.

Both species of sage will work nicely. But *Salvia officinalis* will likely do a little better than *Salvia lavandulaefolia*.

Rosemary

Rosemary (*Rosmarinus officinalis*) is an evergreen shrub and a member of the mint family. It has been used for thousands of years as a medicinal herb. The Egyptians, Greeks and Romans used it more than 3,500 years ago.

It is said the name was ascribed to Mother Mary's use of it. It grows profusely in temperate climates of North America, the Medi-terranean region and temperate climates of Asia and Southern Europe.

Rosemary is also an herb with numerous benefits. Rosemary boosts memory, even for Alzheimer's disease sufferers. But clinical research also indicates that Rosemary also reduces symptoms of anxiety and depression, and improves sleep. These in addition to improving memory even in younger people.

Most of us know that students can experience a significant amount of anxiety and depression. A clinical study from the Kerman University of Medical Sciences (Nematolahi *et al.* 2018) included 68 medical students. The study was double-blinded and randomized. The students were aged between 20 and 25 years old.

The researchers divided the students into two groups. One group was given 500 milligrams a day of dry powdered rosemary in a capsule. The other group was given a placebo – the capsules looked identical to the rosemary capsules.

The treatment period was 30 days.

The rosemary was collected as fresh leaves and flowers. After picking, it was dried and crushed into the powder and encapsulated.

The researchers used the Hospital Anxiety and Depression Scale (HADS) to measure relative anxiety and depression among the students. Anxiety and depression are scored differently from the test. Each has the following scale:

- Normal = 0 to 7 points
- Mild = 8 to 10 points
- Moderate = 11 to 15 points
- Severe = 16 to 21 points

Anxiety scores improved after Rosemary treatment

Prior to the treatment, 64.71 percent of the students has normal scores, while 17.65 percent had mild anxiety. And 14.71 percent had moderate anxiety, while 2.94 percent had severe anxiety.

After the treatment with Rosemary, 82.35 percent of the students had normal scores (up from 64.71). None of the students had severe anxiety scores, while only 11.77 percent (down from 17.65) had moderate scores. Only 5.88 percent had mild anxiety scores, down from 17.65 percent.

Meanwhile, the placebo scores were mostly unchanged after the 30 days, with similar scores in the beginning of the study.

The researchers also found that depression scores improved after the 30 days of Rosemary treatment. The researchers saw the moderate depression scores go down from 5.88 percent to 2.94 and mild depression from 14.71 to 8.83 percent. Meanwhile, the normal scores went up from 79.41 to 88.23.

The placebo group had similar scores in the beginning of the study, but saw no improvement at the end of 30 days.

Sleep also improved with Rosemary

The researchers also found that sleep improved among the Rosemary students. Students reporting good sleep went up from 47 percent to 62 percent at the end of the 30 days of Rosemary supplementation.

Students reporting poor sleep went down from 53 percent to 38 percent after the 30 days of Rosemary.

The researchers also found that memory scores went up among the students taking the Rosemary. Prospective and retrospective memory scores improved by about 14 percent.

Meanwhile, memory scores didn't change much for the placebo group.

Anxiety reduced with Rosemary aromatherapy

Other research has found that Rosemary essential oil can also reduce anxiety.

For example, a study from Srinakharinwirot University in Thailand (Hongratanaworakit *et al.* 2009) found that a massage with Rosemary oil significantly improved the moods of healthy adults. The researchers found the subjects felt, "more attentive, more alert, more vigorous and more cheerful" after receiving the Rosemary oil massage.

Research from Western Oregon University (Burnett *et al.* 2004) studied 73 adults. They tested each with anxiety-producing situations, using Rosemary, Lavender or water scents. They used the Profile of Mood States to gauge their mood changes.

The researchers found that Rosemary resulted in the highest scores of reducing tension and anxiety, compared to the Lavender and water scents.

Ashwagandha

Research has found that Ashwagandha (*Withania somnifera*) is effective for depression and anxiety, as well as bipolar disorder.

A hospital study (Chandrasekhar *et al.* 2012) of 64 people with chronic stress found that 2 months of Ashwagandha therapy reduced anxiety and insomnia by 68%, reduced severe depression by 79 percent, and reduced stress by 44%.

A 2019 study from the Western Psychiatric Institute and Clinic at the University of Pittsburgh Medical Center (Gannon *et al.*) studied 66 schizophrenia patients. They were either given a placebo or 1,000 milligrams of Ashwagandha for 12 weeks in this double-blind study. The patients were tested before and after the treatment period.

After the 12 weeks, the Ashwagandha significantly reduced anxiety and depression scores among the patients. The researchers concluded:

> *"Our findings suggest that WSE may hold promise in the treatment of depression and anxiety symptoms in schizophrenia."*

A number of other studies have confirmed that Ashwagandha can significantly calm the mind and boost moods.

A 2020 review of research from the School of Medicine at National University of Singapore (Ng *et al.*) found that Ashwagandha is able to curb cognitive dysfunction along with boosting moods and suppressing bipolar disorder. The researchers stated:

> *"Overall, there is some early clinical evidence, in the form of randomized, placebo-controlled, double-blind trials, to support the cognitive benefits of W. somnifera supplementation. However, a rather heterogeneous study population was sampled, including older adults with mild cognitive impairment and adults with schizophrenia, schizoaffective disorder, or bipolar disorder. In most instances, W. somnifera extract improved performance on cognitive tasks, executive function, attention, and reaction time. It also appears to be well tolerated, with good adherence and minimal side effects."*

Another placebo-controlled double-blind study (Katz *et al.* 2010) of 120 children diagnosed with Attention Deficit Hyperactivity Disorder (ADHD) found that Ashwagandha treatment improved *"attention, cognition, and impulse control"* among the ADHD children.

Still other studies have shown that Ashwagandha reduces oxidation among brain regions, and can significantly treat symptoms of bipolar disorder.

Doctors from the University of Pittsburgh's Western Psychiatric Institute and Clinic (Chengappa *et al.* 2013) randomly divided 60

DSM-IV bipolar patients into two groups. 53 patients completed the study. For eight weeks they gave 24 patients 500 milligrams per day of Ashwagandha herb extract, and 29 patients a placebo.

The researchers gave the patients a series of bipolar tests to gauge cognition, response time, social cognition response and others.

After the eight weeks, the researchers found the Ashwagandha group had significantly improved in the digit span backward test, the Flanker neutral response time, and the Penn Emotional Acuity Test for social cognition response.

The digital span backward test is conduced by having the patient repeat back a series of numbers backward. Other memory span tests use letters or words for a reverse recall. Recalling in reverse measures the ability of the brain's cognitive potential together with its functional memory.

The researchers concluded:

> "Although results are preliminary, Ashwagandha extract appears to improve auditory-verbal working memory (digit span backward), a measure of reaction time, and a measure of social cognition in bipolar disorder."

The researchers also noted that the treatment was safe with few side effects.

Chamomile

The research continues to prove that chamomile is not only relaxing to drink in a tea. It can also significantly decrease anxiety and fight depression. And the effects of chamomile continue with long-term use.

Several species are often described as Chamomile. The most commonly used is German Chamomile (*Matricaria chamomilla* or *Matricaria recutita*).

A study from the Perelman School of Medicine at the University of Pennsylvania (Mao *et al.* 2016) investigated long-term chamomile use for generalized anxiety disorder. This particular form of anxiety is the most prevalent form of anxiety treated by doctors.

The researchers treated 93 anxiety patients between 2010 and 2015. Of these, 47 were given a placebo and 46 were given the chamomile. The researchers found that the chamomile group had over 40 percent fewer anxiety relapses during the treatment period.

Also, anxiety relapses occurred an average of every 6.3 weeks for the placebo group and 11.4 weeks for the chamomile group. The risk of relapse was nearly half for the chamomile group compared to the placebo group.

Long-term chamomile use was also safe. Indeed, the chamomile group showed significant weight loss compared to the placebo group. The chamomile group also had lower blood pressure than the placebo group.

Short-term chamomile use also effective. In a study from the UK's University of Nottingham Medical School (Pek *et al.* 2013) researchers found that chamomile significantly relaxed blood vessels and smooth muscle fibers. This effect was indicated specifically with the application of three of chamomile's central constituents, apigenin, luteolin and bisabolol – all hydroxylates.

This effect of chamomile to soothe and calm the system was also showed in a study from the Eulji University Hospital in South Korea (Cho *et al.* 2013). Here 56 patients undergoing coronary treatment and surgery were given aromatherapy with a combination of lavender, chamomile and neroli. A control group was given only nursing care.

The researchers found that the aromatherapy group had significantly lower anxiety and improved sleep compared to the control group.

The fact that chamomile is an anti-anxiety and anti-depression herb was confirmed by a clinical study at the University of Pennsylvania School of Medicine (Amsterdam *et al.* 2009).

The researchers enlisted 19 people diagnosed with anxiety with depression, along with 16 people who were diagnosed as having a history of anxiety and depression. These groups were studied along with a control group of 22 people who had no anxiety or depression – past or present.

The study was randomized, double-blind and placebo-controlled. The researchers gave the subjects either 220 milligrams of chamomile extract (standardized to 1.2% apigenin) or a placebo study, both in capsules.

The treatment period spanned eight weeks. During the first week the subjects were given one capsule a day, and for those receiving less benefit on their anxiety scores, this was increased (if needed) to two capsules the second week, three capsules the third week, four the fourth week and five for the remainder of the eight weeks.

The primary means for judging the success of the treatment was the Hamilton Anxiety Rating (HAM-A) scoring system – which utilizes questionnaires to determine ones level of anxiety. The researchers also used the Beck Anxiety Inventory system and the Psychological Well Being system, as well as the Clinical Global Impression Severity system to confirm their findings.

The researchers found that 57% of the group using the chamomile extract had significantly reduced (greater than 50%) anxiety scores using the HAM-A system.

Three years later, the University of Pennsylvania researchers (Amsterdam *et al.* 2012) undertook another review of the data in this study to determine whether or not treatment with chamomile for the clinically anxious and clinically depressed could be considered "clinically meaningful." This of course enables medical peers to gauge whether or not chamomile could be used as a prescriptive treatment for diagnosed patients.

After reviewing the study and research data in depth, the researchers concluded that the results were "clinically meaningful" and they pointed out:

> *"the research team observed a significantly greater reduction over time in total HAM-D scores for chamomile versus placebo in all participants."*

This of course means that the improvement in their HAM-D scores – taken only over an eight-week period - short for an herbal therapy – continued to increase over the period of the trial.

Chamomile used with other herbs for anxiety

Traditional herbalists will typically recommend the use of anti-anxiety herbs such as chamomile, lavender, St. John's Wort and others over a period of three months to a year in order for them to reach their full effectiveness. After that, they are often recommended to be continued at least periodically or as needed.

The good news about chamomile, as evidenced by this and other studies, is that it has no known adverse side effects and is non-addictive. This is in stark contrast to anti-depressant pharmaceuticals, some of which are known for being significantly addictive in addition to having numerous other adverse effects.

One positive side effect to consider: Chamomile tea has been shown to increase longevity.

Rhodiola

Rhodiola has been used for centuries for a number of ailments including fatigue, anxiety and depression. It was mentioned by the Greek physician Pedanius Dioscorides (born 40 AD) as part of his healing repertoire. Rhodiola is considered an adaptogenic herb more recently made famous by its use by Russian athletes to increase endurance.

A review from researchers at the Philadelphia's Perelman School of Medicine at the University of Pennsylvania School of Medicine (Mao *et al.* 2016) found that Rhodiola was a clinical antidepressant.

The researchers reviewed clinical research of involving 860 patients with depression. 714 of these had stress-induced depression. The results found Rhodiola improved moods and stress levels, changing neurotransmitter function.

The doctors concluded:

> *"Overall, results of these studies suggests a possible antidepressant action for R. rosea extract in adult humans."*

In a study from the North China University of Science and Technology (Yu *et al.* 2019), doctors tested Rhodiola with 90 sleep apnea patients. They split the patients into three groups. These included two ventilator groups and two groups given Rhodiola herb for three months.

The researchers found that Rhodiola treatment reduced depressive symptoms and reduced anxiety and physiological stress levels. The researchers found that levels of superoxide dismutase levels and malondialdehyde levels improved, illustrating their free radical levels were reduced.

The scientists wrote:

"Rhodiola may improve the negative emotions such as anxiety and depression by inhibiting oxygen free radicals and lipid peroxidation in patients with OSA."

Researchers from the Perelman School of Medicine (Mao *et al.* 2015) also determined in a clinical study that Rhodiola can significantly reduce depression symptoms.

The research was led by Dr. Jun Mao, a professor of medicine at the University of Pennsylvania. Dr. Mao and fellow researchers enrolled 57 adults who had received a diagnosis of major depressive disorder (MDD). Major depressive disorder means the patient has exhibited at least two episodes of depression that lasted for two weeks or more. It also includes other symptoms such as impending feelings of death or suicide, sleeping problems, weight loss or gain, or an inability to concentrate.

The patients were divided into three groups. Over a three-month period, the patients received a daily dose from 340 milligrams to 1,360 milligrams of standardized Rhodiola extract, or between 50 and 200 milligrams of the depression drug sertraline, or a placebo.

Before and after the treatment, the patients were given depression symptom tests that included the 17-item Hamilton Depression Rating (HAM-D), the Beck Depression Inventory (BDI), and the Clinical Global Impression Change (CGI/C) test. These tests provide clinicians with a way to gauge the extent of a patient's depression symptoms and whether the patient is improving or sliding downward.

After the three-month treatment period, the patients that took the sertraline drug had the greatest reduction of depression symptoms, with an odds of 90 percent reduced incidence. Meanwhile, the Rhodiola extract also significantly reduced depression symptoms, with an odds factor of 40 percent reduced incidence.

However, the adverse side effects were quite high for the sertraline-treated patients, with a 63 percent adverse effect level, compared to 30 percent among the Rhodiola group and 16 percent among the placebo group.

The researchers concluded:

"Although R. rosea produced less antidepressant effect versus sertraline, it also resulted in significantly fewer adverse events

and was better tolerated. These findings suggest that R. rosea, although less effective than sertraline, may possess a more favorable risk to benefit ratio for individuals with mild to moderate depression."

Researchers from Sweden's Uppsala University (Olsson *et al.* 2009) tested 60 people who were suffering from stress-related chronic fatigue. The researchers gave half the group 576 milligrams of Rhodiola extract per day for 20 days. The other half received a placebo.

The scientists found that the patients given the Rhodiola scored significantly better on fatigue symptom tests, depression tests and attention tests. They also had reduced physiological stress, noted by the levels of cortisol. Their scores on the Pines burnout scale and the mental health scales were also significantly higher after taking the Rhodiola.

What makes Rhodiola work for mood disorders?

Research suggests that Rhodiola affects the hypothalamic-pituitary-adrenocortical axis – which is the link between the body's neurotransmitters and hormones. The herb has an ability referred to as adaptogenic – which means that it helps balance the body's stress response. This was determined clinical by Swedish researchers (Panossian and Wagner) in 2005.

This is apparently accomplished by allowing precursors of serotonin and dopamine through the blood-brain barrier. This in turn allows more of these important neurotransmitters to be produced. Rhodiola also helps increase body levels of endorphins, and has been shown to halt cancer growth.

Rhodiola also increases brain plasticity

Part of Rhodiola's effects may be related to its direct affect on the adaptability of the brain.

A 2018 study from the Hackensack Meridian School of Medicine at Seton Hall University (Concerto *et al.*) tested 28 healthy volunteers. They were given either 500 milligrams of Rhodiola or a placebo. The doctors then tested their brain stimulation and activation levels.

They tested their brains' motor brain function, cortical activity, and intracortical brain function. They also tested nerve conduction and spine activity.

The researchers found that just a single dose of Rhodiola significantly affected their brain plasticity levels. They wrote:

> *"Our findings suggest that a single oral dose of Rhodiola rosea extract intake modulates cortical plasticity in humans preventing the activity-dependent reduction in the efficacy of neuronal synapses. These results suggest that the adaptogenic and antidepressant effects of Rhodiola rosea extract might be based on its modulation of brain plasticity."*

Holy Basil

Holy Basil (*Ocimum tenuiflorum* or *Ocimum sanctum*) is one of the oldest and most used medicinal herbs. It has provided the backbone of many treatments among Ayurvedic physicians from thousands of years ago, as it was used to treat numerous disorders.

It has also been revered for its spiritual potency, and has been dubbed among ancient Ayurvedic texts as "elixir of life." The word Tulsi is translated to "incomparable." The plant grows in warm and tropical regions, but also up to 6,000 feet among mountainous regions. There are actually two general cultivars of the herb: One has green leaves and the other has purple leaves.

One might be tempted to compare Holy Basil to Culinary Basil - *Ocimum basilicum*. Yes, there are some common effects. But Holy Basil is quite different. A 2014 DNA sequencing study was conducted at the CSIR-Central Institute of Medicinal and Aromatic Plants genetically compared the two species. The research found significant genetic differences between the two species. While they may share a few of their constituents, their genetic sequences have significant differences.

In terms of active constituents, Holy Basil's stronger pungency is due to its content of eugenol along with sesquiterpenoids such as beta-caryophyllene. Other medically active constituents of Holy Basil include:

Oleanolic acid, ursolic acid, carvacrol, linalool, rosmarinic acid, myretenal, luteolin, germacrene D, beta-sitosterolorintin, beta-elemene, vicenin, carnosic acid, several apigenins, luteolinglucuronic acids, luteolin-glucopyranosides, glucopyronosyl-hydroxybenzenes, dimethoxy-flavans, methoxyphenoxy-dimethoxyflavans, methoxyphenoxymethyls, methoxyphenyl-dihydrobenzofurans, methoxyphenoxy-methoxyphenyl-methoxypropanes and many others.

Holy Basil is also rich in calcium (25 mg per 100 grams), phosphorus, iron and vitamin C.

Ancient Ayurvedic texts have advised Holy Basil be used to combat a myriad of conditions. These include stress and anxiety. The herb is calming, and considered an anxiolytic.

This has been proven out in the research. For example, a study from India's JB Roy State Ayurvedic Medical College (Bhattacharyya *et al.* 2008) tested 35 adults with generalized anxiety disorder. They were given 1,000 milligrams of Holy Basil (*Ocimum sanctum*) extract for 60 days.

The researchers tested the patients prior to the treatment, after 30 days and after the end of the trial utilizing the Hamilton brief psychiatric rating scale (BPRS) along with examinations. They found that Holy Basil significantly reduced their anxiety scores, as well as stress and depression scores. The researchers wrote in their paper:

> *"The observations exhibited that O. sanctum significantly attenuated generalized anxiety disorders and also attenuated its correlated stress and depression."*

Anxiety and stress are related as we've discussed. A study from India's Central Drug Research Institute (Gupta *et al.* 2007) found that extracted constituents of Holy Basil reduced stress levels. The mechanisms of this included normalizing blood sugar, modulating corticosterone, attenuating the adrenal glands and balancing creatine kinase.

They found that extracted constituents of Holy Basil reduced stress levels. The mechanisms of this included normalizing blood sugar, modulating corticosterone, attenuating the adrenal glands and balancing creatine kinase.

We have discussed how oxidative stress is a typical cause of neuroinflammation, which is significantly related to a disruption in the HPA axis and mood disorders like depression and anxiety.

Oxidative free radicals produce nerve and tissue damage. When lipoprotein fats such as LDL are oxidized, they begin to damage the blood vessels, creating atherosclerosis, high blood pressure and other cardiovascular issues. Free radicals can also damage brain cells, increasing the risk of dementia and mood disorders.

Research from India's Annamalai University (Manikandan *et al.* 2007) found that a whole leaf extract of Holy Basil significantly reduced lipid and protein oxidation. The researchers found that Tulsi exhibited superior antioxidant properties but also lowered phase I enzymes that are found in peroxidation metabolism. The extract also increased the phase II enzymes – which tend to balance and moderate oxidative stress.

Ancient Ayurveda suggests that Holy Basil is useful to reduce pain in various conditions. This ability has been confirmed in a number of studies, as Holy Basil has been shown to inhibit the cyclooxygenase 2 (COX-2) enzyme - the inflammatory enzyme known to stimulate substance P - (P for pain).

Sacred Lotus

The Sacred Lotus (*Nelumbo nucifera*) is not only pleasing to the eyes. The plant contains natural compounds that give it numerous healing powers – to both the body and the mind.

The hypnotically beautiful Sacred Lotus flower is certainly pleasing to the eyes. Depending upon the location and genetics, lotus flowers can be white, pink, yellow or even rainbow-colored.

The leaves, stem, seeds, roots and flowers of the lotus have been used medicinally for thousands of years. The Mandarin name for the Sacred Lotus (seed) is Lian Zi and its Japanese name is Ren-shi, and in Korean, Yoncha.

Ancient Chinese and Ayurvedic texts indicate the stems and leaves of the plant are helpful for stomach aches, ulcers and intestinal cramping, increasing circulation, and improving the condition of the heart (cardiotonic). It is also known for strengthening the spleen.

The seeds and flowers of the lotus flower – and to a lesser degree the leaves - also have a range of other effects. These include being hypnotic and calming. The seeds contain alkaloid constituents that relax the nerves and the muscles. They also promote sleep.

Restlessness and nervousness – even depression – have been treated traditionally using the seeds, flowers and leaves of the Sacred Lotus.

Then you have the roots of the lotus. These have been used to treat numerous infections, including intestinal infections and diarrhea. The dried roots have also been used for various issues of bleeding as well.

These are not theoretical uses either. These are recorded uses of the plant in clinical settings. Science has been recently confirming these uses.

Sacred Lotus' calming effects

Researchers have confirmed the hypnotic and sedative effects of the lotus plant. In one study (Yan *et al.* 2015) published in the *Journal of Agricultural and Food Chemistry*, researchers used lotus extracts to test neurotransmitter production in the brain after the extract.

They found that the alkaloids of the plant increased the production of gamma-amino butyric acid (GABA), along with serotonin, 5-hydroxyindoleacetic acid and dopamine.

The researchers stated:

> *"These data demonstrated that the alkaloids from lotus leaf exert sedative-hypnotic and anxiolytic effects via binding to GABA receptor and activates the monoaminergic system."*

Another study (Kumarihamy *et al.* 2015) found that an extract of the flower of the Sacred Lotus had elements that bound to several key receptors in the brain and nervous system known for encouraging relaxation: two cannabinoid receptors, and four opioid receptors.

A study from several Japanese universities, including the Yokohama College of Pharmacy (Sugimoto *et al.* 2015) extracted two special alkaloids from the Sacred Lotus: liensinine and isoliensinine. Each of these were found to have antidepressant effects.

The researchers concluded:

> *"These data suggest that liensinine and isoliensinine from Nelumbo nucifera Gaertner have antidepressant-like effects and that antidepressant-like effects of liensinine and its analogues are closely related to serotonergic mechanisms."*

Another study (Temviriyanukul *et al.* 2020) found that an extract from Sacred Lotus seeds inhibited acetylcholinesterase and butyrylcholinesterase enzymes. Acetylcholinesterase inhibitors are used to treat a myriad of conditions, from tachycardia, to Alzheimer's and other dementias, to Parkinson's and schizophrenia.

Investigations have also found 19 medicinal constituents in the seeds, including saponins, flavonoids, steroids, alkaloids, terpenoids and cardiac glycosides.

Gotu Kola

Gotu kola is referred scientifically as *Centella asiatica*. It has been an herb used throughout China, Thailand, India, Indonesia and other Asian countries in their respective traditional medicines for thousands of years. The herb grows around the world in tropical and moist regions.

It has a number of reputed uses in Ayurveda, Traditional Chinese Medicine and others, including reducing anxiety and stress.

A 2010 study from India's JB Roy State Ayurvedic Medical College and Hospital (Jana *et al.* 2010) tested 33 adults suffering from anxiety disorders and stress. The patients were given 500 milligrams twice a day of a Gotu Kola extract.

After 60 days, the researchers found the Gotu Kola significantly reduced anxiety and stress among the patients.

A study from Canada's Royal Ottawa Hospital and the Department of Psychiatry at the University of Ottawa (Bradwejn *et al.* 2000) tested 40 healthy adults. Half the subjects were given Gotu Kola while the other 20 were given a placebo.

After 30 minutes and 60 minutes after the dose, the subjects were tested for their acoustic startle response (ASR). The researchers found that the Gotu Kola had significantly reduced the ASR peak among the patients. This is evidence for Gotu Kola's physiological response of calming the nervous system.

The researchers concluded their study found *"that Gotu Kola has anxiolytic activity in humans as revealed by the ASR."*

Bacopa

Bacopa monieri is an herbal medicine used for thousands of years in Ayurveda for a variety of mood-related, memory-related and cognitive-related disorders.

Now we find modern clinical research proves the effectiveness of Bacopa to boost memory, improve moods, increase multi-tasking, reduce stress and boost cognition in general.

In a study from the National College of Natural Medicine (Calabrese *et al.* 2008) researchers tested 48 adults for 12 weeks. They gave half 300 milligrams a day of Bacopa herb and the other half were given a placebo.

All the subjects were given a battery of tests before and after, including the State-Trait Anxiety Inventory, Center for Epidemiologic Studies Depression scale (CESD)-10 depression scale, and the Profile of Mood State.

The researchers found those who received the Bacopa had significantly improved depression scores. They also had reduced anxiety scores after the 12 weeks.

The Bacopa-treated group had increased word recall, less anxiety, decreased average heart rate and cognitive increases. The researchers concluded:

> *"This study provides further evidence that B. monnieri has potential for safely enhancing cognitive performance in the aging."*

Laboratory and animal research has concluded similar findings, using Bacopa and its constituents.

This result of better memory for Bacopa has also been discovered in other research.

Research from Australia's Swinburne University of Technology (Benson *et al.* 2014) showed that Bacopa monnieri helps multitasking and stress reduction along with cognitive improvements.

The researchers, from Swinburne's Center for Human Psychopharmacology, conducted a placebo-controlled, double-blind study of 17 healthy adult volunteers.

They utilized what is called a cross-over design, meaning each of the subjects was tested on both the placebo and treatment doses separated by a washout period – a period of time enough to allow the system to be cleared.

The subjects were given multitasking framework testing, and then underwent the testing one and two hours after taking two different doses of the Bacopa or a placebo.

The subjects were also tested for moods and salivary cortisol levels – which will indicate levels of stress and/or anxiety – before and after the dosing of the Bacopa or placebo.

Each of the subjects underwent the multitasking framework testing separated by a week – called the washout period. The first week the subjects were given the test, then given the placebo, and then tested again a week later before and after being given 320 milligrams of a commercial extract of Bacopa called CDRI 08.

After another washout period of seven days, the subjects returned to receive 640 milligrams of the CDRI 08 – followed and proceeded by a round of multitasking framework testing.

The results of the study determined the subjects' memory was enhanced by the Bacopa, but not with the placebo. The research also found the Bacopa elevated mood levels and reduced stress levels – indicated by the reduction of salivary cortisol levels. These also indicated adaptogenic effects of the Bacopa extract.

Studies have also found that Bacopa prevented neurological damage related to oxidative damage. In a study conducted by India's National Institute of Mental Health and Neurosciences (George *et al.* 2012) researchers concluded:

> *"We infer that BM displays prophylactic effects against ACR induced oxidative damage and neurotoxicity with potential therapeutic application in human pathology associated with neuropathy."*

The overriding conclusion of this peer-reviewed amalgam of research by different researchers using different methods is clear: The Ayurvedic herb, *Bacopa monnieri*, long held as a way to increase cognition, reduce anxiety and prevent dementia, does precisely that, along with potentially being one of the first known herbal treatments of Alzheimer's disease, as we investigated in our book on the subject.

Echinacea

Echinacea angustifolia is also called the purple coneflower. The roots of Echinacea (*E. purpura* or *E. angustifolia*) are typically used to boost immunity. But did you know that Echinacea can also reduce anxiety?

Researchers from Hungary's Institute of Experimental Medicine in Budapest (Haller *et al.* 2019) studied 64 adults who had high levels of anxiety.

Anxiety scores were measured using the Beck Depression Inventory (BDI) and the Perceived Stress Scale (PSS). The test subjects were given either 80 milligrams of Echinacea root extract for seven days, or a placebo.

After only taking Echinacea for seven days, those taking the Echinacea had significantly reduced anxiety scores. Their scores decreased by about 11 points.

The researchers concluded:

> *"These findings suggest that particular Echinacea preparations have significant beneficial effects on anxiety in humans."*

Mechanism of action

The researchers suggested that the alkamides in Echinacea may bind to a cannabinoid receptor called CB1.

This can inhibit the activity of a fat enzyme called FAAH (fatty acid amide hydrolase). This, in turn, will decrease anandamide levels in the brain, which has been linked to higher anxiety levels.

Inhibiting the FAAH enzyme has been a target for drug development.

But Echinacea was found in this study to have practically no side effects:

> *"Adverse effects were rare and mild, and all were observed in the placebo group."*

A 2013 study (Haller *et al.*) tested healthy humans with Echinacea for one week. But this time, the dose was 40 milligrams per day and the volunteers were tested using the State-Trait Anxiety Inventory (STAI) test. They found that after the seven days, the subjects scored higher on the STAI test.

Other Anti-anxiety Herbs

Researchers from Australia's University of Melbourne (Sarris *et al.* 2013) conducted a Cochrane review of medicinal herbs for anxiety disorders. They concluded that in addition to the herbs we've discussed in this book, these herbs proved useful for various anxiety disorders:

- *Galphimia glauca*
- *Ginkgo biloba*
- Lemon Balm (*Melissa officinalis*)
- Milk thistle (*Silybum marianum*)
- Passionflower (*Passiflora incarnate*)
- Red feathers (*Echium amoenum*)
- Skullcap (*Scutellaria lateriflora*)

Motherwort for Postpartum Depression and Anxiety

This natural therapy has been used in traditional medicines for childbirth for at least 1,800 years.

Hundreds of thousands of women die every year from complications giving birth. In 2015, for example, about 830 women died every day on average, of pregnancy or childbirth complications. That adds up to over 300,000 women dying around the world each year.

Yes, many of these occurred in second and third-world countries. But women do still die from childbirth in first-world countries.

Most of these deaths – approximately two-thirds – will die as a result of what is called postpartum hemorrhage. Postpartum hemorrhage simply refers to bleeding that occurs directly after the baby is delivered.

The motherwort herb (*Leonurus* sp.) has been used by traditional medicines – primarily in Asia – specifically to reduce postpartum bleeding, and complications in general. The herb has hundreds of medicinal constituents, and thus works in a multifaceted way to reduce anxiety and increase blood clotting at the same time.

The use of motherwort for reducing bleeding and complications has been researched with positive results.

But the traditional use of motherwort has also been used for postpartum anxiety and depression for centuries. This was illustrated by a 2016 study from Germany's Ruhr University (Hoffmann *et al.*). The researchers found that motherwort was effective in binding with GABAA receptors, notably the 5-HT receptor.

This means that motherwort reduces anxiety and depressive symptoms.

In a study from Russia's Saint-Petersburg Institute of Pharmacy (Shikov *et al.* 2011) researchers studied 50 patients for a month. They gave them 1200 milligrams of motherwort extract oil. At the end of the month, 32 percent of the patients showed significant improvement in anxiety and depression symptoms, and 48 percent showed moderate improvement.

The patients also showed improvements in their blood pressure.

Only 12 percent did not respond to the therapy. Side effects were minimal according to the researchers.

One of the amazing things about herbs is their complexity. While pharmaceutical medicines might have one or two active constituents, medicinal herbs can have hundreds.

In a study from China's Chengdu University of Traditional Chinese Medicine (Miao *et al.* 2019) researchers analyzed motherwort herb in the laboratory and found it contained no less than 280 medicinal compounds.

Cypress

Have you walked through a Cypress forest lately? If so, you undoubtedly became intoxicated with the sweet aroma. One of the most amazing things about the Cypress tree is its production of essential oils. These give the Cypress tree a strong aroma, which provides the richest of breathing air for anyone blessed with walking through such a forest.

In fact, the fragrant aroma produced by Cypress trees is not simply great to breathe as we walk through a forest: Breathing this aroma from its essential oils actually has curative effects upon the body. Anecdotal, you say? Read on.

Cypress trees from the genus Chamaecyparis (*Chamecyparis obtuse*) can grow from about 50 feet to 200 feet depending upon the species and location. These evergreen trees can pack densely into a forested area. The Cypress produces cones and is treasured for its rich rot-resistant wood. For this reason we find fine furniture made from Cypress.

In the U.S., we have two species of Cypress trees that adorn some of our forests. These are *Chamaecyparis thyoides* (Atlantic white cedar or cypress) and *Chamaecyparis lawsoniana* (cedar or Lawson Cypress). Atlantic white cedars grow up and down the Eastern Seaboard. Lawson Cypress trees grow throughout Oregon and California. Each of these will also grow sparsely in forested areas of the Southwest and Southeast as well.

In Asia, the predominant Cypress species are *Chamecyparis formosensis* (called Meniki) and *Chamecyparis obtusa* (called Hinoki). These two conifers grow among the forests of Asia and Japan.

Each of the species above produces a similar mix of essential oils that produce the aromas known to these Cypress forests. These have not only been thought to be therapeutic for centuries: Aromatherapy has been utilizing their essential oils medicinally for over a thousand years.

Note these species of Cypresses are not the same as Cupressus species such as *Cupresses sempervirens* – also called the Italian Cypress or the Mediterranean Cypress. But in fact, Chamecyparis species of Cypress do belong in the family Cupressaceae - which is shared with Cupressus species of Cypresses. Thus we can say with confidence that they are related species. Confirming this, their essential oils also share some of the same medicinal benefits - including those mentioned in this article.

Cypress aromatherapy

One clinical study (Chen *et al.* 2015) tested essential oils from two of these Asian Cypress trees: Meniki (*Chamecyparis formosensis*) and Hinoki (*Chamecyparis obtusa*).

The researchers extracted the essential oils from the wood of these two trees. Then they tested the two essential oils on 16 healthy adult volunteers.

They allowed each volunteer to inhale each essential oil for five minutes on separate occasions. This is what we might call a dose of aromatherapy.

Before and after the inhalation, the researchers tested the heart rate, blood pressure, heart rate variability and other vital signs of the subjects before and after inhalation of each essential oil. They also examined each subjects' state of nervous system activity – including their parasympathetic activity and their sympathetic activity.

In addition, the researchers studied the subjects using several psychological tests: This included the internationally recognized Profile of Mood States (POMS) test.

The POMS test, designed in 1971, has the subject respond to a long list of reactionary states. These responses are then calculated, categorized and rated for six different mood profiles: anger, confusion, depression, fatigue, tension and vigor.

As the subjects' responses are calculated into these mood profiles, this establishes the subjects' general mood levels. This of course includes levels of anxiety, depression and so on.

Both Meniki and Hinoki essential oils improved the cardiovascular condition of all the subjects.

The researchers found that breathing the aroma of both essential oils reduced systolic blood pressure. It also reduced heart rate and decreased the parasympathetic nervous system while increasing sympathetic nervous system activity.

These are all positive signs for the heart. Stress on the heart is reduced, while its vitality and function are increased.

Furthermore, both essential oils increased heart rate variability (HRV). Heart rate variability has been shown in a number of studies to reduce the risk of death from cardiovascular events. Increased HRV means the heart is beating stronger and more responsively with respect to its needs.

The above cardiovascular signs – especially the reduced parasympathetic nervous system and the increased sympathetic nervous system – that stress levels were decreased. This was also consistent with the results of the Profile of Mood States testing.

These tests indicated that both the Meniki and Hinoki essential oils stimulated what they classified as a "pleasant mood status." These POMS results indicated reduced stress, increased positive moods and increased optimism among the subjects.

The researchers concluded:

> *"Our results strongly suggest that Meniki and Hinoki essential oils could be suitable agents for the development of regulators of sympathetic nervous system dysfunctions."*

This all means that Cypress aromatherapy can help those who have indigestion, high blood pressure or any number of other maladies related to an over-engaged 'fight or flight' stress response.

Cypress inhibits inflammation

Another study (An *et al.* 2013) tested *Chamaecyparis obtusa* essential oil in the laboratory among cells. They found that the oil inhibited a number of components involved in inflammation.

These included tumor necrosis factor (TNF-alpha), IL-6, IL-1, pro IL-1beta, NO, iNOS, ERKI/2, JNKI/2 and p38.

The researchers concluded:

> *"Thus, the overall results indicated that C. obtusa wood oil had very good anti-inflammatory efficacies."*

Another study – from South Korea's Chungbuk National University (Chen *et al.* 11) - had similar findings. Here *C. obtusa* was used, and found to reduce inflammation produced by prostaglandin E2. The researchers concluded:

> *"These findings suggest that C. obtusa essential oil may constitute a novel source of anti-inflammatory drugs."*

The researchers also chemically analyzed the Cypress essential oils carefully. They found many active components, including limonene, cadinene, cadinene, cadinol, muurolene, calamenene, linalyl acetate, myrtenol, terpineol, pinene, borneol and terpinolene.

In all, they identified 36 active constituents in the Meniki essential oil, and 29 constituents in the Hinoki essential oil.

Other research has found Cypress essential oils also contain thujopsene and terpinyl acetate, along with elemol, thujopsenal, erpineol, tau-muurolol and borneol.

Not surprising, since most plants produce hundreds of biochemicals – many medicinal in one respect or another.

Herbal Aromatherapy

As we discussed individual herbs, we included some research proving that aromatherapy can reduce depression symptoms. To these we can add research showing that a number of other essential oils can significantly curb depressive symptoms with aromatherapy.

While scientific and clinical research evidence for aromatherapy is growing, many still believe their effects are anecdotal. Yet research studies we have discussed here establish their scientific basis.

How does aromatherapy change moods?

The relationship between smelling and hormone and neurotransmitter levels has been made scientifically. For example, a study from the University of California at Berkeley (Wyart et al. 2007) studied smelling chemosignals. They found that smelling a compound found in male sweat (androstadienone) significantly boosted levels of cortisol hormone in women.

Plants also produce chemicals that modulate our moods when we smell them. There are so many plant species, and most of them produce some kind of aromatic essential oil. Thus we find literally thousands of essential oils to choose from.

Yet practically every plant's essential oil produces a different medicinal effect when used aromatherapeutically.

There is a good collection of literature to draw from in order to establish the effects of particular essential oils. Matching this with whatever clinical research is available is still prudent, however.

Multiple studies prove this

A review of research published in the *Evidence-Based Complementary and Alternative Medicine* journal (Sánchez-Vidaña *et al.* 2017) found over 500 studies on the topic during their investigation. After screening out studies that were not clinically based or qualified for other reasons, they found 12 randomized clinical trials that tested aromatherapy for depression.

The 12 studies included a total of 1,226 men and women. Some of the participants had other conditions such as cancer, pregnancy or menopause. Some of the women included in the research had postpartum depression.

The treatments of the studies included the following essential oil formulations:
- Lavender, Bergamot and Cedarwood
- Rose and Lavender
- Lavender, Pititgrain and Bergamot
- Yuzu (Japanese citrus fruit)

- Lavender alone
- Bergamot, Lemon Clary Sage, Lavender, Roman Chamomile, Geranium, Rose, Sandalwood and Jasmine
- Melissa, Juniper and Rosemary
- Rose and Lavender
- Lavender, Geranium, Rose and Rosemary
- Lavender and Geranium

Treatments ranged from every day to once every two weeks weekly. Some of the treatments included inhalation therapy alone. Others included aromatherapy massage. This is when a small amount of the essential oils are blended with a massage oil.

For the inhalation aromatherapy, the diffuser timing ranged between 5 and 20 minutes.

The researchers concluded after their meta-analysis:

> *"In the overall analysis carried out, aromatherapy showed potential to be used as an effective therapeutic option for the relief of depressive symptoms in a wide variety of subjects."*

Let's discuss the two types of aromatherapy in more detail:

Inhalation aromatherapy

Two studies that used inhalation therapy decreased depressive symptoms. This means they simply breathed in diffused essential oils for a few minutes each session. One was a 2014 study (Matsumoto *et al.*) that used the Yuzu citrus fruit essential oil among 20 women.

A 2012 study (Conrad *et al.*) on 28 women who were postpartum found that a blend of *Rose otto* and *Lavandula angustifolia* essential oils significantly improved their depression and anxiety scores.

Using undiluted essential oils on the skin should be done with caution and only after careful spot testing for sensitivities. The easiest and safest way to utilize an essential oil is with aromatherapy — in which there is no physical consumption or application.

An aromatherapy diffuser can be used. To make a quick and simple one, simply shake a few drops of the oil onto a crumpled paper towel and set this on a plate. Put the plate close by and simply breathe the air for awhile.

The typical way of utilizing aromatherapy is with a diffuser. Just a few drops (3-4) of an essential oil onto a diffusing element can quickly deliver its therapeutic scents throughout the room.

Other types of diffusers are available - including some that utilize heat to diffuse the scent. An essential oil may be diffused by dropping into boiled water as well - this will diffuse the scent via the vapor - but less oil should probably be used in this case.

Aromatherapy scents may also be diffused via candles and lamp rings - but be careful because essential oils are also flammable.

Another way is to simply make the effort to walk or run through a lavender field or pine forest. This will render some of the same aromatherapy as a diffuser will. And it will have long-term benefits when this is done regularly.

Massage Aromatherapy

Massage aromatherapy consists of mixing a few drops of an essential oil to a base massage oil such as coconut oil or almond oil. Once blended, it should be tested on the a small patch of skin before massaging over a considerable amount of the body.

Five of the studies using massage aromatherapy significantly decreased depression symptoms. This means they were given massages using massage oils that were blended with essential oils.

In one, 32 depression patients were treated at the Surrey Oaklands NHS Trust's Day Hospital (Lemon 2014). The essential oils were chosen based on each patient's symptoms, and used in a daily massage. Their test results were compared to a control group.

Those receiving the aromatherapy massage had a significant improvement of depression scores. These included the Montgomery-Asberg Depression Rating Scale (MADRS) and the Tyrer Brief Anxiety Scale (TBAS).

In a 2011 study (Wu *et al.*) aromatherapy massage was used with cognitive behavioral therapy with 63 patients with depression and/or anxiety. The treatment resulted in significant improvement in scores among the patients receiving the aromatherapy.

In a 2013 study (Taavoni *et al.*) 90 menopause patients with depressive symptoms were treated with aromatherapy massage or massage without aromatherapy. The massage-only group showed some improvement in symptoms. But the aromatherapy massage group showed significantly more improvement in psychological scores.

In a 2014 study (Wu *et al.*) of 25 depressed patients, some received aromatherapy massage for 40 minutes twice a week for four weeks. Those patients scored significantly higher on the Stat-Trait Anxiety Index, Beck Depression Inventory and the Short Form of Psychosocial Well-being Index. They also showed improvements in their brain waves, cortisol levels and levels of brain-derived neurotrophic factor (BDNF).

The results of these studies illustrate that aromatherapy can produce serious changes to our moods, yes. But they also show aromatherapy affects the production of particular hormones and neurotransmitters. More importantly, those that adjust and regulate our moods. In the 2014 study above, the researchers concluded:

> *"These results suggest that aromatherapy massage could exert significant influences on multiple neurobiological indices such as EEG pattern, salivary cortisol and plasma BDNF levels as well as psychological assessments."*

Using essential oils

The research has illustrated that some essential oils are better for certain issues. Their analysis found that lavender, bergamot and sandalwood provided significant benefit for depressive symptoms. And the Yuzu citrus oil "alleviates negative emotional stress." Most of the other oils used in the various studies have been found to have anti-anxiety and sedative properties.

Certainly, trying out several different types of essential oils for inhalation comes with little risk. Blending essential oils into a massage oil should be considered carefully, because of the contact with our skin. Using a very tiny amount with a base oil is advisable. One or two drop into a few ounces of jojoba or grapeseed oil should suffice. If multiple oils are used, one drop is better. Blending more than two or three essential oils together can also be problematic for a massage oil. Unless you really know what you are doing.

It's also best to test the blended oil on a small area of skin before using it to do a full massage. Let it sit for several hours to make sure you don't react to that oil.

Note that we've also discussed the evidence for St. John's Wort and depression.

All of this is best done after discussions with your doctor or other health professional. And don't stop any medications without first talking with the doctor who prescribed them.

Herbal Combinations for Depression

For thousands of years, herbalists have been creating formulations made of different herbs to produce healing effects that may not be produced by single herbs. Some of these combinations come from the ancient healing modalities of Ayurveda and Traditional Chinese Medicine, as illustrated below.

Manasamitra Vataka Herbal Formula

Manasamitra Vataka is an ancient and complex Ayurvedic formula. The Manasamitra Vataka formula consists of up to 73 natural ingredients including many herbal extracts. According to leading Ayurvedic remedy producer, Kottakkal Arya Vaidya Sala (AVS), these include:

- Bala (*Sida acuta*)
- Nagabala
- Bilva (*Aegle marmelos*)
- Dhavanimula
- *Vidruma pisti*
- Sankhapuspi (*Evolvulus alsinoides*)
- Tamracudapadika
- Hema
- *Puskara mula*
- *Mrgasrnga bhasma*
- Vaca (*Acorus calamus*)
- *Tapya bhasma*
- *Sveta chandana*
- *Rakta chandana*
- Mauktika
- *Kalaloha bhasma*
- Madhuka (Honey)
- Tvak (*Cinnamomum zeylanicum* bark)
- Magadhi

- Ghanasara
- Aileya
- Visala (*Cucurbita trigonus*)
- Arkaraga
- *Nirgundika mula*
- Plava
- Rasna (*Vanda roxburghii*)
- Rajata bhasma
- Saileya
- Gojihva
- Padmakesara
- Jivaka (*Malaxis acuminata*)
- Rsabhaka (*Malaxis muscifera*)
- Kakoli (*Lilium polyphyllum*)
- Ksirakakoli (*Gymnema lactiferum*)
- Brhati (*Solanum indicum*)
- Ksudra
- Sravani
- Mahasravani
- Bhunimba
- *Krtamala tvak*
- *Parusaka mula*
- Haritaki (*Terminalia chebula*)
- Bibhitaka (*Terminalia belerica*)
- Amalaki/Amla (*Emblica officinalis*)
- Amrita/Guduchi (*Tinospora cordifolia*)
- Sweta sariva (*Hemidesmus indicus* Anantmool - White)
- Krishna sariva (Anantmool – Black)
- Jivanti (*Leptadenia reticulata*)
- Somavlli
- Hayagandha
- Nisa
- Usira (*Vetiveria zizanioides*)
- Draksha (*Vitis vinifera*)
- Vastyahavaya
- Riddhi (*Habenaria intermedia*)
- Durva (*Desmostachya bipinnata*)
- Hamsapadi

- *Bhadra mula*
- Lavariga
- Tulasidala
- Kasturi
- Kunkuma
- *Trayanti svarasa*
- Shankhapuspi (*Evolvulus alsinoides*)
- Vacatoya
- Ananta
- Laksmana
- Bilva (*Aegle marmelos*)
- Blamula Goksira
- Somavallivari
- Stanya

(Note that some of the above are Ayurvedic names of herbal extracts).

Ayurveda is the world's oldest ongoing medicine, with a 5,000-year plus history of treating patients with various diseases. The first recorded surgery was also done by Ayurvedic physicians.

Manasamitra Vataka tested against pharma drug

A 2012 clinical study proved that an ancient Ayurveda remedy for anxiety outperforms the benzodiazepine drug Clonazepam (Konopin) in relieving anxiety.

The researchers, from India's National Institute of Mental Health and Neurosciences (Tubaki *et al.* 2012) tested 72 patients in a hospital setting who were diagnosed with severe generalized anxiety disorder using the Hamilton Anxiety Rating Scale (HARS).

The test subjects were all adults between 20 and 55 years old of both sexes and most had experienced their anxiety disorder for seven years or more. They were also diagnosed with comorbid generalized social phobia.

The researchers randomly divided the patients into three groups. One group was given the standard anti-anxiety medication Clonazepam (Klonopin) at the standard prescriptive dose of .75 milligrams per day (.25mg in the morning, .50mg at night). Another group received 200 milligrams of an Ayurvedic herbal remedy called Manasamitra Vataka (also Manasamitra Vatakam) – in two doses (100 mg each).

A third group was given the same dosage of Manasamitra Vataka but this was added to the patients' receiving an Ayurvedic treatment called Shirodhara therapy – where warmed Brahmi taila oil is poured onto the forehead of the patient.

The patients each continued their treatments for 30 days, and were evaluated at day 15 and day 30. Beck Depression Inventory (BDI) and Beck Anxiety Inventory (BAI) testing was conducted along with Hamilton Anxiety Rating Scale (HARS) analysis of the patients' progress.

At the end of thirty days' treatment, the researchers found that the Manasamitra Vataka group on average had a 73% improved disposition according to the BAI testing, while the Clonazepam group on average improved 67% using the same scale. Using the HARS test scale, those patients receiving the Manasamitra Vataka plus the Shirodhara therapy saw a 91% average improvement in symptoms, while the Clonazepam group experienced a 76% improvement.

The researchers concluded that the Ayurvedic treatment not only exceeded the performance of the benzodiazepine, but came with no side effects. The researchers noted:

> *"Thirty days of treatment with Manasamitra Vataka reduced the anxiety, severity of the disease, increased quality of life and improved clinical profile significantly. Shirodhara as an add-on therapy to Manasamitra Vataka decreased the daytime sleepiness and improved the quality of life in the patients."*

Lixujieyu Herbal Formula

Traditional Chinese Medicine is one of the oldest forms of medicine. It is also one of the more sophisticated traditional medicines, with herbal formulations that have undergone thousands of years of use.

One TCM formula that has been used for moods contains specific plant parts of several herbs. Here is the Lixujieyu formula plant list with species, common names and the plant part used:

• Astragalus root - Huangqi (Radix Astragali Mongolici – root of *Astragalus membranaceus*)

• Kudzu root - Ge-gen (Radix Puerariae Lobatae – root of *Pueraria Lobata*)

• Ginseng root - Sanqi (Radix Noto ginseng – *Panex ginseng*)

• Epimedium Barrenwort leaves - Yinyanghuo (*Epimedii Brevicornus*)

• *Curcuma wenyujin* root - Yujin (Radix Curcumae Wenyujin)

• *Acorus gramineus* bud - Acori Tatarinowii - Shichangpu (Rhizoma Acori Tatarinowii)

A clinical study from Shanghai University (Wu *et al.* 2012) studied 120 patients with chronic fatigue syndrome. The doctors treated the patients with either the Lixujieyu formula or vitamin B plus oryzanol tablets (another TCM formula) twice a day. This study found that symptoms of fatigue, depression, anxiety and other scores were improved in the group treated with the Lixujieyu formula.

Lixujieyu with Five Element Music Therapy

Five-element music therapy means musical tones that harmonize with particular meridians, organs and emotions. These five types of music therapy, together with their respective organ and emotion:

• Jiao – liver – anger - do
• Zhi – heart – joy - re
• Gong – spleen – anxiety - mi
• Shang – worry – lungs - so
• Yu – kidneys – fear - la

These last phrases apply to the five elements music scale, which corresponds with the musical scales (do, re, mi, so, la).

Five element music will also be soothing and melodious. Other research has found these are helpful for various types of disorders, especially when combined with herbal therapy and/or acupuncture.

The music used in this study was composed by ShiFeng, and came from a compact disc called – you guessed it - Five Element Music. The music was performed by the Philharmonic of the Central Conservatory of Music.

Researchers from China's Shanghai University of Traditional Chinese Medicine (Zhang *et al.* 2015) studied 75 patients diagnosed with chronic fatigue syndrome.

The researchers divided the patients into six groups of 15 each:

• Group one was treated with an herbal blend called Lixujieyu together with a type of five-element music therapy called Gong Tune.

• The second group of 15 was treated with the Lixujieyu formula along with another music therapy called Jiao Tune.

• The third treatment group was given the Lixujieyu herbs together with a music therapy called Yu Tune.

• The fourth group was treated with Lixujieyu and Shang Tune.

• The fifth group was given the Lixujieyu herbs with Zhi Tune.

• The last group was the control group. These 15 patients were treated with the Lixujieyu herbs without the music therapy.

Each patient was given a dose of 300 milliliters of the Lixujieyu decoction twice a day. The decoction was prepared by the university pharmacy.

Each patient was tested and then treated for four weeks. They were then tested again after the four weeks of treatment.

The music therapy patients listened to the music each week for five days with two days off. They started at either noon or 7 pm each day. They listened to the music for 45 minutes each session at a volume of between 55 and 65 decibels.

The researchers used three ways to judge the success of the treatments. These included the Fatigue Scale, a standard criteria as approved by the U.S. Centers for Disease Control to assess chronic fatigue syndrome.

The researchers also utilized the Hamilton Depression Scale or HAMD, along with the Hamilton Anxiety Scale (HAMA) to assess depression and anxiety.

All the treatment groups experienced reduced symptoms after the treatment period. But the researchers found that two of the treatment groups had a more significant reduction in their symptoms, compared to the other groups.

The two successful treatments were achieved in groups one and two. These were given the Lixujieyu formula with the Gong Tune, and the Lixujieyu with the Jiao Tune.

The control group's fatigue scale went from 22.6 to 20.2. This was just from the herb formula alone – which is a respectable drop of nearly 11 percent from the beginning of the study.

But group one's fatigue scale dropped from 19.8 to 12.5 – a drop of nearly 37 percent.

And group two's fatigue scale dropped from 22.1 to 14.2 – a drop of 36 percent.

These two groups used the Gong Tune and Jiao Tune respectively. These correspond to the organs of the liver and spleen and anxiety and anger, respectively.

This is not the first time that the Lixujieyu - or Lixu jieyu - formula has been proven successful in the treatment of fatigue and depression-related disorders.

Another study from Shanghai University (Wu et al. 2012) studied 120 patients with chronic fatigue syndrome. This 2012 study treated the patients with either the Lixujieyu formula or vitamin B plus oryzanol tablets (another TCM formula) twice a day.

The study found that symptoms of fatigue, depression, anxiety and other scores were improved in the group treated with the Lixujieyu formula.

Another study (Zhang et al. 2009) of 75 chronic fatigue syndrome patients treated the patients with either the Lixujieyu formula or vitamin B plus oryzanol tablets twice a day. Both groups were treated for three months.

In this study, the researchers tested fatigue scores along with various immune cells. They found that not only were fatigue scores lower after the Lixujieyu treatment, but Th-cells, T-cells and CD4/CD8 cell ratios were significantly lower in the Lixujieyu group.

But as seen with the most recent study, a combination of the herbal formula with the music therapy resulted in an even greater response.

Herbal Combo for ADHD Children with Depressive Symptoms

Before prescribing medications to children, conventional doctors need to ask themselves whether or not we want to expose our children to a possible lifetime of drug-dependency.

What will the children do when their prescriptions run out? Will they necessarily stop? The evidence shows that many will reach for illegal drugs. What kind of illegal drugs will they take - and potentially become addicted to?

A large team of doctors (Trompetter *et al.* 2013) determined that a formula of three herbs successfully treats children with learning difficulties, behavioral problems, anxiety, depression and attention deficit issues.

The researchers, consisting of 17 physicians - including 15 pediatricians and a neurologist – studied 114 children from multiple hospitals throughout Germany.

The children were between six and 12 years old, with an average age of 9.4 years old among the study population. The children had been diagnosed with an emotional or behavioral disorder an average of 2.3 years previous to the study.

The symptoms of the children included anxiety, depression, learning disorders, speech disorders, lack of concentration, fatigue, sleepiness, problems falling asleep, headaches, and hyperkinesias. In the U.S., these symptoms are typically diagnosed as attention deficit/hyperactivity disorder or ADHD.

The children were also qualified for the study for having been given conventional treatment without success. These were, in other words, difficult cases.

The above symptoms were measured by a physician prior to the beginning of the treatment, after two weeks of the treatment and after four weeks of treatment. The physicians were given the option of continuing the treatment and submitting final documentation later.

The children were treated with a combination of three herbal extracts - extracts from St. John's Wort (*Hypericum perforatum*), Passionflower (*Passiflora incarnata*), and Valerian (*Valeriana officinalis*).

The researchers discussed the synergistic effects of this combination and compared therapeutic effects to that of Prozac:

> *"The experimentally verified synergistic effect of Passiflora on Hypericum enables application of a small amount of Hypericum with a simultaneous high efficacy. This reduces the probability of side effects and leads to effects more comparable to the impact of Fluoxetine [Prozac] than to the impact of*

St. John's Wort extract alone. Passiflora is traditionally used in combination with other herbs as a mild sedative. The third plant, Valerian, is traditionally used in medical conditions of sleep disorders and nervous agitation. The combination of all the three medical plants act on gamma-amino butyric acid (GABA) and serotonin (5-HT) receptors, which are recognized targets of pharmacological antidepressant treatment."

Contrasting conventional medicine in the U.S., European physicians are increasingly concerned about the prospect of children taking drugs like Prozac which have been shown to have numerous side effects in addition to being potentially addictive. The researchers noted this in their paper:

"The broad range of interventions for anxieties, nervousness, and depression involve cognitive behavioral therapy as well as mostly chemical antidepressants, anxiolytics, and hypnotics. Especially, treatment with traditional allopathic medication is controversially discussed addressing efficacy and safety of psychotropic agents in pediatrics. Due to the potential for side effects and addiction, prolonged treatment with chemical drugs as it is recommended by the WHO is often accompanied by simultaneous impairment of quality of life. As a result, there is a clear increasing demand for complementary and alternative medicine..."

The herbal treatment therapy was successful in most of the cases. The researchers stated that:

"The majority of children were stabilized in a normal behavior under the treatment."

As the data is analyzed, the researchers found that children with these disorders at the beginning of the treatment had no symptoms or mild symptoms at the end of the herb treatment period (remember these were difficult-to-treat cases):

- Over 80% of those who had depression had no symptoms or mild symptoms after the herbal treatment.
- More than 80% of those with school and/or exam anxiety had no or mild symptoms.

- Nearly 70% of those with other anxiety disorders had no or mild symptoms.
- Over two-thirds of those with aggressiveness and/or irritability had no or mild symptoms.
- More than half of those children with learning disorders had no or mild symptoms.
- More than 85% who had speech disorders had no or mild symptoms.
- Over 70% of those with hyperkinesias had no or mild symptoms.
- Over 80% of those who had problems falling asleep or staying asleep had no or mild symptoms.
- Nine of ten children who had headaches and/or abdominal/stomach pain had no or mild symptoms at the end of the study.

These were the effective rates among the children treated with the herbal combination. In addition, improvement in family life was experienced among 86.7% of the children.

The researchers found that the treatment with the remedy was highly successful. More than 97% of the children tolerated the treatment well.

In 53 cases, the children continued the treatment under the doctor's supervision.

The researchers commented about the alternatives and why treatment with conventional medicine can be problematic for children:

> "...approximately 40–50 % of children with these disorders do not have a response to medication or behavioral therapy alone, and a combination of both is more effective. On the other hand, psychotropic medications are used too early and about 25 % of depressive adolescents develop substance abuse. So, parents prefer non-medical therapies as initial treatment because of the higher risk of side effects in therapies with chemical medication. For these families, the tested herbal combination of St. John's Wort, Valerian, and Passionflower offers a good alternative and fulfills the requested aspects."

Other research has shown that these herbs can reduce anxiety. A large review of research from the Global Neuroscience Initiative found that among 24 studies involving 2,619 people, 71% of the subjects tested had positive results to their natural treatments, many of which received one or a combination of those herbs used in the German study.

Chapter Five

Lifestyle Strategies

Flotation Therapy

Research confirms that flotation therapy can reduce pain, lower depression, and soothe anxiety. It can also improve our sleep.

Flotation therapy is just what it sounds like: Therapeutic floating in a tank of water or in nature. But there is more to it than this.

The water should be at the right temperature with some salt content to allow for good floating suspension. And in order to provide the best healing results, stressful sensory stimuli should be removed from the tank and surroundings.

This latter point is called "sensory isolation." And it is an integral component of flotation therapy. Sometimes soothing music – typically with no lyrics - is added to increase relaxation.

First applied in 1954 by Dr. John Lilly, a neuropsychologist, the floating sensory isolation chamber was tested for its ability to mimic sleep. Flotation therapy has come along way since, but the isolation element is implemented in most systems for good reason.

Just imagine, for example, if you were floating – say in a swimming pool on a mattress. Someone yells from over the fence that they were being robbed. Are you feeling very relaxed as you floated? You'd probably become more stressed and anxious due to the fact that you could not respond immediately – as you were floating!

Flotation is a proven therapy

Today we find scattered around Europe and the Americas, a few flotation therapy businesses. Most of these have dedicated sensory isolation chambers to float in. Some of these simply include the flotation tank having an enclosure that seals off the client – while providing enough air and ambiance – from the rest of the environment.

Flotation therapy is being used by many, including elite athletes to increase their performance. And there is very good reasons for this new therapy – it works.

Passers-by to these centers – including myself - often wonder if the therapy really makes a difference upon our health. Yes, it actually does.

Research from Sweden's Human Performance Laboratory at Karlstad University says yes – in fact, flotation therapy may actually be have significant effects upon our health.

The researchers (Kjellgren *et al.* 2014) tested 65 people. They were randomly divided and given either flotation therapy treatment or were put on a waiting list as a control group.

The flotation group was given seven weeks of a flotation program, which added up to 12 flotation sessions.

Their flotation sessions were done with three flotation therapy centers. The centers each utilized the flotation tanks with sensory isolation. Each of the sessions were 45 minutes long, followed by a half-hour to shower and relax.

The subjects were tested for stress levels, energy levels, anxiety and depression, as well as pain, stress and sleep quality.

They were also tested for other psychological measures such as optimism and mindfulness.

Compared with the control group, those who were given flotation therapy had significantly reduced levels of pain, anxiety, depression and stress. The flotation group also experienced significantly better sleep quality than the control group after completing the flotation therapy.

For example, the flotation group's average depression scores went from 4.42 to 2.25 – close to half - during the twelve week period, while the control group's average depression scores went from 4.00 points to 4.30 points during the twelve weeks.

Stress levels went from 1.86 to 0.95 – over half – during the twelve weeks, while the control group's stress levels stayed about the same.

Anxiety levels among the flotation group went from 7.92 to 4.28 during the testing period, while the control group's levels were also about the same.

The control group's sleep quality also remained about the same, while the sleep quality of the flotation group went up from a 23.72 score to a 29.69 score – a significant increase.

Pain levels among the flotation group also went down significantly, as mentioned. The worst pain went from 64.29 down to 39.70 in the flotation group, and the normal pain went from 27.32 to 15.00 among the flotation group. The control group also reported slightly reduced pain, but reductions were about a third of the flotation group.

The research highlights what is referred to as the relaxation response – a relief of stress found when someone achieves deep relaxation. This contrasts with what is referred to in stress medicine as the fight-or-flight response.

The fight-or-flight response stimulates the release of cortisol, ACTH and epinephrine, and a dramatic change in many of the body's parasympathetic operations such as digestion – which slows - and heart rate – which speeds up. The fight-or-flight response also reduces the body's focus upon healing – which means the body does not repair itself the way it should.

This often coincides with reduced sleep. Sleep is typically reduced when a person has significant stress.

Stress also reduces our serotonin and dopamine levels, which lead to greater levels of long term anxiety and depression.

When this fight-or-flight response takes place in the body over an extended period, the body increases levels of oxidation - which can produce free radicals and reduced healing and repair. Sleep is a necessary part of healing – as the body does much of its repair work while we sleep.

Flotation therapy mimics sleep

As mentioned with Dr. Lilly's research, one of the reasons flotation therapy may be so beneficial is that it puts much of the body into suspension. That is, the body can completely relax, which is also what takes place when we drift into deep sleep.

This of course allows the body to conduct repairs and healing strategies. These include hiking up the immune response and clearing toxins.

Allowing the mind to drift is also one of the things we do when we sleep. This allows the mind and brain to consolidate memories and reflect upon issues – and often solve problems.

This is good for the mind – as well as anxiety, stress and depression – because it allows us to resolve things that we might be stressed over. This problem-solving element is also one of the characteristics of sleeping.

Of course – actually falling asleep in the flotation tank is not unheard of. Just ask a flotation therapist.

Can we get the same benefit by just floating in water?

Certainly, flotation therapy doesn't necessarily require a complex float tank with sensory isolation. But it certainly helps. The water has to be kept at a certain temperature – not too hot and not too cold – to encourage complete relaxation.

This means the temperature must be kept close to but a little less than body temperature – something that may be difficult to do in a home flotation setup.

That said, there are some places in the world where floating can be done in nature - such as in the Dead Sea or on some tropical beaches. The Dead Sea has a greater salt content, however, allowing for better suspension.

Many flotation therapy centers achieve the ability to float - leaving the face above water to breathe - with Epsom salts - though other chemicals are also used in some tank setups.

The isolation float chamber blocks out excitable sensory stimuli, and this might be hard to create at home.

Especially if we have people, cell phones, computers and other sources of external stress surrounding us.

I surf, and sometimes I will lay back flat on my board in the water and simply float on the board – though I have to keep one eye out for the next set wave. And in the past I have laid on a mattress in a private pool. So I can attest that these and other low cost floating strategies can also be very productive in terms of reducing stress.

So if you have available any means of floating – completely suspending the body in water at the right temperature, with a minimum of interruptions – give it a shot. Or give a flotation therapy center a try if you pass by one. You're sure to find yourself floating away to a new frame of mind - and better health.

Saunas

Taking a sauna can do a lot more than help sweat out toxins. It can also reduce our risk of Alzheimer's disease and other forms of dementia. And it can reduce anxiety and the risk of depression. Saunas also improve the cardiovascular system and brain circulation according to the research.

Lowers anxiety and depression

A study from Japan's Hamamatsu University School of Medicine (Hayasaka *et al.* 2008) studied 45 people. They tested each using shortened versions of the Profile of Mood States (POMS) and State-Trait Anxiety Inventory (STAI) tests.

Then each of the patients took charcoal kiln saunas. After the saunas, the subjects were tested again. The research found they had significantly improved moods and reduced anxiety levels according to the testing.

A study from Japan's Kagoshima University School of Medicine (Soejima *et al.* 2015) found that infrared sauna therapy reduced anxiety, fatigue and depression levels. It also improved moods.

The researchers wrote:

> *"Perceived fatigue significantly decreased after therapy, although no significant reductions were observed during therapy. In addition, a negative mood, including anxiety, depression and fatigue, and the performance status significantly improved after therapy."*

What is a sauna?

For those who are not sure, the sauna is a method of deep perspiration (profusion). The traditional dry sauna is a Finnish invention. Today, infrared saunas have become popular for personal and commercial use due to the lower cost and additional benefits.

The sauna is basically a dry heated room set up for the purpose of sweating.

This is similar to Native American Indian sweat lodges – which use covered shelters and hot rocks from a nearby fire.

The traditional Finnish sauna is usually built of wood such as fir or pine, with wooden benches. This allows for insulation as well as absorbance. Wood will absorb sweat but will also dry out easily. This helps neutralize the toxins from sweat.

Traditional Finnish saunas were heated with wood stove furnaces. Now radiant sauna heaters are usually electric. Rocks are often placed on top of the heater. This helps transmit and retain heat. Some rock heaters also allow for water to be poured on in order to add some moisture to the dry sauna.

A dry sauna will typically be heated to between 140 degrees Fahrenheit (60 Celsius) and 195 degrees Fahrenheit (90 Celsius). The upper range can become intolerable. But this is often controlled by keeping the sauna dryer (less humidity).

A steam room will feel hotter at lower temperatures. For this reason, water is used judiciously in a dry sauna. When the sauna feels a little too hot on the skin a little water is poured on the rocks.

A newer form of dry sauna is the infrared sauna. These saunas are also typically built of wood. But instead of being heated with a radiant furnace, they contain multiple panels of infrared heaters.

Besides this, the infrared sauna will also maintain a much lower heat temperature – ranging between 110 and 125 degrees Fahrenheit. But it will heat the body just as much if not more.

Outside of the heat difference, the primary difference between the infrared sauna and the dry sauna is the effect of infrared radiation. Both saunas work by making us sweat profusely. But the infrared radiation will penetrate the tissues and dilate the blood vessels.

Saunas also reduce dementia

Researchers from the University of Eastern Finland (Laukkanen *et al.* 2016) followed 2,315 healthy men for over 20 years. They were 42 to 60 years old at the beginning of the study.

Saunas are used so frequently by Finnish men. So the researchers broke the men into three groups:
- Those who took saunas 4 to 7 times a week
- Those who took saunas 2 to 3 times a week
- Those who took a sauna on average once a week

The researchers found that those men who took between 4 and 7 saunas a week had two-thirds (65 percent) less incidence of Alzheimer's disease compared to those who took a sauna once a week.

Saunas also reduced the incidence of all types of dementia.

Those who took a sauna between 4 and 7 times a week had 66 less incidence of all dementia. Again, this is compared to those who took a sauna once a week.

With this kind of significant result for taking a sauna more frequently, we can also assume an even greater difference between those who don't take saunas.

Compared to the once-a-week sauna users, the 2-3 times/week sauna users had a 22 percent decreased incidence of dementia. They also had 20 percent less incidence of Alzheimer's disease. This type of decreasing difference indicates that taking a sauna even once a week has significant effects.

The researchers concluded:

> *"In this male population, moderate to high frequency of sauna bathing was associated with lowered risks of dementia and Alzheimer's disease."*

In a study from Finland's University of Eastern Finland (Knekt *et al.* 2020) researchers followed over 13,000 men and women for 39 years. They found that those taking a sauna 9-12 times per month were 53 percent less likely to have dementia compared to those who took a sauna for less than four times a month.

They also decrease chronic pain

A study from Japan's Nishi Kyusyu University (Masuda *et al.* 2005) tested 46 patients with chronic pain. The researchers gave 22 patients a daily sauna for four weeks in addition to other therapy. The remaining group was treated with the other treatments along with cognitive therapy.

The researchers found that infrared sauna therapy significantly reduced pain scores among the sauna group. It also allowed more people to return to work.

They concluded:

> *"These results suggest that a combination of multidisciplinary treatment and repeated thermal therapy may be a promising method for treatment of chronic pain."*

Saunas reduces recovery time and fatigue too

A study from Finland's University of Jyväskylä (Mero *et al.* 2015) tested 10 healthy men after they worked out. The research found the infrared sauna penetrated about 3-4 centimeters into the tissues and neuromuscular system. It helped the men's recovery rates and decreased lactate concentrations.

Cleanses toxins

A review of sauna research from the Southwest College of Naturopathic Medicine concluded that regular sauna use offered a number of benefits, including cleansing of toxins. The research concluded that:

> *"Existing evidence supports the use of saunas as a component of depuration (purification or cleansing) protocols for environmentally-induced illness."*

What these studies tell us about saunas

The research clearly proves that saunas can significantly improve our health. If we consider the excellent benefits of exercise, we find that saunas have a similar effect.

The above studies also tell us that it isn't about taking a sauna once in awhile. Taking saunas regularly is the key ingredient.

This is quite possibly why Finland's life expectancy is two years higher than the U.S. – 81 years compared to 79 years.

These studies also tell us that taking a sauna is tremendously good for the health of our heart and blood vessels.

It also improves circulation, and increases the removal of toxins.

By increasing the removal of toxins, we lighten our body's burden. This allows our immune system to more easily remove other pathogens. These include cancerous cells.

A word of caution

Saunas do have their risks. A 1976 study of saunas tested 60 people before and during their saunas. They found that during the sauna their core body temperatures increased to more than 101 degrees Fahrenheit (38.6 Celsius). During the sauna, their heartbeat levels jumped to more than 140 BPM – and more than 160 BPM in about a third of the group. They also found that blood pressure increased during the sauna.

Of course, these levels are also seen during intense physical exercise. So these temporary increases may not be concerning for many of us. But for those who might have a pre-existing heart condition or are otherwise not used to taking a sauna, it is a different matter.

Don't drink alcohol in or before a sauna – especially in the Finnish dry sauna. It is thus advisable to talk to your doctor before you embark on a sauna routine. Even after that, easing into a sauna routine is a good idea. This means starting with lower temperatures for a short time. Infrared saunas may be safer because of the lower temperatures. Again, talk to your doctor. Be wise.

Outdoor Therapy

We discussed in an earlier chapter how getting natural sunlight is an effective and proven way to improve our moods and reduce depression. But it turns out that going outside in itself also can benefit our moods.

Researchers from Japan's Kyoto University (Nakau *et al.* 2013) tested 22 cancer patients for four months. The patients were given weekly sessions of four central protocols: They worked in the garden, planting seeds and caring for plants – termed horticultural therapy. They engaged in walking in the forest.

They were also engaged in yoga meditation exercises. And they attended weekly support group therapy sessions.

The researchers assessed the patients before and after the therapy using several assessments. Quality of life was assessed using the Short Form-36 Health Survey Questionnaire.

Fatigue was assessed using the Cancer Fatigue Scale. Psychological moods and state of mind was assessed using the Profile of Mood States index and State-Trait Anxiety Inventory. Spiritual well-being was assessed using the Functional Assessment of Chronic Illness Therapy-Spiritual. And their immune system was assessed through testing for natural killer cell (NK cells) activity.

The researchers found that the therapy significantly increased quality of life scores. They also found reduced cancer-related fatigue and increased functional well-being scores among the patients.

The outdoor therapy also improved moods and emotions among the patients after the twelve week testing period.

Other research has shown the success of some of these measures. Other evidence shows that forest walking has heart benefits and improves quality of life.

Being outdoors has a number of benefits, ranging from sunshine to increased negative ions to better air quality. Nature's colors also improve moods and wellness.

Forest walking

A team of international researchers confirmed in 2014 that walking in the forest – compared to walking in an urban setting – produces medicinal benefits.

The researchers, from Finland, Japan and Korea (Lee *et al.* 2014) compared the effects of walking among 48 healthy adult men. During their enlistment process, the researchers excluded smokers and anyone diagnosed with heart disease, allergies or mental conditions from the study.

During the two days of the study, the remaining 48 men did not drink alcohol, exercise vigorously nor smoke.

The researchers utilized a physiological parameter called heart rate variability. This was measured by portable electrocardiograph machine (ECG).

The ECG allows researchers to measure autonomic nervous activity.

Measurement of high frequency and low frequency heart rate variability levels were also measured to indicate sympathetic nervous activity.

Heart rate frequency measurements were recorded while the subjects were walking. These frequency measurements indicate metabolic health and nervous condition – anxiety and stress.

In addition, the researchers measured blood pressure using a portable blood pressure monitor. Blood pressure readings were taken three times during each walk, and before and after each walk.

Questionnaires were also given to the subjects to measure their moods and psychological conditions. In all there were four questionnaires given. Scales used included the Profile of Mood States

(POMS) index and the Spielberger State-Trait Anxiety Inventory (STAI) index.

The walking test protocol

The test subjects walked at their own pace, among forest environments that included four different locations in Japan. Each forest walk was matched with an urban walk in the same region. The walks were all more or less flat, and the walking distances were the same.

Each walk lasted from twelve to fifteen minutes. The groups were randomly split and half walked in the forest and the other half walked in the urban center.

The next day, the forest group walked in the urban center and the urban group took the forest walk.

The researchers found that the walking speeds between the forest walks and the urban walks were about the same.

High-frequency heart rate variability – also called HF-HRV - indicates fluctuations of the heart's rhythms that illustrate general health.

Low High-frequency heart rate variability has been seen among those with higher anxiety, reduced cardiovascular health, and tendencies toward depression and hostility according to previous research. Research has also found greater high-frequency HRV scores relate to better sleep (Tobaldini *et al.* 2013).

This study found that while the forest and the urban walks took the same length of time and were physiologically the same, the forest walk resulted in significantly higher levels of high-frequency heart rate variability.

Heart rates were also significantly lower during the forest walks compared to the urban walks. The average heart rates during the forest walk were 87 BPM (beats per minute) while the urban walk average was nearly 92 BPM.

And systolic blood pressure during the forest walk was significantly lower than during the urban walk. Blood pressure during the forest walk averaged 114 mmHg and averaged 116 mmHg during the urban walk.

Note that these are among the same people taking two similar walks – the only difference being the surrounding of each walk.

Regarding the questionnaires, the forest walks resulted in significantly better scores among the men.

This included the tension-anxiety score – 36 versus 42 points; the anger-hostility score – 37.7 versus 39 points; fatigue – 36 versus 41; and confusion – 42 versus 44.

The forest walking also "refreshed" the subjects more than the urban walk did – with a score of 65 versus 50.

The researchers wrote:

> *"Subjective evaluation using the SD method revealed that the participants felt more comfortable, soothed, and natural after forest walking than after urban walking both before and after activities."*

One of the most meaningful differences was in the anxiety levels. The forest walkers scored 33 after the walk, while the urban walkers scored 45 on the anxiety scale.

In their discussion, the researchers concluded:

> *"We performed field experiments in four different local areas to evaluate the physiological benefits of forest walking. Our data indicated that the forest walking program has a positive influence on cardiovascular relaxation."*

The researchers added that the benefits of forest walkers compare favorably with those that have been accomplished with research on meditation:

> *"These trends in heart rate variability response are often detected in meditation or yoga therapies."*

Exercise

Numerous studies have proven that aerobic and resistance exercise can significantly reduce anxiety and depression. The studies are so numerous, in fact, that studies reviewing all the studies provide the best proof. Let's take a quick look at some of the evidence.

A 2016 study from the Department of Clinical Psychology at Norway's University of Bergen (Kvam et al. 2016) analyzed 23 randomized controlled trials on 977 patients that tested exercise and depression.

The studies found that physical exercise had a moderate to large effect on depression. It also had a significant effect compared to usual care and was effective even with medication. The researchers concluded:

"Physical exercise is an effective intervention for depression."

A 2020 study from scientists at the University of Oxford and Australia's Federation University (Miller *et al.*) conducted a systematic review of research that compared aerobic, resistance and mind-body exercise for depression in those over 65 years old.

The researchers analyzed 69 studies that tested 5,379 people. They pooled their results and found that all three forms of exercise produced significant reductions in depression symptoms.

Exercise is also helpful for anxiety. A study from the Institute of Psychiatry at the UK's King's College London (Stubbs et al. 2017) analyzed six randomized and controlled clinical trials that included 262 adults. The data indicated that exercise significantly decreased symptoms of anxiety compared to controls.

The researchers concluded:

"Our data suggest that exercise is effective in improving anxiety symptoms in people with a current diagnosis of anxiety and/ or stress-related disorders. Taken together with the wider benefits of exercise on wellbeing and cardiovascular health, these findings reinforce exercise as an important treatment option in people with anxiety/stress disorders."

A meta-analysis of research from Germany's MSH Medical School Hamburg (Wegner et al. 2014) analyzed 37 studies that included a total of 42,264 anxiety patients and 48,207 depression patients. This study found that exercise decreased both anxiety and depression symptoms, though it had a greater effect upon depression than anxiety when compared.

The connection between exercise and mood disorders also means the brain is improved with exercise. This aspect was researched by doctors at the Department of Psychology at the University of Pittsburgh and the Center for Neural Basis of Cognition at Carnegie Mellon University (Gujral et al. 2017).

Their research indicated that exercise increases the volume of the hippocampus, which is often decreased in mood disorders.

Aerobic training for five days a week for 30 minutes a day was enough to boost the volume of the hippocampus in as little as six weeks. But they also found that after six weeks of inactivity, the hippocampus size decreased back to the original size before the gain in volume as a result of exercise.

The results also showed that exercise boosted hippocampal plasticity and density and increased cerebral blood volume into the region. All this points to a more productive hippocampus, which means better production and balance of neurotransmitters and hormones production.

The research also found that depression was associated with reduced prefrontal cortex and anterior cingulated cortex regions of the brain. The research also found that regular exercise, even walking, increased the volume of both the prefrontal or anterior cingulated cortices within six months.

Their research also found that physical exercise increased levels of white matter and the volume of the cortical striatal – which are both decreased in depression patients.

The researchers stated in their paper:

> *"The prefrontal cortex, anterior cingulate cortex, hippocampus, and corpus callosum emerged as structural neural markers that may serve as targets for exercise-based treatments for depression."*

What this means is that the type of exercise is not as important as the consistency of exercising regularly. Whether your favorite exercise is playing tennis, basketball, or running, biking, walking or even mind-body exercises like Tai Chi, any of these can balance moods and the neurotransmitters that relate to them.

With that in mind, let's examine some of the mind-body exercises that can also provide a spiritual dimension for curbing depression and anxiety.

Tai chi and Qigong

Depression is a condition that has for the most part, escaped efforts by conventional medicine to provide a lasting solution. Now we find that two ancient meditative exercises, Tai chi and Qigong, can significantly reduce symptoms of depression.

Tai chi is a meditative exercise that promotes spiritual contemplation. This is proven out in its ability to treat depressed patients.

Tai consists of a series of slow, gentle and relaxed body movements. These are combined with deep focused breathing and a mental focus within.

These exercises, once the basic moves are learned, result in a contemplative meditation. The exercises are best done outside in a natural environment where the air is fresh.

Researchers from the Harvard Medical School and Massachusetts General Hospital (Yeung *et al.* 2017) conducted a study using 67 adults diagnosed with depression.

The researchers divided the patients into three groups. One group practiced Tai chi exercise three times a week for 12 weeks. Another group participated in education discussions about depression, stress, passive control and mental health during the same period. The third group remained on a waitlist for both during the same period.

The researchers tested each of the patients prior to the clinical trial. Then after 24 weeks, the researchers again tested each patient again. The doctors used the 17-item Hamilton Rating Scale for Depression to test the patients.

The researchers found those who practiced the Tai chi had significant reduction in depressive symptoms compared to the other two groups.

The Tai chi exercise treatments resulted in a 56 percent response rate and a 50 percent remission rate. Yes, just three months of Tai chi cured depression in half of the patients. This was three and four times more than those in the waitlist and education "control" groups.

In a paper on the study published in *the Journal of Clinical Psychiatry*, the researchers (Wu *et al.* 2017) concluded that,

> *"As the primary treatment, Tai chi improved [depression] treatment outcomes..."*

Furthermore, there were no negative side effects in the Tai chi treatment.

Qigong

Qigong is a very similar meditative exercise system. It has many similarities with Tai chi.

There have been multiple studies testing Qigong with depression in humans.

Researchers from the Australian National University and the University of Queensland (Liu *et al.* 2015) conducted a systematic review of the research.

The researchers analyzed 30 studies that treated a total of 2,328 depressed patients using Qigong exercises. The analysis found a significant improvement effect in 48 percent of the patients who underwent Qigong treatments.

Acupuncture

A number of studies have found that acupuncture can reduce the severity of anxiety and depression. In a Cochrane review of clinical research from Australia's Western Sydney University (Smith *et al.* 2018), 64 studies that included 7,104 people were analyzed.

The researchers tested for a number of variables. The research found that acupuncture can moderately reduce depression severity. Tests that compared acupuncture to sham acupuncture also found that acupuncture reduced depression severity.

In studies that tested acupuncture with medications against acupuncture alone found that acupuncture is *"highly beneficial in reducing the severity of depression by end of treatment."*

This study also found that different modes of acupuncture stimulation have also been shown to be helpful for depression.

For example, one study (Liang *et al.* 2014) found that electroacupuncture and ear acupuncture – also called auricular acupuncture – can reduce depression and anxiety symptoms.

The researchers tested 90 patients who were attempting to withdraw from methamphetamine use. For four weeks the patients received either electroacupuncture, ear acupuncture or no treatment.

The electroacupuncture and ear acupuncture groups had significantly better scores for anxiety, depression and withdrawal symptom scores compared with the control group. The electroacupuncture group had better scores than the auricular group.

Yoga and Meditation

The word *yoga* is derived from ancient Sanskrit which literally means 'union with God.' This ancient practice has now been proven scientifically to help reduce depression symptoms.

This may or may not scientifically establish the traditional healer's assumption of the integration between the body, the mind and the spirit. But it goes a long way towards providing some assurance that there is some form of spiritual connection in depression. In terms of the science alone, studies of the effect of meditation on the brain appear to provide some interesting associations.

In a healthy person, each of our brain regions – each cortex – will be thick with gray matter. Areas where gray matter is critical include the cerebral cortex, the cerebellum, the cuneal and precuneal cortices, the motor cortices and the somatosensory cortex among others.

Having normal levels of gray matter is critical to our brain's proper functioning, which includes decision-making, executive cognitive functions, retaining memories and so on. They are also critical for the brain's sensory and motor responses.

Why is this important? Because brain scan research has found that people with depression will typically also have abnormal levels of gray matter among different cortices of the brain.

Chronic pain, for example, has been linked to a reduction of gray matter in the cerebral cortex. And chronic fatigue syndrome patients have been found to have less gray matter in prefrontal and occipital cortices of the brain.

Meditation and the brain

In a 2016 study from the King's College in London and the University of the Laguna in Spain (Hernández *et al.*) doctors measured the brain volumes of 46 adults.

Half of the group (23 adults) were experienced practitioners in Sahaja Yoga Meditation. They had meditated using the system for between five and 26 years. They practiced meditation for between 34 and 150 minutes per day. The other 34 people were matched for age, sex and education. They did not meditate.

The researchers found that the whole brain grey matter volume was significantly greater among those who meditated. Brain regions with more volume included the insula, orbitofrontal cortex, inferior temporal cortex, parietal cortex and ventrolateral prefrontal cortex.

Other research has found similar results. Scientists from the Brain Imaging and Analysis Center at Duke University Medical Center (Froeliger *et al.* 2012) tested seven hatha yoga meditation practitioners and seven people who did not have a history of hatha yoga or meditation. They were all between the ages of 18 and 55.

The researchers gave each of the subjects a battery of tests, including those on symptoms of depression, anxiety and mood states. They also tested cognition and of course, conducted MRI brain scans on each.

The meditation practitioners had significantly greater gray matter volumes in a number of brain regions. These included the bilateral orbital frontal cortex, the right middle frontal and the left precentral region. The meditation practitioners also had higher levels of gray matter among the cerebellum, the temporal cortices, the occipital cortex and the hippocampus.

One of the most important findings was the significant increase in gray matter among the prefrontal cortex regions of the meditation practitioners. These have correlated with better moods and emotional responses.

Meditation has also been found to relieve anxiety, depression and even pain. Researchers from St. Mary's College (Ando *et al.* 2009) found in a study of 28 cancer patients that mindfulness meditation reduced pain scores as well as depression and anxiety after only two weeks of meditation therapy - which included yoga postures, breathing and meditation.

Gray matter content is increased with meditation. This is also confirmed by other research that has indeed found that hatha yoga and mindfulness meditation in general not only affect brainwave content within the brain, but also boost gray matter content within the brain.

Other research has in fact seen this type of 'intervention' effect - increasing gray matter. Researchers from India's National Institute of Mental Health and Neurosciences (Hariprasad *et al.* 2013) studied seven elderly persons who added hatha yoga practice to their lives for six months. The research found significant increases in gray matter within the hippocampus of the test subjects.

Furthermore, researchers from the University of Illinois at Chicago (Dasai *et al.* 2013) investigated no less than 15 studies that examined yoga interventions and the brain. The researchers found that yoga practices significantly produced immediate and lasting changes within the brain:

> *"It was concluded that breathing, meditation, and posture-based yoga increased overall brain wave activity. Increases in gray matter along with increases in amygdala and frontal cortex activation were evident after a yoga intervention. Yoga practice may be an effective adjunctive treatment for a clinical and healthy aging population. Further research can examine the effects of specific branches of yoga on a designated clinical population."*

A review of a broader swath of research led by Dr. John de Castro (2015) from the Sam Houston State University also found that the associations of yoga practice with the brain were also similar to those found from mindfulness meditation as well as prayer. Dr. Castro concluded that both mindfulness and prayer had a foundation within the context of meditation.

Hatha yoga is a series of exercises that are done meditatively. This meditative aspect may or may not be focused on during the practice, but the original art from India included it as part of the meditative yoga practice.

A study from the University of California San Francisco (Prathikanti *et al.* 2017) tested 38 adults with mild to moderate depression. The doctors had 20 people take a 90-minute hatha yoga class twice a week. The other 18 people attended an education class for 90 minutes for twice a week. The yoga participants saw a significant reduction in their depression scores.

A mindfulness meditation routine

There are many mindfulness meditation types and routines out there. But my favorite, which I call *mind-body-spirit meditation*, brings into focus the connection between the mind, body and spirit:

- Sit quietly in a comfortable position that can be maintained without falling asleep. Arch the back a bit to allow the chest and abdomen to expand with the breath.

- Now begin breathing in from the bottom of the abdomen. Push the abdomen slightly out to relax the diaphragm. As you breathe in, slowly push out the rest of the abdomen and after it is full, begin to lift the chest as you fill the top of your lungs with fresh air.

- Now empty the top of the chest first, and then slowly push the rest of the air out by contracting the abdomen. When you reach the bottom and the air is out, relax for a second and begin the process again with another breath.

- After several breaths, keep maintaining this breathing, but begin focusing your mind on your feet. On the first inward breath, relax the toes, and heel. On the first outward breath, relax the upper foot muscles and ligaments. On the second breath, remind yourself that you are the spirit and not your feet. You might whisper or say to yourself quietly: *I am not the feet.*

- Now move your mind to your lower legs. Relax the calves on the first inward breath, and the shin side on the outward breath. On the second breath, see yourself as spirit, and say to yourself: *I am not my lower legs.*

- Now move your mind to the upper legs – thighs and hamstrings. Relax the thighs, then relax the hamstrings on the first breath. On the second breath, see yourself as spirit and say to yourself: *I am not the legs.*

- Now move to your groin and buttocks region. On the inward breath, relax the groin region. On the outward breath, relax the buttocks and the hips. On the second breath, see yourself as spirit and say to yourself: *I am not the groin, hips or buttocks.*

- Now move your mind to your abdomen and lower back region. On the inward breath relax your abdomen as you are breathing in. On the outward breath, relax your back muscles. On the second breath, see yourself as spirit and say to yourself: *I am not the abdomen or lower back.*

- Now move your mind to your chest region and upper back. On the inward breath, relax your chest and rib cage. On the outward breath, relax your upper back. Now see yourself as spirit and say to yourself: *I am not the chest, lungs, heart or upper back.*

- Now move your mind to your neck region. On the inward breath, relax your throat region and front neck muscles. On the outward breath relax the back of the next and those muscles at the base of the head in the back. On the second breath, see yourself as spirit and say to yourself: *I am not the neck.*

- Now move your mind to your head. On the inward breath, relax your face muscles, your eyes, your chin, your jaw. On the outward breath, relax the back of your head, and the brain. Now see yourself as spirit and say to yourself: *I am not the face or the brain.*

You can expand this meditation to separate more of the body parts, and even do different organs and body parts as you wish separately. For example, the focus could be on the eyes, ears, mouth, lungs, heart, stomach and so on, in addition to the regions.

This can be helpful especially if you have pain or issues in one region or organ. For example, a person with hip pain might want to do some separate breathing on just the hips, breathing in and out on relaxing the hips and then on the second breath, seeing yourself as spirit and saying: *I am not the hips.*

This mindfulness exercise brings us the ability to not only relax the body and breath slowly to oxidize the system. It can also focus the mind on the deeper elements of our existence, namely our spiritual side. This allows our mind to remove itself from the mundane elements of our existence and focus on the higher self more and more.

Loving Kindness Meditation

Research has also found that a type of meditation called loving-kindness meditation will increase what is called vagal tone. And this in turn reduces depression and PTSD symptoms.

Vagal tone relates to the vagus nerve. This tenth's cranial nerve's origin is in the lower portion of the brainstem – in an area called the medulla. This region of the brain controls many of the body's the autonomic functions, including those of the blood vessels, the heart, the digestive tract and the lungs.

In other words, our respiratory health, our digestive health and our respiratory health is closely tied to the activities of the vagus nerve.

This is because the vagus nerve descends from the brainstem down through the neck and heart and lung region through the thorax and down to the diaphragm. Here it regulates the rhythms of digestion – called peristalsis.

For these reasons, better vagal tone is linked with better overall health.

In a study published in the Association for Psychological Science's journal *Psychological Science*, (Kok *et al.* 2013) researchers at the University of North Carolina and the Max Planck Institute for Human Cognitive and Brain Sciences divided 65 men and women into two groups.

For two months, one group was guided through loving-kindness meditation and the other group was put on a waiting list.

Both groups were examined with regard to their vagal tone at the beginning and compared vagal tone with the intervention group and the control group – the 'waiting list' group.

The research found the meditation significantly increased vagal tone.

The researchers also found the effect was increased through social connections. With increased social connections came increased vagal tone. Even those with greater vagal tone in the beginning of the study had increases in the vagal tone after undergoing the meditation and applying it within their social connections.

A study by researchers from the Veteran's Administration in Seattle (Kearney *et al.* 2013) tested Loving-Kindness meditation for cases of veterans with post-traumatic stress disorder (PTSD). The researchers conducted a three-month course with weekly classes, and found that attendance was high – 74%.

In a three-month follow-up of the effects of the meditation course, the researchers found that the meditation significantly reduced depression and other PTSD symptoms among the veterans.

Researchers from Stanford University tested whether loving-kindness meditation could increase practical feelings of social connections between people and improve their view of each other. The study found the affirmative.

The connection between depression and heart rate variability is also discussed in the forest walking section. Better heart rate variability has been linked with better emotional control and adaptability.

Heart rate variability is a variation in the intervals between beats. Reduced HRV has been linked to increased heart attack risk.

Increased heart rate variability has also been linked with longer lifespans and reduced stress in general. Several studies have linked increased tone of the vagus nerve - vagal tone - with increased heart rate variability.

What is loving-kindness meditation?

The meditation has its roots in Buddhism and it seeks to produce within the heart, four experiences:

- Friendliness (metta)
- Compassion (karuna)
- Appreciative Joy (mudita)
- Equanimity (upekkha)

Typically the meditation is to be directed at someone who the person respects greatly, and traditionally in Buddhism this has been used with respect to ones spiritual teacher and the Buddha. More modern/secular versions of this practice will direct ones loving-kindness meditation towards a friend, family member or even a person where there is a disagreement with – or multiple parties. It is typically not done with those of the opposite sex as that can provoke the opposite effect.

Modern techniques suggest a self-love technique but the traditional meditation focused upon oneself in a humble manner, and seeking forgiveness for oneself.

The meditation brings ones focus towards the positive aspects of the person or persons – thinking of the person's achievements, their personality qualities and directing appreciation towards the person(s). This can include visualizing the person in a kind exchange.

The meditation then progresses to sending out positive feelings – positive intentions for the person(s) and their own life and future.

How to practice loving-kindness meditation

Loving-kindness meditation can be practiced in cases of difficulties with work or personal relationships as well as building our overall feelings towards others. The meditation itself can done lying down, sitting or walking.

Deep breathing with eyes closed is often suggested to minimize outside interruptions.

It can be guided by others or self-guided. It is helpful to organize and even write down the positive areas and intentions towards the person(s) that will be focused upon prior to the meditation.

This unburdens the meditation to enable better focus.

It is more successful when personalizing the experience rather than be guided through rote repetition.

Finding Challenges as Learning Experiences

How we handle adversity is key to whether we succumb to negative moods and emotions.

A study from Warsaw's University of Social Sciences and Humanities (Braniecka *et al.* 2014) found that a combination of positive and negative emotions mixed with nostalgia – called *secondary mixed emotions* – provides increased ability to deal with adversity.

Researchers conducted three successive studies to test the effects of positive and negative moods. The three studies tested 111, 96 and 118 men and women between 20 and 26 years old. The researchers conducted tests using the Positive and Negative Affect Schedule (PANAS), the General Health Questionnaire and the State-Trait Anxiety Inventory among others to assess the subjects' ability to cope with challenges.

Test subjects were divided into groups that included secondary mixed emotions compared to sequential positive and negative emotions – where the test subjects were tested with positive and negative moods consecutively.

Compared with both positive and negative moods, the research found that secondary mixed emotions were more natural responses to stress, and resulted in less depressive symptoms later.

Anxiety levels were also lower among those with secondary mixed emotions. Furthermore, the secondary mixed emotion group had a greater tendency to cope with challenges using solution-oriented action, with 78 percent choosing actions that provided solutions.

Another way to look at secondary mixed emotional responses is to consider events that play out in our lives as learning experiences.

Seeing events as learning experiences allows us to step back and be an observer, removing us just a little from the fray. Seeing these learning experiences as challenges allows us to participate, but with the understanding that we are spirit and our participation will be temporary.

One may be faced with a challenge that can be tremendously inconvenient, and even painful. The first realization is that the challenge is, in the long term, temporary. We are only on this earth, at least in this lifetime, for a few decades. Then our spirit will move on, taking with it our learning experiences that arose from our challenges.

If we understand these challenges are essentially learning experiences and we will at some point get through them, we can realize that we can grow and evolve from each challenge and experience.

Such an attitude can change our outlook as we face so many challenges that come at us during our lifetime. If we can approach each as a test and learning experience, we can keep them from ruining our quest to grow and evolve. This attitude can, coupled with some of the constructive physiological strategies examined in this book, boost our enthusiasm for accomplishing our goals in life.

(To help you find, organize and establish your short-term and lifetime goals, consider my book, *"Your Plan for Life."*)

A New Vision of Depression and Anxiety

This book has covered a vision of depression and anxiety that opens up a significant opportunity for our society. That opportunity is to approach these conditions as temporary lapses of the body's abilities to produce the right natural balance of hormones and neurotransmitters that keep our moods and emotional responses balanced, coupled with establishing our identity as spirit.

This new vision embraces, firstly, an understanding that mood disorders are not a fault in the person. There is no potential for embarrassment for the sufferer, nor an assumption that these conditions are permanent.

The scientific evidence reveals that depression and anxiety may have a spiritual connection at some level, but their physiological causes relate to neuroinflammation produced by some combination of physical and lifestyle stressors that change our body's output and maintenance of hormones and neurotransmitters through a disruption of our hypothalamus-pituitary-adrenal (HPA) axis.

Such an alteration in our HPA axis may have occurred as a result of something as simple as a lack of proper sleep and sunlight, and the exposure of bright (blue) light from our screens during late nights, disrupting our body's hormone-neurotransmitter cycles. This may be exasperated by our dietary choices and lack of outdoor activities.

Elements of our diet may have deprived our body of the nutrients needed to detoxify free radicals, and supply or balance these hormones and neurotransmitters. And the lack of exercise and outdoor activities can deprive our bodies of the challenges and stimulation that provide natural rhythms to our life.

This text has examined evidence showing that our lack of certain phytonutrients may be exasperating our levels of neuroinflammation. This is because phytonutrients provide the antidote to free radical toxins that may be surging in our body and nervous system.

Indeed, we have also examined how specific medicinal herbs have been shown scientifically to rebalance the body's production of mood-altering hormones and neurotransmitters. These herbs come with a history of safety and when used under the supervision of a doctor can provide a significant ray of hope for those who have been suffering from mood disorders for many years.

On top of these strategies we have discussed the evidence showing that practical lifestyle strategies can significantly reduce the severity of mood conditions such as depression and bipolar disorder. These have included outdoor exercise, forest walking, yoga, meditation, taking saunas and flotation therapy among others.

The research providing this evidence has studied regimented versions of these lifestyles. But it is quite easy for us to apply all of these types of lifestyle therapies to our life in a more casual way. Most of them are available to us in different forms, during our everyday lifestyle without causing significant sacrifice.

Taking time during the day to take a walk in the forest or beach in the sun, for example, is a pleasant way to keep our life grounded. And/or taking a few minutes to meditate in a natural setting where we can get some natural light and breathe some fresh air. Or taking our exercise routines outside whenever possible.

Indeed, most of the strategies proven out in this text can actually provide numerous enhancements to our life that open the avenues for our internal growth and personal evolution.

That is the magic of natural approaches. They are not one-dimensional. They typically provide a myriad of benefits. That's because nature is smart.

References and Bibliography

Aan het Rot M, Benkelfat C, Boivin DB, Young SN. Bright light exposure during acute tryptophan depletion prevents a lowering of mood in mildly seasonal women. Eur Neuropsychopharmacol. 2008 Jan;18(1):14-23.

Abdou AM, Higashiguchi S, Horie K, Kim M, Hatta H, Yokogoshi H. Relaxation and immunity enhancement effects of gamma-aminobutyric acid GABA. Biofactors. 2006;26(3):201-8.

Abreu T, Bragança M. The bipolarity of light and dark: A review on Bipolar Disorder and circadian cycles. J Affect Disord. 2015 Oct 1;185:219-29. doi: 10.1016/j.jad.2015.07.017.

Ackerman D. A Natural History of the Senses. New York: Vintage, 1991.

Adams C. Probiotics - Protection Against Infection: Using Nature's Tiny Warriors To Stem Infection and Fight Disease. Logical Books, 2016.

Addelman M. Healthy diet can ease symptoms of depression. Univ Manchester, 2019; Feb 5.

Agarwal U, Mishra S, Xu J, Levin S, Gonzales J, Barnard ND. A Multicenter Randomized Controlled Trial of a Nutrition Intervention Program in a Multiethnic Adult Population in the Corporate Setting Reduces Depression and Anxiety and Improves Quality of Life: The GEICO study. Am J Health Promot. 2014 Feb 13.

Ahn YJ, Park SJ, Woo H, Lee HE, Kim HJ, Kwon G, Gao Q, Jang DS, Ryu JH. Effects of allantoin on cognitive function and hippocampal neurogenesis. Food Chem Toxicol. 2014 Feb;64:210-6. doi: 10.1016/j.fct.2013.11.033.

Airola P. How to Get Well. Phoenix, AZ: Health Plus, 1974.

Akhondzadeh S, Noroozian M, Mohammadi M, Ohadinia S, Jamshidi AH, Khani M. Salvia officinalis extract in the treatment of Alzheimer's disease: a double blind, randomized and placebo-controlled trial. J Clin Pharm Ther. 2003;28(1):53–9.

Akihiro T., Koike S., Tani R., Tominaga T., Watanabe S., Iijima Y., Aoki K., Shibata D., Ashihara H., Matsukura C. Biochemical mechanism on GABA accumulation in tomato. Plant Cell Physiol. 2008;49:1378–1389. doi: 10.1093/pcp/pcn113.

Amassian VE, Cracco RQ, Maccabee PJ, Cracco JB, Rudell A, Eberle L. Suppression of visual perception by magnetic coil stimulation of human occipital cortex. Electroencephalogr Clin Neurophysiol. 1989 Nov-Dec;74(6):458-62.

American Academy of Neurology. Can therapy help improve mood in people with concussion? American Academy of Neurology's 72nd Annual Meeting in Toronto, Canada, April 25 to May 1, 2020.

Amsterdam JD, Li Y, Soeller I, Rockwell K, Mao JJ, Shults J. A randomized, double-blind, placebo-controlled trial of oral Matricaria recutita (chamomile) extract therapy for generalized anxiety disorder. J Clin Psychopharmacol. 2009 Aug;29(4):378-82.

Amsterdam JD, Panossian AG. Rhodiola rosea L. as a putative botanical antidepressant. Phytomedicine. 2016 Jun 15;23(7):770-83. doi: 10.1016/j.phymed.2016.02.009.

Amsterdam JD, Shults J, Soeller I, Mao JJ, Rockwell K, Newberg AB. Chamomile (Matricaria recutita) may provide antidepressant activity in anxious, depressed humans: an exploratory study. Altern Ther Health Med. 2012 Sep-Oct;18(5):44-9.

An BS, Kang JH, Yang H, Jung EM, Kang HS, Choi IG, Park MJ, Jeung EB. Anti-inflammatory effects of essential oils from Chamaecyparis obtusa via the cyclooxygenase-2 pathway in rats. Mol Med Rep. 2013 Jul;8(1):255-9. doi: 10.3892/mmr.2013.1459.

Anderson DR, Huston AC, Schmitt KL, Linebarger DL, Wright JC. Early childhood television viewing and adolescent behavior: the recontact study. Monogr Soc Res Child Dev. 2001;66(1):I-VIII, 1-147.

Anderson MJ, Petros TV, Beckwith BE, Mitchell WW, Fritz S. Individual differences in the effect of time of day on long-term memory access. Am J Psych. 1991;104:241–255.

Ando M, Morita T, Akechi T, Ito S, Tanaka M, Ifuku Y, Nakayama T. The efficacy of mindfulness-based meditation therapy on anxiety, depression, and spirituality in Japanese patients with cancer. J Palliat Med. 2009 Dec;12(12):1091-4. doi: 10.1089/jpm.2009.0143.

Apaydin EA, Maher AR, Shanman R, Booth MS, Miles JN, Sorbero ME, Hempel S. A systematic review of St. John's wort for major depressive disorder. Syst Rev. 2016 Sep 2;5(1):148. doi: 10.1186/s13643-016-0325-2.

Armas LA, Hollis BW, Heaney RP. Vitamin D2 is much less effective than vitamin D3 in humans. J Clin Endocrinol Metab. 2004 Nov;89(11):5387-91.

Aton SJ, Colwell CS, Harmar AJ, Waschek J, Herzog ED. Vasoactive intestinal polypeptide mediates circadian rhythmicity and synchrony in mammalian clock neurons. Nat Neurosci. 2005 Apr;8(4):476-83.

Autier P, Gandini S, Mullie P. A systematic review: influence of vitamin D supplementation on serum 25-hydroxyvitamin D concentration. J Clin Endocrinol Metab. 2012 Aug;97(8):2606-13. doi: 10.1210/jc.2012-1238.

Autier P, Gandini S. Vitamin D supplementation and total mortality: a meta-analysis of randomized controlled trials. Arch Intern Med. 2007 Sep 10;167(16):1730-7.

Axelson M. 25-Hydroxyvitamin D3 3-sulphate is a major circulating form of vitamin D in man. FEBS Lett. 1985 Oct 28;191(2):171-5.

Azar JA, Conroy T. Measuring the effectiveness of horticultural therapy at a veterans administration medical center: experimental design issues. In Relf, D. (ed) The Role of Horticulture in Human Well-Being and Social Development: A National Symposium. Portland: Timber Press. 1992:169-171.

Ballentine R. Diet & Nutrition: A holistic approach. Honesdale, PA: Himalayan Int., 1978.

Ballentine R. Radical Healing. New York: Harmony Books, 1999.

Baran D, Apostol I. Signification of biorhythms for human performance assessment. Rev Med Chir Soc Med Nat Iasi. 2007 Jan-Mar;111(1):295-302.

Barron M. Light exposure, melatonin secretion, and menstrual cycle parameters: an integrative review. Biol Res Nurs. 2007 Jul;9(1):49-69.

Bazrafshan MR, Jokar M, Shokrpour N, Delam H. The effect of lavender herbal tea on the anxiety and depression of the elderly: A randomized clinical trial. Complement Ther Med. 2020 May;50:102393. doi: 10.1016/j.ctim.2020.102393.

Becker R. Cross Currents. Los Angeles: Tarcher, 1990.

Becker R. The Body Electric. New York: Morrow, Inc., 1985.

Beecher GR. Phytonutrients' role in metabolism: effects on resistance to degenerative processes. Nutr Rev. 1999 Sep;57(9 Pt 2):S3-6.

Benedetti F, Radaelli D, Bernasconi A, Dallaspezia S, Falini A, Scotti G, Lorenzi C, Colombo C, Smeraldi E. Clock genes beyond the clock: CLOCK genotype biases neural correlates of moral valence decision in depressed humans. Genes Brain Behav. 2007 Mar 26.

Bennet LW, Cardone S, Jarczyk J. Effects of therapeutic camping program on addiction recovery. Journal of Substance Abuse Treatment. 1998;15(5):469-474.

Bensky D, Gable A, Kaptchuk T (transl.). Chinese Herbal Medicine Materia Medica. Seattle: Eastland Press, 1986.

Bensky D, Gamble A, Kaptehuk T. Chinese Herbal Medicine: Materia Medica. Eastland Press, 1986.

Benson S, Downey LA, Stough C, Wetherell M, Zangara A, Scholey A. An acute, double-blind, placebo-controlled cross-over study of 320 mg and 640 mg doses of Bacopa monnieri (CDRI 08) on multitasking stress reactivity and mood. Phytother Res. 2014 Apr;28(4):551-9. doi: 10.1002/ptr.5029.

Bentley E. Awareness: Biorhythms, Sleep and Dreaming. London: Routledge, 2000.

Berk M, Dodd S, Henry M. Do ambient electromagnetic fields affect behaviour? A demonstration of the relationship between geomagnetic storm activity and suicide. Bioelectromagnetics. 2006 Feb;27(2):151-5.

Berk M, Sanders KM, Pasco JA, Jacka FN, Williams LJ, Hayles AL, Dodd S. Vitamin D deficiency may play a role in depression. Med Hypotheses. 2007;69(6):1316-9.

Berk M, Williams LJ, Jacka FN, O'Neil A, Pasco JA, Moylan S, Allen NB, Stuart AL, Hayley AC, Byrne ML, Maes M. So depression is an inflammatory disease, but where does the inflammation come from? BMC Med. 2013 Sep 12;11:200. doi: 10.1186/1741-7015-11-200.

Berman S, Fein G, Jewett D, Ashford F. Luminance-controlled pupil size affects Landolt C task performance. J Illumin Engng Soc. 1993;22:150-165.

Berman S, Jewett D, Fein G, Saika G, Ashford F. Photopic luminance does not always predict perceived room brightness. Light Resch and Techn. 1990;22:37-41.

Berry J. Work efficiency and mood states of electronic assembly workers exposed to full-spectrum and conventional fluorescent illumination. Diss Abstr Internl. 1983;44:635B.

Berry-Bibee EN, Kim MJ, Tepper NK, Riley HE, Curtis KM. Co-administration of St. John's wort and hormonal contraceptives: a systematic review. Contraception. 2016 Jul 18. pii: S0010-7824(16)30164-0. doi: 10.1016/j.contraception.2016.07.010.

Bhasin M. Ocimum- Taxonomy, medicinal potentialities and economic value of essential oil. Journal of Biosphere. 2012;1:48–50.

Bhattacharyya D, Sur TK, Jana U, Debnath PK. Controlled programmed trial of Ocimum sanctum leaf on generalized anxiety disorders. Nepal Med Coll J. 2008 Sep;10(3):176-9.

Bickham DS, Rich M. Is television viewing associated with social isolation? Roles of exposure time, viewing context, and violent content. Arch Pediatr Adolesc Med. 2006 Apr;160(4):387-92.

Bishop ID, Rohrmann B. Subjective responses to simulated and real environments: a comparison. Landscape and Urban Planning. 2003;65(4):261-277.

Boivin DB, Czeisler CA. Resetting of circadian melatonin and cortisol rhythms in humans by ordinary room light. Neuroreport. 1998 Mar 30;9(5):779-82.

Boivin DB, Duffy JF, Kronauer RE, Czeisler CA. Dose-response relationships for resetting of human circadian clock by light. Nature. 1996 Feb 8;379(6565):540-2.

Bollani L, Dolci C, Gerola O, Montaruli A, Rondini G, Carandente F. The early maturation of the circadian system in newborns. Chronobiologia. 1994 Jan-Jun;21(1-2):105-8.

REFERENCES AND BIBLIOGRAPHY

Boray P, Gifford R, Rosenblood L. Effects of warm white, cool white and full-spectrum fluorescent lighting on simple cognitive performance, mood and ratings of others. J Environl Psychol. 1989;9:297-308.

Boudebesse C, Henry C. Emotional hyper-reactivity and sleep disturbances in remitted patients with bipolar disorders. Encephale. 2012 Dec;38 Suppl 4:S173-8. doi: 10.1016/S0013-7006(12)70096-9.

Boyce P, Rea M. A field evaluation of full-spectrum, polarized lighting. Paper presented at the 1993 Annual Convention of the Illuminating Engineering Society of North America, Houston, TX. 1993 Aug.

Boyce P. Investigations of the subjective balance between illuminance and lamp colour properties. Light Resch and Technol. 1977;9:11-24.

Bradwejn J, Zhou Y, Koszycki D, Shlik J. A double-blind, placebo-controlled study on the effects of Gotu Kola (Centella asiatica) on acoustic startle response in healthy subjects. J Clin Psychopharmacol. 2000 Dec;20(6):680-4. doi: 10.1097/00004714-200012000-00015.

Brainard GC, Hanifin JP, Warfield B, Stone MK, James ME, Ayers M, Kubey A, Byrne B, Rollag M. Short-wavelength enrichment of polychromatic light enhances human melatonin suppression potency. J Pineal Res. 2015 Apr;58(3):352-61. doi: 10.1111/jpi.12221

Braniecka A, Trzebińska E, Dowgiert A, Wytykowska A. Mixed emotions and coping: the benefits of secondary emotions. PLoS One. 2014 Aug 1;9(8):e103940. doi: 10.1371/journal.pone.0103940.

Bravo JA, Forsythe P, Chew MV, Escaravage E, Savignac HM, Dinan TG, Bienenstock J, Cryan JF. Ingestion of Lactobacillus strain regulates emotional behavior and central GABA receptor expression in a mouse via the vagus nerve. Proc Natl Acad Sci U S A. 2011 Sep 20;108(38):16050-5.

Breslau N, Novak SP, Kessler RC. Psychiatric disorders and stages of smoking. Biol Psychiatry. 2004 Jan 1;55(1):69-76.

Briguglio M, Dell'Osso B, Panzica G, Malgaroli A, Banfi G, Zanaboni Dina C, Galentino R, Porta M. Dietary Neurotransmitters: A Narrative Review on Current Knowledge. Nutrients. 2018 May 10;10(5). pii: E591. doi:10.3390/nu10050591.

Brodeur P. Currents of Death. New York: Simon and Schuster, 1989.

Brookie KL, Best GI, Conner TS. Intake of Raw Fruits and Vegetables Is Associated With Better Mental Health Than Intake of Processed Fruits and Vegetables. Front Psychol. 2018 Apr 10;9:487. doi: 10.3389/fpsyg.2018.00487.

Buijs RM, Scheer FA, Kreier F, Yi C, Bos N, Goncharuk VD, Kalsbeek A. Organization of circadian functions: interaction with the body. Prog Brain Res. 2006;153:341-60.

Burnett KM, Solterbeck LA, Strapp CM. Scent and mood state following an anxiety-provoking task. Psychol Rep. 2004 Oct;95(2):707-22.

Buscemi N, Vandermeer B, Pandya R, Hooton N, Tjosvold L, Hartling L, Baker G, Vohra S, Klassen T. Melatonin for treatment of sleep disorders. Evid Rep Technol Assess. 2004 Nov;(108):1-7.

Buzsaki G. Theta rhythm of navigation: link between path integration and landmark navigation, episodic and semantic memory. Hippocampus. 2005;15(7):827-40.

Cajochen C, Jewett ME, Dijk DJ. Human circadian melatonin rhythm phase delay during a fixed sleep-wake schedule interspersed with nights of sleep deprivation. J Pineal Res. 2003 Oct;35(3):149-57.

Cajochen C, Zeitzer JM, Czeisler CA, Dijk DJ. Dose-response relationship for light intensity and ocular and electroencephalographic correlates of human alertness. Behav Brain Res. 2000 Oct;115(1):75-83.

Calabrese C, Gregory WL, Leo M, Kraemer D, Bone K, Oken B. Effects of a standardized Bacopa monnieri extract on cognitive performance, anxiety, and depression in the elderly: a randomized, double-blind, placebo-controlled trial. J Altern Complement Med. 2008 Jul;14(6):707-13.

Celec P. Analysis of rhythmic variance – ANORVA. A new simple method for detecting rhythms in biological time series. Biol Res. 2004;37(4 Suppl A):777-82.

Centers for Disease Control and Prevention. Chronic Fatigue Syndrome. Accessed March 7, 2016.

Chandrasekhar K, Kapoor J, Anishetty S. A prospective, randomized double-blind, placebo-controlled study of safety and efficacy of a high-concentration full-spectrum extract of Ashwagandha root in reducing stress and anxiety in adults. Ind Jnl Psych Med. 2012 34(3): 255-262.

Chandrasekhar K, Kapoor J, Anishetty S. A prospective, randomized double-blind, placebo-controlled study of safety and efficacy of a high-concentration full-spectrum extract of Ashwagandha root in reducing stress and anxiety in adults. Ind Jnl Psych Med. 2012 34(3): 255-262.

Chang AM, Aeschbach D, Duffy JF, Czeisler CA. Evening use of light-emitting eReaders negatively affects sleep, circadian timing, and next-morning alertness. Proc Natl Acad Sci U S A. 2015 Jan 27;112(4):1232-7. doi: 10.1073/pnas.1418490112.

Chatterjee M, Verma P, Maurya R, Palit G. Evaluation of ethanol leaf extract of Ocimum sanctum in experimental models of anxiety and depression. Pharm Biol. 2011 May;49(5):477-83. doi: 10.3109/13880209.2010.523832.

Chen CJ, Kumar KJ, Chen YT, Tsao NW, Chien SC, Chang ST, Chu FH, Wang SY. Effect of Hinoki and Meniki Essential Oils on Human Autonomic Nervous System Activity and Mood States. Nat Prod Commun. 2015 Jul;10(7):1305-8.

Chen HH, Chen CY, Chow LP, Chen CH, Lee YT, Smith CV, Yang CY. Iron-catalyzed oxidation of Trp residues in low-density lipoprotein. Biol Chem. 2011 Aug 18.

Chen SJ, Chao YL, Chen CY, Chang CM, Wu EC, Wu CS, Yeh HH, Chen CH, Tsai HJ. Prevalence of autoimmune diseases in in-patients with schizophrenia: nationwide population-based study. Br J Psychiatry. 2012 May;200(5):374-80.

Chen Y, Guillemin GJ. Kynurenine Pathway Metabolites in Humans: Disease and Healthy States. Internl Jnl Trypt Res. 2009:2 1-19.

Chen YJ, Lin CY, Cheng SS, Chang ST. Phylogenetic relationships of the genus Chamaecyparis inferred from leaf essential oil. Chem Biodivers. 2011 Jun;8(6):1083-97.

Chengappa KN, Bowie CR, Schlicht PJ, Fleet D, Brar JS, Jindal R. Randomized placebo-controlled adjunctive study of an extract of withania somnifera for cognitive dysfunction in bipolar disorder. J Clin Psychiatry. 2013 Nov;74(11):1076-83. doi: 10.4088/JCP.13m08413.

Chien LW, Cheng SL, Liu CF. The effect of Lavender aromatherapy on autonomic nervous system in midlife women with insomnia. Evid Based Complement Alternat Med. 2012;2012:740813.

Chien TC, Lo SF, Ho CL. Chemical composition and anti-inflammatory activity of Chamaecyparis obtusa f.formosana wood essential oil from Taiwan. Nat Prod Commun. 2014 May;9(5):723-6.

Chirkova EN, Suslov LS, Avramenko MM, Krivoruchko GE. Monthly and daily biorhythms of amylase in the blood of healthy men and their relation with the rhythms in the external environment. Lab Delo. 1990;(4):40-4.

Cho MY, Min ES, Hur MH, Lee MS. Effects of aromatherapy on the anxiety, vital signs, and sleep quality of percutaneous coronary intervention patients in intensive care units. Evid Based Complement Alternat Med. 2013;2013:381381.

Chong NW, Codd V, Chan D, Samani NJ. Circadian clock genes cause activation of the human PAI-1 gene promoter with 4G/5G allelic preference. FEBS Lett. 2006 Aug 7;580(18):4469-72.

Christensen MA, Bettencourt L, Kaye L, Moturu ST, Nguyen KT, Olgin JE,Pletcher MJ, Marcus GM. Direct Measurements of Smartphone Screen-Time:Relationships with Demographics and Sleep. PLoS One. 2016 Nov 9;11(11):e0165331.doi: 10.1371/journal.pone.0165331.

Cocilovo A. Colored light therapy: overview of its history, theory, recent developments and clinical applications combined with acupuncture. Am J Acupunct. 1999;27(1-2):71-83.

Cohen MM. Tulsi - Ocimum sanctum: A herb for all reasons. J Ayurveda Integr Med. 2014 Oct-Dec;5(4):251-9. doi: 10.4103/0975-9476.146554.

Coles JA, Yamane S. Effects of adapting lights on the time course of the receptor potential of the anuran retinal rod. J Physiol. 1975 May;247(1):189-207.

Compas BE, Jaser SS, Dunn MJ, Rodriguez EM. Coping with chronic illness in childhood and adolescence. Annu Rev Clin Psy-chol. 2012;8:455-80.

Concerto C, Infortuna C, Muscatello MRA, Bruno A, Zoccali R, Chusid E, Aguglia E, Battaglia F. Exploring the effect of adaptogenic Rhodiola Rosea extract on neuroplasticity in humans. Complement Ther Med. 2018 Dec;41:141-146. doi: 10.1016/j.ctim.2018.09.013.

Conrad P, Adams C. The effects of clinical aromatherapy for anxiety and depression in the high risk postpartum woman - a pilot study. Complement Ther Clin Pract. 2012 Aug;18(3):164-8. doi: 10.1016/j.ctcp.2012.05.002.

Corry J, Green M, Roberts G, Frankland A, Wright A, Lau P, Loo C, Breakspear M, Mitchell PB. Anxiety, stress and perfectionism in bipolar disorder. J Affect Disord. 2013 Dec;151(3):1016-24. doi: 10.1016/j.jad.2013.08.029.

Cox NJ, Oostendorp GM, Folgering HT, van Herwaarden CL. Sauna to transiently improve pulmonary function in patients with obstructive lung disease. Arch Phys Med Rehabil 1989;70:911-913.

Crawley J. The Biorhythm Book. Boston: Journey Editions, 1996.

Creinin MD, Keverline S, Meyn LA. How regular is regular? An analysis of menstrual cycle regularity. Contraception. 2004 Oct;70(4):289-92.

Crinnion WJ. Sauna as a valuable clinical tool for cardiovascular, autoimmune, toxicant- induced and other chronic health problems. Altern Med Rev. 2011 Sep;16(3):215-25.

Cryan JF, Dinan TG. Mind-altering microorganisms: the impact of the gut microbiota on brain and behaviour. Nat Rev Neurosci. 2012 Oct;13(10):701-12. doi: 10.1038/nrn3346. Luna RA, Foster JA. Gut brain axis: diet microbiota interactions and implications for modulation of anxiety and depression. Curr Opin Biotechnol. 2015 Apr;32:35-41. doi: 10.1016/j.copbio.2014.10.007.

Davies G. Timetables of Medicine. New York: Black Dog & Leventhal, 2000.

Davinelli S, Scapagnini G, Marzatico F, Nobile V, Ferrara N, Corbi G. Influence of equol and resveratrol supplementation on health-related quality of life in menopausal women: A randomized, placebo-controlled study. Maturitas. 2017 Feb;96:77-83. doi: 10.1016/j.maturitas.2016.11.016.

Davis GE Jr, Lowell WE. Chaotic solar cycles modulate the incidence and severity of mental illness. Med Hypotheses. 2004;62(2):207-14.

Davis GE Jr, Lowell WE. The Sun determines human longevity: teratogenic effects of chaotic solar radiation. Med Hypotheses. 2004;63(4):574-81.

Davis S, Mirick DK, Stevens RG. Night shift work, light at night, and risk of breast cancer. J Natl Cancer Inst. 2001 Oct 17;93(20):1557-62.

Davis-Berman J, Berman DS. The wilderness therapy program: an empirical study of its effects with adolescents in an outpatient setting. Journal of Contemporary Psychotherapy. 1989;19 (4):271-281.

Davison KM, Hyland CE, West ML, Lin SL, Tong H, Kobayashi KM, Fuller-Thomson E. Post-traumatic stress disorder (PTSD) in mid-age and older adults differs by immigrant status and ethnicity, nutrition, and other determinants of health in the Canadian Longitudinal Study on Aging (CLSA). Soc Psychiatry Psychiatr Epidemiol. 2021 Feb 3. doi: 10.1007/s00127-020-02003-7

Davison KM, Lin SL, Tong H, Kobayashi KM, Mora-Almanza JG, Fuller-Thomson E. Nutritional Factors, Physical Health and Immigrant Status Are Associated with Anxiety Disorders among Middle-Aged and Older Adults: Findings from Baseline Data of The Canadian Longitudinal Study on Aging (CLSA). Int J Environ Res Public Health. 2020 Feb 26;17(5):1493. doi: 10.3390/ijerph17051493.

Davison KM, Lung Y, Lin SL, Tong H, Kobayashi KM, Fuller-Thomson E. Depression in middle and older adulthood: the role of immigration, nutrition, and other determinants of health in the Canadian longitudinal study on aging. BMC Psychiatry. 2019 Nov 6;19(1):329. doi: 10.1186/s12888-019-2309-y.

de Castro JM. Meditation has stronger relationships with mindfulness, kundalini, and mystical experiences than yoga or prayer. Conscious Cogn. 2015 May 20;35:115-127. doi: 10.1016/j.concog.2015.04.022.

de Koning EJ, Lips P, Penninx BWJH, Elders PJM, Heijboer AC, den Heijer M, Bet PM, van Marwijk HWJ, van Schoor NM. Vitamin D supplementation for the prevention of depression and poor physical function in older persons: the D-Vitaal study, a randomized clinical trial. Am J Clin Nutr. 2019 Nov 1;110(5):1119-1130. doi: 10.1093/ajcn/nqz141.

de Koning EJ, van Schoor NM, Penninx BW, Elders PJ, Heijboer AC, Smit JH, Bet PM, van Tulder MW, den Heijer M, van Marwijk HW, Lips P. Vitamin D supplementation to prevent depression and poor physical function in older adults: Study protocol of the D-Vitaal study, a randomized placebo-controlled clinical trial. BMC Geriatr. 2015 Nov 19;15:151. doi: 10.1186/s12877-015-0148-3.

De Leo V, La Marca A, Lanzetta D, Palazzi S, Torricelli M, Facchini C, Morgante G. Assessment of the association of Kava-Kava extract and hormone replacement therapy in the treatment of postmenopause anxiety. Minerva Ginecol. 2000 Jun;52(6):263-7.

Dement W, Vaughan C. The Promise of Sleep. New York: Dell, 1999.

Desai R, Tailor A, Bhatt T. Effects of yoga on brain waves and structural activation: A review. Complement Ther Clin Pract. 2015 May;21(2):112-118. doi: 10.1016/j.ctcp.2015.02.002.

Desbonnet L, Garrett L, Clarke G, Bienenstock J, Dinan TG. The probiotic Bifidobacteria infantis: An assessment of potential antidepressant properties in the rat. J Psychiatr Res. 2008 Dec;43(2):164-74.

Dickerson F, Adamos M, Katsafanas E, Khushalani S, Origoni A, Savage C, Schweinfurth L, Stallings C, Sweeney K, Goga J, Yolken RH. Adjunctive probiotic microorganisms to prevent rehospitalization in patients with acute mania: A randomized controlled trial. Bipolar Disord. 2018 Nov;20(7):614-621. doi: 10.1111/bdi.12652. Epub 2018 Apr 25.

Diop L, Guillou S, Durand H. Probiotic food supplement reduces stress-induced gastrointestinal symptoms in volunteers: a double-blind, placebo-controlled, randomized trial. Nutr Res. 2008 Jan;28(1):1-5.

Downey LA, Kean J, Nemeh F, Lau A, Poll A, Gregory R, Murray M, Rourke J, Patak B, Pase MP, Zangara A, Lomas J, Scholey A, Stough C. An Acute, Double-Blind, Placebo-Controlled Crossover Study of 320 mg and 640 mg Doses of a Special Extract of Bacopa monnieri (CDRI 08) on Sustained Cognitive Performance. Phytother Res. 2012 Dec 19.

Downey LA, Kean J, Nemeh F, Lau A, Poll A, Gregory R, Murray M, Rourke J, Patak B, Pase MP, Zangara A, Lomas J, Scholey A, Stough C. An acute, double-blind, placebo-controlled crossover study of 320 mg and 640 mg doses of a special extract of Bacopa monnieri (CDRI 08) on sustained cognitive performance. Phytother Res. 2013 Sep;27(9):1407-13. doi: 10.1002/ptr.4864.

Ebbesen F, Agati G, Pratesi R. Phototherapy with turquoise versus blue light. Arch Dis Child Fetal Neonatal Ed. 2003 Sep;88(5):F430-1.

Edwards R, Ibison M, Jessel-Kenyon J, Taylor R. Light emission from the human body. Comple Med Res. 1989;3(2):16-19.

Edwards R, Ibison M, Jessel-Kenyon J, Taylor R. Measurements of human bioluminescence. Acup Elect Res, Intl Jnl, 1990;15:85-94.

Eriksson O, Wall A, Marteinsdottir I, Agren H, Hartvig P, Blomqvist G, Långström B, Naessén T. Mood changes correlate to changes in brain serotonin precursor trapping in women with pre-menstrual dysphoria. Psychiatry Res. 2006 Mar 31;146(2):107-16.

Ernst E, Pecho E, Wirz P, Saradeth T. Regular sauna bathing and the incidence of common colds. Ann Med 1990;22:225-227.

Evans P, Forte D, Jacobs C, Fredhoi C, Aitchison E, Hucklebridge F, Clow A. Cortisol secretory activity in older people in relation to positive and negative well-being. Psychoneuroendocrinology. 2007 Aug 7.

FDA. Risk of drug interactions with St. John's wort.

Fehring RJ, Schneider M, Raviele K. Variability in the phases of the menstrual cycle. J Obstet Gynecol Neonatal Nurs. 2006 May-Jun;35(3):376-84.

Firth J, Gangwisch JE, Borisini A, Wootton RE, Mayer EA. Food and mood: how do diet and nutrition affect mental wellbeing? BMJ. 2020 Jun 29;369:m2382. doi: 10.1136/bmj.m2382. Erratum in: BMJ. 2020 Nov 9;371:m4269.

Firth J, Marx W, Dash S, Carney R, Teasdale SB, Solmi M, Stubbs B, Schuch FB, Carvalho AF, Jacka F, Sarris J. The Effects of Dietary Improvement on Symptoms of Depression and Anxiety: A Meta-Analysis of Randomized Controlled Trials. Psychosom Med. 2019 Apr;81(3):265-280. doi: 10.1097/PSY.0000000000000673.

Fitzpatrick AM, Baena-Cagnani CE, Bacharier LB. Severe asthma in childhood: recent advances in phenotyping and pathogenesis. Curr Opin Allergy Clin Immunol. 2012 Apr;12(2):193-201.

Francis HM, Stevenson RJ, Chambers JR, Gupta D, Newey B, Lim CK. A brief diet intervention can reduce symptoms of depression in young adults - A randomised controlled trial. PLoS One. 2019 Oct 9;14(10):e0222768. doi: 10.1371/journal.pone.0222768.

Freeman HL, Stansfield SA. Psychosocial effects of urban environments, noise, and crowding. In Lundberg, A. (ed) Environment and Mental Health. London: Lawrence Erlbaum. 1998:147-173.

Frey A. Electromagnetic field interactions with biological systems. FASEB Jnl. 1993;7:272-28.

Froeliger BE, Garland EL, Modlin LA, McClernon FJ. Neurocognitive correlates of the effects of yoga meditation practice on emotion and cognition: a pilot study. Front Integr Neurosci. 2012 Jul 26;6:48. doi: 10.3389/fnint.2012.00048.

Fukada Y, Okano T. Circadian clock system in the pineal gland. Mol Neurobiol. 2002 Feb;25(1):19-30.

Gambini JP, Velluti RA, Pedemonte M. Hippocampal theta rhythm synchronizes visual neurons in sleep and waking. Brain Res. 2002 Feb 1;926(1-2):137-41.

Gange R. UVA sunbeds - are there longterm hazards. In Cronley-Dillon J, Rosen E, Marshall J (Eds.):Hazards of Light, Myths and Realities. Oxford, U.K.: Pergamon Press, 1986.

Gannon JM, Brar J, Rai A, Chengappa KNR. Effects of a standardized extract of Withania somnifera (Ashwagandha) on depression and anxiety symptoms in persons with schizophrenia participating in a randomized, placebo-controlled clinical trial. Ann Clin Psychiatry. 2019 May;31(2):123-129.

Gardner A. U.S. has highest bipolar rate in 11-nation study. CNN Health.

Gardner MP, Wansink B, Kim J, Park SB. Better moods for better eating?: How mood influences food choice. Jour Cons Psych. 2014 Jan 25.

Garma L. (2003) Insomnias associated with psychiatric disorders. In: Billiard M. (eds) Sleep. Springer, Boston, MA. 2003. doi: 10.1007/978-1-4615-0217-3_19

Garma L. Insomnias associated with psychiatric disorders. In: Billiard M. (eds) Sleep. Springer, Boston, MA 2003.

Gau SS, Soong WT, Merikangas KR. Correlates of sleep-wake patterns among children and young adolescents in Taiwan. Sleep. 2004 May 1;27(3):512-9.

Gehlich KH, Beller J, Lange-Asschenfeldt B, Köcher W, Meinke MC, Lademann J. Consumption of fruits and vegetables: improved physical health, mental health, physical functioning and cognitive health in older adults from 11 European countries. Aging Ment Health. 2019 Feb 7:1-8. doi: 10.1080/13607863.2019.1571011.

Geller SE, Studee L. Botanical and dietary supplements for mood and anxiety in menopausal women. Menopause. 2007 May-Jun;14(3 Pt 1):541-9.

Geoffroy PA, Boudebesse C, Henrion A, Jamain S, Henry C, Leboyer M, Bellivier F, Etain B. An ASMT variant associated with bipolar disorder influences sleep and circadian rhythms: a pilot study(1.). Genes Brain Behav. 2013 Nov 14. doi: 10.1111/gbb.12103.

George KS, Raghunath N, Bharath MM, Muralidhara. Prophylaxis with Bacopa monnieri attenuates Acrylamide induced neurotoxicity and oxidative damage via elevated antioxidant function. Cent Nerv Syst Agents Med Chem. 2012 Oct 17.

Gesler WM. Therapeutic landscapes: medical issues in light of the new cultural geography. Soc Sci Med. 1992 Apr;34(7):735-46.

Ghadioungui P. (transl.) The Ebers Papyrus. Academy of Scientific Research. Cairo, 1987.

Gleason CE, Dowling NM, Wharton W, Manson JE, Miller VM, Atwood CS, Brinton EA, Cedars MI, Lobo RA, Merriam GR, Neal-Perry G, Santoro NF, Taylor HS, Black DM, Budoff MJ, Hodis HN, Naftolin F, Harman SM, Asthana S. Effects of Hormone Therapy on Cognition and Mood in Recently Postmenopausal Women: Findings from the Randomized, Controlled KEEPS-Cognitive and Affective Study. PLoS Med. 2015 Jun 2;12(6):e1001833.

Gomez-Abellan P, Hernandez-Morante JJ, Lujan JA, Madrid JA, Garaulet M. Clock genes are implicated in the human metabolic syndrome. Int J Obes. 2007 Jul 24.

REFERENCES AND BIBLIOGRAPHY

Gopinath B, Flood VM, Burlutksy G, Louie JC, Mitchell P. Association between carbohydrate nutrition and prevalence of depressive symptoms in older adults. Br J Nutr. 2016 Dec;116(12):2109-2114. doi: 10.1017/S0007114516004311.

Gryka D, Pilch W, Szarek M, Szygula Z, Tota Ł. The effect of sauna bathing on lipid profile in young, physically active, male subjects. Int J Occup Med Environ Health. 2014 Aug;27(4):608-18. doi: 10.2478/s13382-014-0281-9

Gu Q, Dillon CF, Burt VL. Prescription Drug Use Continues to Increase: US Prescription Drug Data for 2007-2008. NCHS/CDC. Sept. 2010.

Gupta P, Yadav DK, Siripurapu KB, Palit G, Maurya R. Constituents of Ocimum sanctum with antistress activity. J Nat Prod. 2007 Sep;70(9):1410-6.

Gupta YK, Gupta M, Kohli K. Neuroprotective role of melatonin in oxidative stress vulnerable brain. Indian J Physiol Pharmacol. 2003 Oct;47(4):373-86.

Gujral S, Aizenstein H, Reynolds CF 3rd, Butters MA, Erickson KI. Exercise effects on depression: Possible neural mechanisms. Gen Hosp Psychiatry. 2017 Nov;49:2-10.

Hagins WA, Penn RD, Yoshikami S. Dark current and photocurrent in retinal rods. Biophys J. 1970 May;10(5):380-412.

Hagins WA, Robinson WE, Yoshikami S. Ionic aspects of excitation in rod outer segments. Ciba Found Symp. 1975;(31):169-89.

Hagins WA, Yoshikami S. Proceedings: A role for Ca2+ in excitation of retinal rods and cones. Exp Eye Res. 1974 Mar;18(3):299-305.

Hagins WA. The visual process: Excitatory mechanisms in the primary receptor cells. Annu Rev Biophys Bioeng. 1972;1:131-58.

Haller J, Freund TF, Pelczer KG, Füredi J, Krecsak L, Zámbori J. The anxiolytic potential and psychotropic side effects of an echinacea preparation in laboratory animals and healthy volunteers. Phytother Res. 2013 Jan;27(1):54-61. doi: 10.1002/ptr.4677.

Haller J, Krecsak L, Zámbori J. Double-blind placebo controlled trial of the anxiolytic effects of a standardized Echinacea extract. Phytother Res. 2019 Dec 25. doi: 10.1002/ptr.6558.

Halpern S. Tuning the Human Instrument. Palo Alto, CA: Spectrum Research Institute, 1978.

Hammermeister J, Brock B, Winterstein D, Page R. Life without TV? cultivation theory and psychosocial health characteristics of television-free individuals and their television-viewing counterparts. Health Commun. 2005;17(3):253-64.

Hammitt WE. The relation between being away and privacy in urban forest recreation environments. Environment and Behaviour. 2000;32 (4):521-540.

Hancox RJ, Milne BJ, Poulton R. Association of television viewing during childhood with poor educational achievement. Arch Pediatr Adolesc Med. 2005 Jul;159(7):614-8.

Hanifin JP, Stewart KT, Smith P, Tanner R, Rollag M, Brainard GC. High-intensity red light suppresses melatonin. Chronobiol Int. 2006;23(1-2):251-68.

Hans J. The Structure and Dynamics of Waves and Vibrations. New York:.Schocken and Co., 1975.

Hansen SN, Ipsen DH, Schou-Pedersen AM, Lykkesfeldt J, Tveden-Nyborg P. Long term Westernized diet leads to region-specific changes in brain signaling mechanisms. Neurosci Lett. 2018 May 29;676:85-91. doi: 10.1016/j.neulet.2018.04.014

Hardin P. Transcription regulation within the circadian clock: the E-box and beyond. J Biol Rhythms. 2004 Oct;19(5):348-60.

Hariprasad VR, Varambally S, Shivakumar V, Kalmady SV, Venkatasubramanian G, Gangadhar BN. Yoga increases the volume of the hippocampus in elderly subjects. Indian J Psychiatry. 2013 Jul;55(Suppl 3):S394-6. doi: 10.4103/0019-5545.116309.

Hartz AJ, Bentler S, Noyes R, Hoehns J, Logemann C, Sinift S, Butani Y, Wang W, Brake K, Ernst M, Kautzman H. Randomized controlled trial of Siberian Ginseng for chronic fatigue. Psychol Med. 2004 Jan;34(1):51-61.

Hayasaka S, Nakamura Y, Kajii E, Ide M, Shibata Y, Noda T, Murata C, Nagata K, Ojima T. Effects of charcoal kiln saunas (Jjimjilbang) on psychological states. Complement Ther Clin Pract. 2008 May;14(2):143-8. doi: 10.1016/j.ctcp.2007.12.004.

He Q, Yang L, et al. Smoking and Major Depressive Disorder in Chinese Women. PLoS One. 2014 Sep 2;9(9):e106287. doi: 10.1371/journal.pone.0106287.

He Q, Yang L, et al. Smoking and Major Depressive Disorder in Chinese Women. PLoS One. 2014 Sep 2;9(9):e106287. doi: 10.1371/journal.pone.0106287.

Hernández SE, Suero J, Barros A, González-Mora JL, Rubia K. Increased Grey Matter Associated with Long-Term Sahaja Yoga Meditation: A Voxel-Based Morphometry Study. PLoS One. 2016 Mar 3;11(3):e0150757. doi: 10.1371/journal.pone.0150757.

Hewitt PL, Flett GL. Perfectionism and stress processes in psychopathology. (Perfectionism: Theory, Research and Treatment) American Psychological Association, Wash., 2002.

189

Hoffmann KM, Herbrechter R, Ziemba PM, Lepke P, Beltrán L, Hatt H, Werner M, Gisselmann G. Kampo Medicine: Evaluation of the Pharmacological Activity of 121 Herbal Drugs on GABAA and 5-HT3A Receptors. Front Pharmacol. 2016 Jul 29;7:219.

Holick MF. Sunlight and vitamin D for bone health and prevention of autoimmune diseases, cancers, and cardiovascular disease. Am J Clin Nutr. 2004 Dec;80(6 Suppl):1678S-88S.

Holick MF. Vitamin D status: measurement, interpretation, and clinical application. Ann Epidemiol. 2009 Feb;19(2):73-8.

Holick MF. Vitamin D. In: Shils ME, Shike M, Ross AC, Caballero B, Cousins RJ, eds. Modern Nutrition in Health and Disease, 10th ed. Philadelphia: Lippincott Williams & Wilkins, 2006.

Hollfoth K. Effect of color therapy on health and wellbeing: colors are more than just physics. Pflege.Z 2000;53(2):111-112.

Hollwich F, Dieckhues B, Schrameyer B. The effect of natural and artificial light via the eye on the hormonal and metabolic balance of man. Klin Monbl Augenheilkd. 1977 Jul;171(1):98-104.

Hollwich F, Dieckhues B. Effect of light on the eye on metabolism and hormones. Klin Monbl Augenheilkd. 1989 Nov;195(5):284-90.

Hollwich F, Hartmann C. Influence of light through the eyes on metabolism and hormones. Ophtalmologie. 1990 Jul-Aug;4(4):385-9.

Hollwich F. The influence of ocular light perception on metabolism in man and in animal. NY: Springer-Verlag, 1979.

Honeyman MK. Vegetation and stress: a comparison study of varying amounts of vegetation in countryside and urban scenes. In Relf, D. (ed) The Role of Horticulture in Human Well-Being and Social Development: A National Symposium. Portland: Timber Press. 1992:143-145.

Hongratanaworakit, T. Simultaneous aromatherapy massage with rosemary oil on humans. Scientia Pharmaceutica. Volume 77, Issue 2, 2009, Pages 375-387

Horne JA, Donlon J, Arendt J. Green light attenuates melatonin output and sleepiness during sleep deprivation. Sleep. 1991 Jun;14(3):233-40.

Hou Q, He WJ, Chen L, Hao HJ, Liu JJ, Dong L, Tong C, Li MR, Zhou ZZ, Han WD, Fu XB. Effects of the Four-Herb Compound ANBP on Wound Healing Promotion in Diabetic Mice. Int J Low Extrem Wounds. 2015 Mar 20. pii: 1534734615575244

Hsiao CC, Liu CY, Hsiao MC. No correlation of depression and anxiety to plasma estrogen and progesterone levels in patients with premenstrual dysphoric disorder. Psychiatry Clin Neurosci. 2004 Dec;58(6):593-9. doi: 10.1111/j.1440-1819.2004.01308.x.

Huesmann LR, Moise-Titus J, Podolski CL, Eron LD. Longitudinal relations between children's exposure to TV violence and their aggressive and violent behavior in young adulthood: 1977-1992. Dev Psychol. 2003 Mar;39(2):201-21.

Hutcherson CA, Seppala EM, Gross JJ. Loving-kindness meditation increases social connectedness. Emotion. 2008 Oct;8(5):720-4. doi: 10.1037/a0013237.

Igarashi T. Physical and psychologic effects of aromatherapy inhalation on pregnant women: a randomized controlled trial. Journal of Alternative and Complementary Medicine, vol. 19, no. 10, pp. 805–810, 2013.

Ikeda M, Toyoshima R, Inoue Y, Yamada N, Mishima K, Nomura M, Ozaki N, Okawa M, Takahashi K, Yamauchi T. Mutation screening of the human Clock gene in circadian rhythm sleep disorders. Psychiatry Res. 2002 Mar 15;109(2):121-8.

Ikonomov OC, Stoynev AG. Gene expression in suprachiasmatic nucleus and circadian rhythms. Neurosci Biobehav Rev. 1994 Fall;18(3):305-12.

Ishaque S, Shamseer L, Bukutu C, Vohra S. Rhodiola rosea for physical and mental fatigue: a systematic review. BMC Complement Altern Med. 2012 May 29;12:70. doi: 10.1186/1472-6882-12-70.

Jana U, Sur TK, Maity LN, Debnath PK, Bhattacharyya D. A clinical study on the management of generalized anxiety disorder with Centella asiatica. Nepal Med Coll J. 2010 Mar;12(1):8-11.

Jankowski KS. Morningness-eveningness and depressive symptoms: Test on the components level with CES-D in Polish students. J Affect Disord. 2016 May 15;196:47-53. doi: 10.1016/j.jad.2016.02.015.

Jensen B. Foods that Heal. Garden City Park, NY: Avery Publ, 1988, 1993.

Jensen B. Nature Has a Remedy. Los Angeles: Keats, 2001.

Jiajie Yu, Yujia Cai, Guanyue Su, and Youping Li, "Motherwort Injection for Preventing Postpartum Hemorrhage in Women with Vaginal Delivery: A Systematic Review and Meta-Analysis of Randomized Evidence," Evidence-Based Complementary and Alternative Medicine, vol. 2019, Article ID 1803876, 9 pages, 2019.

Johari H. Ayurvedic Massage: Traditional Indian Techniques for Balancing Body and Mind. Roch: Healing Arts, 1996.

Johari H. Chakras. Rochester, VT: Destiny, 1987.

Kalsbeek A, Perreau-Lenz S, Buijs RM. A network of (autonomic) clock outputs. Chronobiol Int. 2006;23(1-2):201-15.

Kamide Y. We reside in the sun's atmosphere. Biomed Pharmacother. 2005 Oct;59 Suppl 1:S1-4.

Kanagarajan K, Gou K, Antinora C, Buyukkurt A, Crescenzi O, Beaulieu S, Storch KF, Mantere O. Morn-ingness-Eveningness questionnaire in bipolar disorder. Psychiatry Res. 2018 Apr;262:102-107. doi: 10.1016/j.psychres.2018.02.004.

Kandel E, Siegelbaum S, Schwartz J. Synaptic transmission. Principles of Neural Science. New York: El-sevier, 1991.

Kantor ED, Rehm CD, Haas JS, Chan AT, Giovannucci EL. Trends in Prescription Drug Use Among Adults in the United States From 1999-2012. JAMA. 2015 Nov 3;314(17):1818-31. doi: 10.1001/jama.2015.13766.

Kaplan R. The psychological benefits of nearby nature. In: Relf, D. (ed) The Role of Horticulture in Human Well-Being and Social Development: A National Symposium. Portland: Timber Press. 1992:125-133.

Kaplan S. The restorative environment: nature and human experience. In: Relf, D. (ed) The Role of Horti-culture in Human Well-Being and Social Development: A National Symposium. Portland: Timber Press. 1992:134-142.

Katz M, Levine AA, Kol-Degani H, Kav-Venaki L. A compound herbal preparation (CHP) in the treatment of children with ADHD: a randomized controlled trial. J Atten Disord. 2010 Nov;14(3):281-91. doi: 10.1177/1087054709356388.

Kawamura KY, Frost RO, Harmatz MG. The relationship to perceived parenting styles to perfectionism. Personality and Individual Differences. 2002;32:317–327.

Kearney DJ, Malte CA, McManus C, Martinez ME, Felleman B, Simpson TL. Loving-kindness meditation for posttraumatic stress disorder: a pilot study. J Trauma Stress. 2013 Aug;26(4):426-34. doi: 10.1002/jts.21832.

Kelly TL, Neri DF, Grill JT, Ryman D, Hunt PD, Dijk DJ, Shanahan TL, Czeisler CA. Nonentrained circadian rhythms of melatonin in submariners scheduled to an 18-hour day. J Biol Rhythms. 1999 Jun;14(3):190-6.

Kennedy DO, Pace S, Haskell C, Okello EJ, Milne A, Scholey AB. Effects of cholinesterase inhibiting sage (Salvia officinalis) on mood, anxiety and performance on a psychological stressor battery. Neuropsy-chopharmacology. 2006;31(4):845–52.

Kent ST, McClure LA, Crosson WL, Arnett DK, Wadley VG, Sathiakumar N. Effect of sunlight exposure on cognitive function among depressed and non-depressed participants: a REGARDS cross-sectional study. Environ Health. 2009 Jul 28;8:34.

Kesse-Guyot E, Andreeva VA, Jeandel C, Ferry M, Hercberg S, Galan P. A healthy dietary pattern at midlife is associated with subsequent cognitive performance. J Nutr. 2012 May;142(5):909-15.

Kianpour M, Mansouri A, Mehrabi T, Asghari G. Effect of lavender scent inhalation on prevention of stress, anxiety and depression in the postpartum period. Iran J Nurs Midwifery Res. 2016 Mar-Apr;21(2):197-201. doi: 10.4103/1735-9066.178248.

Kim ES, Delaney SW, Tay L, Chen Y, Diener ED, Vanderweele TJ. Life Satisfaction and Subsequent Physical, Behavioral, and Psychosocial Health in Older Adults. Milbank Q. 2021 Mar;99(1):209-239. doi: 10.1111/1468-0009.12497.

Kim ES, Weon JB, Yun BR, Lee J, Eom MR, Oh KH, Ma CJ. Cognitive Enhancing and Neuroprotective Effect of the Embryo of the Nelumbo nucifera Seed. Evid Based Complement Alternat Med. 2014;2014:869831. doi: 10.1155/2014/869831.

Kim H, Kim J, Loggia ML, Cahalan C, Garcia RG, Vangel MG, Wasan AD, Edwards RR, Napadow V. Fibromyalgia is characterized by altered frontal and cerebellar structural covariance brain networks. Neuroimage Clin. 2015 Mar 4;7:667-77. doi: 10.1016/j.nicl.2015.02.022.

Kim H, Kim J, Loggia ML, Cahalan C, Garcia RG, Vangel MG, Wasan AD, Edwards RR, Napadow V. Fibromyalgia is characterized by altered frontal and cerebellar structural covariance brain networks. Neuroimage Clin. 2015 Mar 4;7:667-77. doi: 10.1016/j.nicl.2015.02.022.

Kjellgren A, Westman J. Beneficial effects of treatment with sensory isolation in flotation-tank as a preven-tive healthcare intervention - a randomized controlled pilot trial. BMC Complement Altern Med. 2014 Oct 25;14:417. doi: 10.1186/1472-6882-14-417.

Kleitman N. Sleep and Wakefulness. Univ Chicago Press, 1963.

Kloss J. Back to Eden. Twin Oaks, WI: Lotus Press, 1939-1999.

Klungsøyr O, Nygård JF, Sørensen T, Sandanger I. Cigarette smoking and incidence of first depressive episode: an 11-year, population-based follow-up study. Am J Epidemiol. 2006 Mar 1;163(5):421-32.

Knekt P, Järvinen R, Rissanen H, Heliövaara M, Aromaa A. Does sauna bathing protect against dementia? Prev Med Rep. 2020 Oct 2;20:101221. doi: 10.1016/j.pmedr.2020.101221.

Knutson KL, von Schantz M. Associations between chronotype, morbidity and mortality in the UK Biobank cohort. Chronobiol Int. 2018 Apr 11:1-9. doi: 10.1080/07420528.2018.1454458.

Kok BE, Coffey KA, Cohn MA, Catalino LI, Vacharkulksem-suk T, Algoe SB, Brantley M, Fredrickson BL. How positive emotions build physical health: perceived positive social connections account for the upward spiral between positive emotions and vagal tone. Psychol Sci. 2013 Jul 1;24(7):1123-32. doi: 10.1177/0956797612470827.

Kowalczyk E, Krzesiński P, Kura M, Niedworok J, Kowalski J, Błaszczyk J. Pharmacological effects of flavonoids from Scutellaria baicalensis. Przegl Lek. 2006;63(2):95-6.

Kremer B, den Hartog HM, Jolles J. Relationship between allergic rhinitis, disturbed cognitive functions and psychological well-being. Clin Exp Allergy. 2002 Sep;32(9):1310-5.

Kuchta K, Schmidt M, Nahrstedt A. German Kava Ban Lifted by Court: The Alleged Hepatotoxicity of Kava (Piper methysticum) as a Case of Ill-Defined Herbal Drug Identity, Lacking Quality Control, and Misguided Regulatory Politics. Planta Med. 2015 Dec;81(18):1647-53.

Küller R, Laike T. The impact of flicker from fluorescent lighting on well-being, performance and physiological arousal. Ergonomics. 1998 Apr;41(4):433-47.

Kumarihamy M, León F, Pettaway S, Wilson L, Lambert JA, Wang M, Hill C, McCurdy CR, ElSohly MA, Cutler SJ, Muhammad I. In vitro opioid receptor affinity and in vivo behavioral studies of Nelumbo nucifera flower. J Ethnopharmacol. 2015 Aug 7:JEPD1501341. doi: 10.1016/j.jep.2015.08.006.

Kuuler R, Ballal S, Laike T Mikellides B, Tonello G. The impact of light and colour on psychological mood: a cross-cultural study of indoor work environments. Ergonomics. 2006 Nov 15;49(14):1496.

Kvam S, Kleppe CL, Nordhus IH, Hovland A. Exercise as a treatment for depression: A meta-analysis. J Affect Disord. 2016 Sep 15;202:67-86. doi: 10.1016/j.jad.2016.03.063.

Lad V. Ayurveda: The Science of Self-Healing. Twin Lakes, WI: Lotus Press.

Lakhan SE, Vieira KF. Nutritional and herbal supplements for anxiety and anxiety-related disorders: systematic review. Nutr J. 2010 Oct 7;9:42. doi:10.1186/1475-2891-9-42.

Lamport DJ, Saunders C, Butler LT, Spencer JP. Fruits, vegetables, 100% juices, and cognitive function. Nutr Rev. 2014 Dec;72(12):774-89. doi: 10.1111/nure.12149.

LaPorte E, Sarris J, Stough C, Scholey A. Neurocognitive effects of kava (Piper methysticum): a systematic review. Hum Psychopharmacol. 2011 Mar;26(2):102-11. doi: 10.1002/hup.1180.

Larun L, Brurberg KG, Odgaard-Jensen J, Price JR. Exercise therapy for chronic fatigue syndrome. Cochrane Database Syst Rev. 2019 Oct 2;10: CD003200. doi:10.1002/ 14651858. CD003200. pub8.

Laukkanen T, Khan H, Zaccardi F, Laukkanen JA. Association between sauna bathing and fatal cardiovascular mortality events. JAMA Intern Med. 2015 Apr;175(4):542-8. doi: 10.1001/jamainternmed.2014.8187.

Laukkanen T, Kunutsor S, Kauhanen J, Laukkanen JA. Sauna bathing is inversely associated with dementia and Alzheimer's disease in middle-aged Finnish men. Age Ageing. 2016 Dec 7.

Lee DB, Kim DH, Je JY. Antioxidant and Cytoprotective Effects of Lotus (Nelumbo nucifera) Leaves Phenolic Fraction. Prev Nutr Food Sci. 2015 Mar;20(1):22-8. doi: 10.3746/pnf.2015.20.1.22.

Lee J, Tsunetsugu Y, Takayama N, et al. Influence of Forest therapy on Cardiovascular Relaxation in Young Adults. Evidence-Based Complementary and Alternative Medicine, vol. 2014, Article ID 834360, 2014. doi: 10.1155/2014/834360

Lee JS, Shukla S, Kim JA, Kim M. Anti-angiogenic effect of Nelumbo nucifera leaf extracts in human umbilical vein endothelial cells with antioxidant potential. PLoS One. 2015 Feb 25;10(2):e0118552. doi: 10.1371/journal.pone.0118552.

Lemon K. An assessment of treating depression and anxiety with aromatherapy. Intl Jnl Aromath, vol. 14, no. 2, pp. 63–69, 2004.

Leng Y, Wainwright NW, Cappuccio FP, Surtees PG, Hayat S, Luben R, Brayne C, Khaw KT. Daytime Napping and the Risk of All-Cause and Cause-Specific Mortality: A 13-Year Follow-up of a British Population. Am J Epidemiol. 2014 May 1;179(9):1115-24. doi: 10.1093/aje/kwu036.

Leong PK, Wong HS, Chen J, Ko KM. Yang/Qi invigoration: an herbal therapy for chronic fatigue syndrome with yang deficiency? Evid Based Complement lternat Med. 2015;2015:945901. doi: 10.1155/2015/945901.

Li XZ, Ramzan I. Role of ethanol in kava hepatotoxicity. Phytother Res. 2010 Apr;24(4):475-80. doi: 10.1002/ptr.3046.

Liang Y, Xu B, Zhang XC, Zong L, Chen YL. [Comparative study on effects between electroacupuncture and auricular acupuncture for methamphetamine withdrawal syndrome]. Zhongguo Zhen Jiu. 2014 Mar;34(3):219-24.

Liggins J, Bluck LJ, Runswick S, Atkinson C, Coward WA, Bingham SA. Daidzein and genistein contents of vegetables. Br J Nutr. 2000 Nov;84(5):717-25.

Light-Emitting E-Readers Before Bedtime Can Adversely Impact Sleep. Press Release.

Lillestøl K, Berstad A, Lind R, Florvaag E, Arslan Lied LG, Tangen T. Anxiety and depression in patients with self-reported food hypersensitivity. Gen Hosp Psychiatry. 2010 Jan-Feb;32(1):42-8.

Limberg JK, Harrell JW, Johansson RE, Eldridge MW, Proctor LT, Sebranek JJ, Schrage WG. Microvascular function in younger adults with obesity and metabolic syndrome: role of oxidative stress. Am J Physiol Heart Circ Physiol. 2013 Oct 15;305(8):H1230-7. doi: 10.1152/ajpheart.00291.2013.

REFERENCES AND BIBLIOGRAPHY

Limpeanchob N, Jaipan S, Rattanakaruna S, Phrompittayarat W, Ingkaninan K. Neuroprotective effect of Bacopa monnieri on beta-amyloid-induced cell death in primary cortical culture. J Ethnopharmacol. 2008 Oct 30;120(1):112-7.

Lin JH, Lin QD, Liu XH, Yan JY, He J, Li L, Gu H, Sun LZ, Zhang JP, Yu S, Ma YY, Niu JM, Xia Y, Zhao SC, Li W, Wang HL, Wang BS. Multi-center study of motherwort injection to prevent postpartum hemorrhage after caesarian section. Zhonghua Fu Chan Ke Za Zhi. 2009 Mar;44(3):175-8.

Linde K, Berner MM, Kriston L. St John's wort for major de-pression. Cochrane Database Syst Rev. 2008 Oct 8;(4):CD000448. doi: 10.1002/14651858.CD000448.pub3.

Lishmanov IuB, Trifonova ZhV, Tsibin AN, Maslova LV, Dement'eva LA. Plasma beta-endorphin and stress hormones in stress and adaptation. Biull Eksp Biol Med. 1987 Apr;103(4):422-4.

Liu CM, Kao CL, Wu HM, Li WJ, Huang CT, Li HT, Chen CY. Antioxidant and anticancer aporphine alkaloids from the leaves of Nelumbo nucifera Gaertn. cv. Rosa-plena. Molecules. 2014 Nov 3;19(11):17829-38. doi: 10.3390/molecules191117829.

Liu SH, Lu TH, Su CC, Lay IS, Lin HY, Fang KM, Ho TJ, Chen KL, Su YC, Chiang WC, Chen YW. Lotus leaf (Nelumbo nucifera) and its active constituents prevent inflammatory responses in macrophages via JNK/NF-xB signaling pathway. Am J Chin Med. 2014;42(4):869-89. doi: 10.1142/S0192415X14500554.

Liu W, Ma S, Pan W, Tan W. Combination of motherwort injection and oxytocin for the prevention of postpartum hemorrhage after cesarean section. J Matern Fetal Neonatal Med. 2016;29(15):2490-3.

Liu X, Clark J, Siskind D, Williams GM, Byrne G, Yang JL, Doi SA. A systematic review and meta-analysis of the effects of Qigong and Tai Chi for depressive symptoms. Complement Ther Med. 2015 Aug;23(4):516-34. doi: 10.1016/j.ctim.2015.05.001.

Liu X, Yue R, Zhang J, Shan L, Wang R, Zhang W. Neuroprotective effects of bacopaside I in ischemic brain injury. Restor Neurol Neurosci. 2012 Nov 16.

Lloyd D, Murray D. Redox rhythmicity: clocks at the core of temporal coherence. BioEss. 2007;29(5):465-473.

Lloyd JU. American Materia Medica, Therapeutics and Pharmacognosy. Portland, OR: Eclect Med Publ, 1989-1983.

Lopresti AL. Salvia (Sage): A Review of its Potential Cognitive-Enhancing and Protective Effects Drugs R D. 2016 Nov 25.

Loving RT, Kripke DF, Knickerbocker NC, Grandner MA. Bright green light treatment of depression for older adults. BMC Psychiatry. 2005 Nov 9;5:42.

Lydic R, Schoene WC, Czeisler CA, Moore-Ede MC. Suprachiasmatic region of the human hypothalamus: homolog to the primate circadian pacemaker? Sleep. 1980;2(3):355-61.

Lythgoe JN. Visual pigments and environmental light. Vision Res. 1984;24(11):1539-50.

Mah CD, Mah KE, Kezirian EJ, Dement WC. The effects of sleep extension on the athletic performance of collegiate basketball players. Sleep. 2011 Jul 1;34(7):943-50. doi: 10.5665/SLEEP.1132.

Majewska A, Hoser G, Furmanowa M, Urbańska N, Pietrosiuk A, Zobel A, Kuraś M. Antiproliferative and antimitotic effect, S phase accumulation and induction of apoptosis and necrosis after treatment of ex-tract from Rhodiola rosea rhizomes on HL-60 cells. J Ethnopharmacol. 2006 Jan 3;103(1):43-52.

Majewska A, Hoser G, Furmanowa M, Urbańska N, Pietrosiuk A, Zobel A, Kuraś M. Antiproliferative and antimitotic effect, S phase accumulation and induction of apoptosis and necrosis after treatment of ex-tract from Rhodiola rosea rhizomes on HL-60 cells. J Ethnopharmacol. 2006 Jan 3;103(1):43-52.

Mamiya T, Kise M, Morikawa K, Aoto H, Ukai M, Noda Y. Effects of pre-germinated brown rice on depression-like behavior in mice. Pharmacol Biochem Behav. 2007 Jan;86(1):62-7.

Manikandan P, Murugan RS, Abbas H, Abraham SK, Nagini S. Ocimum sanctum Linn. (Holy Basil) ethano-lic leaf extract protects against 7,12-dimethylbenz(a)anthracene-induced genotoxicity, oxidative stress, and imbalance in xenobiotic-metabolizing enzymes. J Med Food. 2007 Sep;10(3):495-502.

Mansour HA, Monk TH, Nimgaonkar VL. Circadian genes and bipolar disorder. Ann Med. 2005;37(3):196-205.

Mao JJ, Li QS, Soeller I, Xie SX, Amsterdam JD. Rhodiola rosea therapy for major depressive disorder: a study protocol for a randomized, double-blind, placebo- controlled trial. J Clin Trials. 2014 Jun 20;4:170.

Mao JJ, Xie SX, Keefe JR, Soeller I, Li QS, Amsterdam JD. Long-term chamomile (Matricaria chamomilla L.) treatment for generalized anxiety disorder: A randomized clinical trial. Phytomedicine. 2016 Dec 15;23(14):1735-1742. doi: 10.1016/j.phymed.2016.10.012.

Mao JJ, Xie SX, Zee J, Soeller I, Li QS, Rockwell K, Amsterdam JD. Rhodiola rosea versus sertraline for major depressive disorder: A randomized placebo-controlled trial. Phytomedicine. 2015 Mar 15;22(3):394-9. doi: 10.1016/j.phymed.2015.01.010.

Maqnusson A, Stefánsson JG. Prevalence of seasonal affective disorder in Iceland. Arch Gen Psychiatry. 1993 Dec;50(12):941-6. doi: 10.1001/archpsyc.1993.01820240025002.

Marotta A, Sarno E, Del Casale A, Pane M, Mogna L, Amoruso A, Felis GE, Fiorio M. Effects of Probiotics on Cognitive Reactivity, Mood, and Sleep Quality. Front Psychiatry. 2019 Mar 27;10:164. doi: 10.3389/fpsyt.2019.00164.

Martin MA, Thomas AM, Mosnaim G, Greve M, Swider SM, Rothschild SK. Home Asthma Triggers: Barriers to Asthma Control in Chicago Puerto Rican Children. J Health Care Poor Underserved. 2013;24(2):813-827.

Marwat SK, Rehman F, Khan EA, Khakwani AA, Ullah I, Khan KU, Khan IU. Useful ethnophytomedicinal recipes of angiosperms used against diabetes in South East Asian Countries (India, Pakistan & Sri Lanka). Pak J Pharm Sci. 2014 Sep;27(5):1333-58.

Mastorakos G, Pavlatou M. Exercise as a stress model and the interplay between the hypothalamus-pituitary-adrenal and the hypothalamus-pituitary-thyroid axes. Horm Metab Res. 2005 Sep;37(9):577-84.

Masuda A, Koga Y, Hattanmaru M, Minagoe S, Tei C. The effects of repeated thermal therapy for patients with chronic pain. Psychother Psychosom. 2005;74(5):288-94.

Matsumoto T, Asakura H, Hayashi T. Does Lavender aroatheapy alleviate premenstrual emotional symptoms?: a randomized crossover trial. Biopsychosoc Med. 2013 May 31;7(1):12.

Matsumoto T, Asakura H, Hayashi T. Effects of olfactory stimulation from the fragrance of the Japanese citrus fruit yuzu (Citrus junos Sieb. ex Tanaka) on mood states and salivary chromogranin A as an endocrinologic stress marker. J Altern Complement Med. 2014 Jun;20(6):500-6. doi: 10.1089/acm.2013.0425.

Mayer EA, Gupta A, Kilpatrick LA, Hong JY. Imaging brain mechanisms in chronic visceral pain. Pain. 2015 Apr;156 Suppl 1:S50-63. doi: 10.1097/j.pain.0000000000000106.

Mazloom Z, Ekramzadeh M, Hejazi N. Efficacy of supplementary vitamins C and E on anxiety, depression and stress in type 2 diabetic patients: a randomized, single-blind, placebo-controlled trial. Pak J Biol Sci. 2013 Nov 15;16(22):1597-600.

Mazmanian SK, Round JL, Kasper DL. A microbial symbiosis factor prevents intestinal inflammatory disease. Nature. 2008 May 29;453(7195):620-5. doi: 10.1038/nature07008

McClung CA. Role for the Clock gene in bipolar disorder. Cold Spring Harb Symp Quant Biol. 2007;72:637-44.

McColl SL, Veitch JA. Full-spectrum fluorescent lighting: a review of its effects on physiology and health. Psychol Med. 2001 Aug;31(6):949-64.

McCrimmon RJ, Ryan CM, Frier BM. Diabetes and cognitive dysfunction. Lancet. 2012 Jun 16;379(9833):2291-9.

McCrimmon RJ, Ryan CM, Frier BM. Diabetes and cognitive dysfunction. Lancet. 2012 Jun 16;379(9833):2291-9.

McGillivray JA, Evert HT. Group Cognitive Behavioural Therapy Program Shows Potential in Reducing Symptoms of Depression and Stress Among Young People with ASD. J Autism Dev Disord. 2014 Mar 15.

Mehta VV, Rajesh G, Rao A, Shenoy R, B H MP. Antimicrobial Efficacy of Punica granatum mesocarp, Nelumbo nucifera Leaf, Psidium guajava Leaf and Coffea Canephora Extract on Common Oral Pathogens: An In-vitro Study. J Clin Diagn Res. 2014 Jul;8(7):ZC65-8. doi: 10.7860/JCDR/2014/9122.4629.

Melo MC, Garcia RF, Linhares Neto VB, Sá MB, de Mesquita LM, de Araújo CF, de Bruin VM. Sleep and circadian alterations in people at risk for bipolar disorder: A systematic review. J Psychiatr Res. 2016 Dec;83:211-219. doi: 10.1016/j.jpsychires.2016.09.005.

Melo MCA, Abreu RLC, Linhares Neto VB, de Bruin PFC, de Bruin VMS. Chronotype and circadian rhythm in bipolar disorder: A systematic review. Sleep Med Rev. 2017 Aug;34:46-58. doi: 10.1016/j.smrv.2016.06.007.

Meng W, Li R, Zha N, E L. Efficacy and safety of motherwort injection add-on therapy to carboprost tromethamine for prevention of post-partum blood loss: A meta-analysis of randomized controlled trials. J Obstet Gynaecol Res. 2019 Jan;45(1):47-56.

Mero A, Tornberg J, Mäntykoski M, Puurtinen R. Effects of far-infrared sauna bathing on recovery from strength and endurance training sessions in men. Springerplus. 2015 Jul 7;4:321. doi: 10.1186/s40064-015-1093-5.

Miao LL, Zhou QM, Peng C, Liu ZH, Xiong L. Leonurus japonicus (Chinese motherwort), an excellent traditional medicine for obstetrical and gynecological diseases: A comprehensive overview. Biomed Pharmacother. 2019 Jun 10;117:109060.

Miller KJ, Areerob P, Hennessy D, Gonçalves-Bradley DC, Mesagno C, Grace F. Aerobic, resistance, and mind-body exercise are equivalent to mitigate symptoms of depression in older adults: A systematic review and network meta-analysis of randomised controlled trials. F1000Res. 2020 Nov 13;9:1325. doi: 10.12688/f1000research.27123.1.

Min J, Min K. Outdoor artificial nighttime light and use of hypnotic medications in older adults: a population-based cohort study. J Clin Sleep Med. 2018;14(11):1903–1910.

Miniscalco C, Rudling M, Råstam M, Gillberg C, Johnels JA. Imitation (rather than core language) predicts pragmatic development in young children with ASD: a preliminary longitudinal study using CDI parental reports. Int J Lang Commun Disord. 2014 Mar 31. doi: 10.1111/1460-6984.12085.

Mishra S, Xu J, Agarwal U, Gonzales J, Levin S, Barnard ND. A multicenter randomized controlled trial of a plant-based nutrition program to reduce body weight and cardiovascular risk in the corporate setting: the GEICO study. Eur J Clin Nutr. 2013 Jul;67(7):718-24. doi: 10.1038/ejcn.2013.92.

Mitchell C, Hobcraft J, McLanahan SS, Siegel SR, Berg A, Brooks-Gunn J, Garfinkel I, Notterman D. Social disadvantage, genetic sensitivity, and children's telomere length. Proc Natl Acad Sci U S A. 2014 Apr 22;111(16):5944-9. doi: 10.1073/pnas.1404293111.

Mohammadi AA, Jazayeri S, Khosravi-Darani K, Solati Z, Mohammadpour N, Asemi Z, Adab Z, Djalali M, Tehrani-Doost M, Hosseini M, Eghtesadi S. The effects of probiotics on mental health and hypothalamic-pituitary-adrenal axis: A randomized, double-blind, placebo-controlled trial in petrochemical workers. Nutr Neurosci. 2015 Apr 16.

Mondal S, Mirdha BR, Mahapatra SC. The science behind sacredness of Tulsi (Ocimum sanctum Linn.). Indian J Physiol Pharmacol. 2009 Oct-Dec;53(4):291-306.

Monji A. The neuroinflammation hypothesis of psychiatric disorders. Seishin Shinkeigaku Zasshi. 2012;114(2):124-33.

Moore RY. Neural control of the pineal gland. Behav Brain Res. 1996;73(1-2):125-30.

Morriss R, Sharpe M, Sharpley AL, Cowen PJ, Hawton K, Morris J. Abnormalities of sleep in patients with the chronic fatigue syndrome. BMJ. 1993 May 1;306(6886):1161-4.

Moss L, Rouse M, Wesnes KA, Moss M. Differential effects of the aromas of Differential effects of the aromas of Salvia species on memory and mood. Hum Psychopharmacol. 2010;25(5):388–96.

Mujcic R, Oswald AJ. Does eating fruit and vegetables also reduce the longitudinal risk of depression and anxiety? Social Science & Medicine, Volume 222, February 2019, Pages 346-348.

Mujcic R, Oswald AJ. Evolution of Well-Being and Happiness After Increases in Consumption of Fruit and Vegetables. Am. J. Public Health, 106 2016, pages 1504-1510

Murata T, Takahashi T, Hamada T, Omori M, Kosaka H, Yo-shida H, Wada Y. Individual trait anxiety levels characterizing the properties of zen meditation. Neuropsychobiology. 2004;50(2):189-94.

Nadkarni AK, Nadkarni KM. Indian Materia Medica. (Vols 1 and 2). Bombay: Popular Pradashan, 1908, 1976.

Nadkarni KM. The Indian Materia Medica. Prakashan Private Ltd., 1908-1989.

Nakatani K, Yau KW. Calcium and light adaptation in retinal rods and cones. Nature. 1988 Jul 7;334(6177): 69-71.

Nakau M, Imanishi J, Imanishi J, Watanabe S, Imanishi A, Baba T, Hirai K, Ito T, Chiba W, Morimoto Y. Spiritual care of cancer patients by integrated medicine in urban green space: a pilot study. Explore (NY). 2013 Mar-Apr;9(2):87-90.

Nematolahi P, Mehrabani M, Karami-Mohajeri S, Dabaghzadeh F. Effects of Rosmarinus officinalis L. on memory performance, anxiety, depression, and sleep quality in university students: A randomized clinical trial. Complement Ther Clin Pract. 2018 Feb;30:24-28. doi: 10.1016/j.ctcp.2017.11.004.

Newman AB, Spiekerman CF, Enright P, Lefkowitz D, Manolio T, Reynolds CF, Robbins J. Daytime sleepiness predicts mortality and cardiovascular disease in older adults. The Cardiovascular Health Study Research Group. J Am Geriatr Soc. 2000 Feb;48(2):115-23

Ng QX, Loke W, Foo NX, et al. A systematic review of the clinical use of Withania somnifera (Ashwagandha) to ameliorate cognitive dysfunction Phytother Res. 2020;34(3):583-590. doi:10.1002/ptr.6552

Noonan S, Zaveri M, Macaninch E, Martyn K. Food & mood: a review of supplementary prebiotic and probiotic interventions in the treatment of anxiety and depression in adults. BMJ Nutr Prev Health. 2020 Jul 6;3(2):351-362. doi: 10.1136/bmjnph-2019-000053. PMID: 33521545; PMCID: PMC7841823.

Nur Hanisah Azmi, Maznah Ismail, Norsharina Ismail, Mustapha Umar Imam, Noorjahan Banu Mohammed Alitheen, and Maizaton Atmadini Abdullah, Germinated Brown Rice Alters Aβ(1-42) Aggregation and Modulates Alzheimer's Disease-Related Genes in Differentiated Human SH-SY5Y Cells, Evidence-Based Complementary and Alternative Medicine, vol. 2015, Article ID 153684, 12 pages, 2015. doi:10.1155/2015/153684

Ocean N, Howley P, Ensor J. Lettuce be happy: A longitudinal UK study on the relationship between fruit and vegetable consumption and well-being. Soc Sci Med. 2019 Feb;222:335-345. doi: 10.1016/j.socscimed.2018.12.017.

Ohsie S, Gerney G, Gui D, Kahana D, Martín MG, Cortina G. A paucity of colonic enteroendocrine and/or enterochromaffin cells characterizes a subset of patients with chronic unexplained diarrhea/malabsorption. Hum Pathol. 2009 Jul;40(7):1006-14. doi: 10.1016/j.humpath.2008.12.016.

O'Connor DB, Hendrickx H, Dadd T, Elliman TD, Willis TA, Talbot D, Mayes AE, Thethi K, Powell J, Dye L. Cortisol awakening rise in middle-aged women in relation to psychological stress. Psychoneuroendocrinology. 2009 Nov;34(10):1486-94. doi: 10.1016/j.psyneuen.2009.05.002.

195

O'Leary KD, Rosenbaum A, Hughes PC. Fluorescent lighting: a purported source of hyperactive behavior. J Abnorm Child Psychol. 1978 Sep;6(3):285-9.

Oliveira AI, Pinho C, Sarmento B, Dias AC. Neuroprotective Activity of Hypericum perforatum and Its Major Components. Front Plant Sci. 2016 Jul 11;7:1004. doi: 10.3389/fpls.2016.01004.

O'Loughlin J, Casanova F, Jones SE, Hagenaars SP, Beaumont RN, Freathy RM, Watkins ER, Vetter C, Rutter MK, Cain SW, Phillips AJK, Windred DP, Wood AR, Weedon MN, Tyrrell J. Using Mendelian Randomisation methods to understand whether diurnal preference is causally related to mental health. Mol Psychiatry. 2021 Jun 8. doi: 10.1038/s41380-021-01157-3.

Olsen LR, Grillo MP, Skonberg C. Constituents in kava extracts potentially involved in hepatotoxicity: a review. Chem Res Toxicol. 2011 Jul 18;24(7):992-1002. doi: 10.1021/tx100412m.

Olsson EM, von Schéele B, Panossian AG. A randomised, double-blind, placebo-controlled, parallel-group study of the standardised extract shr-5 of the roots of Rhodiola rosea in the treatment of subjects with stress-related fatigue. Planta Med. 2009 Feb;75(2):105-12. doi: 10.1055/s-0028-1088346.

O'Malley D, Quigley EM, Dinan TG, Cryan JF. Do interactions between stress and immune responses lead to symptom exacerba-tions in irritable bowel syndrome? Brain Behav Immun. 2011 Oct;25(7):1333-41.

Østergaard L, Jørgensen MB, Knudsen GM. Low on energy? An energy supply-demand perspective on stress and depression. Neurosci Biobehav Rev. 2018 Nov;94:248-270. doi: 10.1016/j.neubiorev.2018.08.007.

O'Sullivan E, Barrett E, Grenham S, Fitzgerald P, Stanton C, Ross RP, Quigley EM, Cryan JF, Dinan TG. BDNF expression in the hippocampus of maternally separated rats: does Bifidobacterium breve 6330 alter BDNF levels? Benef Microbes. 2011 Sep 1;2(3):199-207.

Paavonen EJ, Pennonen M, Roine M, Valkonen S, Lahikainen AR. TV exposure associated with sleep disturbances in 5- to 6-year-old children. J Sleep Res. 2006 Jun;15(2):154-61.

Panossian A, Wagner H. Stimulating effect of adaptogens: an overview with particular reference to their efficacy following single dose administration. Phytother Res. 2005 Oct;19(10):819-38.

Park G, Thayer JF. From the heart to the mind: cardiac vagal tone modulates top-down and bottom-up visual perception and attention to emotional stimuli. Front Psychol. 2014 May 1;5:278.

Partonen T, Haukka J, Nevanlinna H, Lönnqvist J. Analysis of the seasonal pattern in suicide. J Affect Disord. 2004 Aug;81(2):133-9.

Partonen T, Haukka J, Viilo K, Hakko H, Pirkola S, Isometsä E, Lönnqvist J, Särkioja T, Väisänen E, Räsänen P. Cyclic time patterns of death from suicide in N. Finland. J Affect Disrd. 2004 Jan;78(1):11-9.

Partonen T. Magnetoreception attributed to the efficacy of light therapy. Med Hypoth. 1998 Nov;51(5):447-8.

Pattanayak P, Behera P, Das D, Panda SK. Ocimum sanctum Linn. A reservoir plant for therapeutic applica-tions: An overview. Pharmacogn Rev. 2010 Jan;4(7):95-105. doi: 10.4103/0973-7847.65323.

Patterson F, Malone SK, Grandner MA, Lozano A, Perkett M, Hanlon A. Interactive effects of sleep dura-tion and morning/evening preference on cardiovascular risk factors. Eur J Public Health. 2018 Feb 1;28(1):155-161. doi: 10.1093/eurpub/ckx029.

Penev PD. Association between sleep and morning testosterone levels in older men. Sleep. 2007 Apr 1;30(4):427-32.

Penn RD, Hagins WA. Kinetics of the photocurrent of retinal rods. Biophys J. 1972 Aug;12(8):1073-94.

Penn RD, Hagins WA. Signal transmission along retinal rods and the origin of the electroretinographic a-wave. Nature. 1969 Jul 12;223(5202):201-4.

Peroxisomes from pepper fruits (Capsicum annuum L.): purification, characterisation and antioxidant activity. J Plant Physiol. 2003 Dec;160(12):1507-16.

Perry NS, Bollen C, Perry EK, Ballard C. Salvia for dementia therapy: review of pharmacological activity and pilot tolerability clinical trial. Pharmacol Biochem Behav. 2003;75(3):651–9.

Persson R, Orbaek P, Kecklund G, Akerstedt T. Impact of an 84-hour workweek on biomarkers for stress, metabolic processes and diurnal rhythm. Scand J Work Environ Health. 2006 Oct;32(5):349-58.

Peth-Nui T, Wattanathorn J, Muchimapura S, Tong-Un T, Piyavhatkul N, Rangseekajee P, Ingkaninan K, Vittaya-Areekul S. Effects of 12-Week Bacopa monnieri Consumption on Attention, Cognitive Proc-essing, Working Memory, and Functions of Both cholinergic and Monoaminergic Systems in Healthy Elderly Volunteers. Evid Based Complement Alternat Med. 2012;2012:606424.

Piggins HD. Human clock genes. Ann Med. 2002;34(5):394-400.

Pollastri MP, Whitty A, Merrill JC, Tang X, Ashton TD, Amar S. Identification and characterization of kava-derived compounds mediating TNF-alpha suppression. Chem Biol Drug Des. 2009 Aug;74(2):121-8. doi: 10.1111/j.1747-0285.2009.00838.x.

Postolache TT, Lapidus M, Sander ER, Langenberg P, Hamilton RG, Soriano JJ, McDonald JS, Furst N, Bai J, Scrandis DA, Cabassa JA, Stiller JW, Balis T, Guzman A, Togias A, Tonelli LH. Changes in allergy symptoms and depression scores are positively correlated in patients with recurrent mood disorders exposed to seasonal peaks in aeroallergens. ScientificWorldJournal. 2007 Dec 17;7:1968-77.

REFERENCES AND BIBLIOGRAPHY

Prathikanti S, Rivera R, Cochran A, Tungol JG, Fayazmanesh N, Weinmann E (2017) Treating major depression with yoga: A prospective, randomized, controlled pilot trial. PLoS ONE 12(3): e0173869.

Pronina TS. Circadian and infradian rhythms of testosterone and aldosterone excretion in children. Probl Endokrinol. 1992 Sep-Oct;38(5):38-42.

Psaltopoulou T, Sergentanis TN, Panagiotakos DB, Sergentanis IN, Kosti R, Scarmeas N. Mediterranean diet, stroke, cognitive impairment, and depression: A meta-analysis. Ann Neurol. 2013 May 30.

Putilov AA. State- and trait-like variation in morning and evening components of morningness-eveningness in winter depression. Nord J Psychiatry. 2017 Nov;71(8):561-569. doi: 10.1080/08039488.2017.1353642.

Rastogi S, Kalra A, Gupta V, Khan F, Lal RK, Tripathi AK, Parameswaran S, Gopalakrishnan C, Ramaswamy G, Shasany AK. Unravelling the genome of Holy basil: an "incomparable" "elixir of life" of traditional Indian medicine. BMC Genomics. 2015 May 28;16:413. doi: 10.1186/s12864-015-1640-z.

Rauwald HW, Savtschenko A, Merten A, Rusch C, Appel K, Kuchta K. GABAA Receptor Binding Assays of Standardized Leonurus cardiaca and Leonurus japonicus Extracts as Well as Their Isolated Constituents. Planta Med. 2015 Aug;81(12-13):1103-10.

Raw fruit and vegetables provide better mental health outcomes: Otago research. Univ of Otago. 2018 April.

Read J, Cartwright C, Gibson K. How many of 1829 antidepressant users report withdrawal effects or addiction? Int J Ment Health Nurs. 2018 Dec;27(6):1805-1815. doi: 10.1111/inm.12488.

Reeves GM, Nijjar GV, Langenberg P, Johnson MA, Khabazghazvini B, Sleemi A, Vaswani D, Lapidus M, Manalai P, Tariq M, Acharya M, Cabassa J, Snitker S, Postolache TT. Improvement in depression scores after 1 hour of light therapy treatment in patients with seasonal affective disorder. J Nerv Ment Dis. 2012 Jan;200(1):51-5.

Regel SJ, Negovetic S, Roosli M, Berdinas V, Schuderer J, Huss A, et al. UMTS base station-like exposure, well-being, and cognitive performance. Environ Health Perspect. 2006 Aug;114(8):1270-5.

Reichrath J. The challenge resulting from positive and negative effects of sunlight: how much solar UV exposure is appropriate to balance between risks of vitamin D deficiency and skin cancer? Prog Biophys Mol Biol. 2006 Sep;92(1):9-16.

Reilly T, Stevenson I. An investigation of the effects of negative air ions on responses to submaximal exercise at different times of day. J Hum Ergol. 1993 Jun;22(1):1-9.

Reiter RJ, Garcia JJ, Pie J. Oxidative toxicity in models of neurodegeneration: responses to melatonin. Restor Neurol Neurosci. 1998 Jun;12(2-3):135-42.

Reiter RJ, Tan DX, Korkmaz A, Erren TC, Piekarski C, Tamura H, Manchester LC. Light at night, chronodisruption, melatonin suppression, and cancer risk: a review. Crit Rev Oncog. 2007;13(4):303-28.

Reiter RJ, Tan DX, Manchester LC, Qi W. Biochemical reactivity of melatonin with reactive oxygen and nitrogen species: a review of the evidence. Cell Biochem Biophys. 2001;34(2):237-56.

Reschetniak VK, Kukushkin ML, Gurko NS. The importance of the cortex and subcortical structures of the brain in the perception of acute and chronic pain. Patol Fiziol Eksp Ter. 2014 Oct-Dec;(4):96-110.

Reuben A, Arseneault L, Beddows A, Beevers SD, Moffitt TE, Ambler A, Latham RM, Newbury JB, Odgers CL, Schaefer JD, Fisher HL. Association of Air Pollution Exposure in Childhood and Adolescence With Psychopathology at the Transition to Adulthood. JAMA Netw Open. 2021 Apr 1;4(4):e217508. doi: 10.1001/jamanetworkopen.2021.7508.

Reutrakul S, Knutson KL. Consequences of Circadian Disruption on Cardiometabolic Health. Sleep Med Clin. 2015 Dec;10(4):455-68. doi: 10.1016/j.jsmc.2015.07.005.

Révész D, Verhoeven JE, Milaneschi Y, de Geus EJ, Wolkowitz OM, Penninx BW. Dysregulated physiological stress systems and accelerated cellular aging. Neurobiol Aging. 2014 Jun;35(6):1422-30. doi: 10.1016/j.neurobiolaging.2013.12.027.

Rhee SH, Pothoulakis C, Mayer EA. Principles and clinical implications of the brain-gut-enteric microbiota axis. Nat Rev Gastroenterol Hepatol. 2009 May;6(5):306-14. doi: 10.1038/nrgastro.2009.35.

Roberts JE. Light and immunomodulation. Ann N Y Acad Sci. 2000;917:435-45.

Roberts RC, Farmer CB, Walker CK. The human brain microbiome; there are bacteria in our brains. Neuroscience Nov. 2018. 594.08 / YY23

Roberts RE, Allen S, Chang AP, Henderson H, Hobson GC, Karania B, Morgan KN, Pek AS, Raghvani K, Shee CY, Shikotra J, Street E, Abbas Z, Ellis K, Heer JK, Alexander SP. Relaxation from chamomile species in porcine isolated blood vessels. Toxicol Appl Pharmacol. 2013 Jul 8.

Robinson TN. Television viewing and childhood obesity. Pediatr Clin North Am. 2001 Aug;48(4):1017-25.

Rodermel SR, Smith-Sonneborn J. Age-correlated changes in expression of micronuclear damage and repair in Paramecium tetraurelia. Genetics. 1977 Oct;87(2):259-74.

Rodhe A, Eriksson BM, Eriksson A. Sauna deaths in Sweden, 1992-2003. Am J Forensic Med Pathol 2008;29:27-31.

Rodriguez E, Valbuena MC, Rey M, Porras de Quintana L. Causal agents of photoallergic contact dermatitis diagnosed in the national institute of dermatology of Colombia. Photodermatol Photoimmunol Photomed. 2006 Aug;22(4):189-92.

Rodriguez-Casado A. The Health Potential of Fruits and Vegetables Phytochemicals: Notable Examples. Crit Rev Food Sci Nutr. 2016 May 18;56(7):1097-107. doi: 10.1080/10408398.2012.755149.

Rosenthal N, Blehar M. Seasonal affective disorders and phototherapy. New York: Guildford Press, 1989.

Rowe A, Ramzan I. Are mould hepatotoxins responsible for kava hepatotoxicity? Phytother Res. 2012 Nov;26(11):1768-70. doi: 10.1002/ptr.4620.

Roy M, Kirschbaum C, Steptoe A. Intraindividual variation in recent stress exposure as a moderator of cortisol and testosterone levels. Ann Behav Med. 2003 Dec;26(3):194-200.

Roybal K, Theobold D, Graham A, DiNieri JA, Russo SJ, Krishnan V, Chakravarty S, Peevey J, Oehrlein N, Birnbaum S, Vitaterna MH, Orsulak P, Takahashi JS, Nestler EJ, Carlezon WA Jr, McClung CA. Mania-like behavior induced by disruption of CLOCK. Proc Natl Acad Sci USA 2007;104(15):6406-6411.

Rubin E., Farber JL. Pathology. 3rd Ed. Philadelphia: Lippincott-Raven, 1999.

Saarijarvi S, Lauerma H, Helenius H, Saarilehto S. Seasonal affective disorders among rural Finns and Lapps. Acta Psychiatr Scand. 1999 Feb;99(2):95-101.

Sabia S, Elbaz A, Dugravot A, Head J, Shipley M, Hagger-Johnson G, Kivimaki M, Singh-Manoux A. Impact of Smoking on Cognitive Decline in Early Old Age: The Whitehall II Cohort Study. Arch Gen Psychiatry. 2012 Feb 6.

Saini N, Mathur R, Agrawal SS. Qualitative and quantitative assessment of four marketed formulations of brahmi. Indian J Pharm Sci. 2012 Jan;74(1):24-8.

Sánchez-Vidaña DI, Ngai SP, He W, Chow JK, Lau BW, Tsang HW. The Effectiveness of Aromatherapy for Depressive Symptoms: A Systematic Review. Evid Based Complement Alternat Med. 2017;2017:5869315. doi: 10.1155/2017/5869315.

Sarkar S, Mishra BR, Praharaj SK, Nizamie SH. Add-on effect of Brahmi in the management of schizophrenia. J Ayurveda Integr Med. 2012 Oct;3(4):223-5.

Sarris J, Kavanagh DJ, Adams J, Bone K, Byrne G. Kava Anxiety Depression Spectrum Study (KADSS): a mixed methods RCT using an aqueous extract of Piper methysticum. Complement Ther Med. 2009 Jun;17(3):176-8. doi: 10.1016/j.ctim.2009.01.001.

Sarris J, Kavanagh DJ, Byrne G, Bone KM, Adams J, Deed G. The Kava Anxiety Depression Spectrum Study (KADSS): a randomized, placebo-controlled crossover trial using an aqueous extract of Piper methysticum. Psychopharmacology (Berl). 2009 Aug;205(3):399-407. doi: 10.1007/s00213-009-1549-9.

Sarris J, LaPorte E, Schweitzer I. Kava: a comprehensive review of efficacy, safety, and psychopharmacology. Aust N Z J Psychiatry. 2011 Jan;45(1):27-35. doi: 10.3109/00048674.2010.522554.

Sarris J, McIntyre E, Camfield DA. Plant-based medicines for anxiety disorders, part 2: a review of clinical studies with supporting preclinical evidence. CNS Drugs. 2013 Apr;27(4):301-19. doi: 10.1007/s40263-013-0059-9.

Sarris J, Scholey A, Schweitzer I, Bousman C, Laporte E, Ng C, Murray G, Stough C. The acute effects of kava and oxazepam on anxiety, mood, neurocognition; and genetic correlates: a randomized, placebo-controlled, double-blind study. Hum Psychopharmacol. 2012 May;27(3):262-9. doi: 10.1002/hup.2216.

Scherrer JF, Salas J, Lustman PJ, Burge S, Schneider FD. Change in opioid dose and change in depression in a longitudinal primary care patient cohort. Pain. 2015 Feb;156(2):348-355. doi: 10.1097/01.j.pain.0000460316.58110.a0.

Schlumpf M, Cotton B, Conscience M, Haller V, Steinmann B, Lichtensteiger W. In vitro and in vivo estrogenicity of UV screens. Environ Health Perspect. 2001 Mar;109(3):239-44.

Schmidt C, Collette F, Cajochen C, Peigneux P. A time to think: circadian rhythms in human cognition. Cogn Neuropsychol. 2007 Oct;24(7):755-89.

Schmidt M, Butterweck V. The mechanisms of action of St. John's wort: an update. Wien Med Wochenschr. 2015 Jun;165(11-12):229-35. doi: 10.1007/s10354-015-0372-7.

Scholey AB, Tildesley NT, Ballard CG, Wesnes KA, Tasker A, Perry EK, et al. An extract of Salvia (sage) with anticholinesterase properties improves memory and attention in healthy older volunteers. Psychopharmacology (Berl). 2008;198(1):127–39.

Scott BO. The history of ultraviolet therapy. in Licht S. ed. Therapeutic Electricity and Ultraviolet Radiation. Phys Med Lib 4. Connecticut: Licht, 1967.

See DM, Broumand N, Sahl L, Tilles JG. In vitro effects of echinacea and ginseng on natural killer and antibody-dependent cell cytotoxicity in healthy subjects and chronic fatigue syndrome or acquired immunodeficiency syndrome patients. Immunopharmacology. 1997 Jan;35(3):229-35.

Seol GH, Shim HS, Kim PJ, Moon HK, Lee KH, Shim I, Suh SH, Min SS. Antidepressant-like effect of Salvia sclarea is explained by modulation of dopamine activities in rats. J Ethnopharmacol. 2010 Jul 6;130(1):187-90. doi: 10.1016/j.jep.2010.04.035.

Shearman LP, Zylka MJ, Weaver DR, Kolakowski LF Jr, Reppert SM. Two period homologs: circadian expression and photic regulation in the suprachiasmatic nuclei. Neuron. 1997 Dec;19(6):1261-9.

Shikov AN, Pozharitskaya ON, Makarov VG, Demchenko DV, Shikh EV. Effect of Leonurus cardiaca oil extract in patients with arterial hypertension accompanied by anxiety and sleep disorders. Phytother Res. 2011 Apr;25(4):540-3.

REFERENCES AND BIBLIOGRAPHY

Singh N, Hoette Y. Tulsi: The Mother Medicine of Nature. Lucknow, India: International Institute of Herbal Medicine; 2002.

Singh-Manoux A, Czernichow S, Elbaz A, Dugravot A, Sabia S, Hagger-Johnson G, Kaffashian S, Zins M, Brunner EJ, Nabi H, Kivimaki M. Obesity phenotypes in midlife and cognition in early old age: The Whitehall II cohort study. Neuro. 2012; 79 (8): 755.

Sit DK, McGowan J, Wiltrout C, Diler RS, Dills JJ, Luther J, Yang A, Ciolino JD, Seltman H, Wisniewski SR, Terman M, Wisner KL. Adjunctive Bright Light Therapy for Bipolar Depression: A Randomized Double-Blind Placebo-Controlled Trial. Am J Psychiatry. 2018 Feb 1;175(2):131-139. doi: 10.1176/appi.ajp.2017.16101200.

SK Whitbourne. Morning Person or Evening Person? It's Time to Find Out. Psy. Today. 2012. June.

Skwerer RG, Jacobsen FM, Duncan CC, Kelly KA, Sack DA, Tamarkin L, Gaist PA, Kasper S, Rosenthal NE. Neurobiology of Seasonal Affective Disorder and Phototherapy. J Biolog Rhyth. 1988;3(2):135-154.

Smith CA, Armour M, Lee MS, Wang LQ, Hay PJ. Acupuncture for depression. Cochrane Database Syst Rev. 2018 Mar 4;3(3):CD004046. doi: 10.1002/14651858.CD004046.pub4.

Sobajima M, Nozawa T, Ihori H, Shida T, Ohori T, Suzuki T, Matsuki A, Yasumura S, Inoue H. Repeated sauna therapy improves myocardial perfusion in patients with chronically occluded coronary artery-related ischemia. Int J Cardiol. 2013 Jul 15;167(1):237-43. doi: 10.1016/j.ijcard.2011.12.064.

Soejima Y, Munemoto T, Masuda A, Uwatoko Y, Miyata M, Tei C. Effects of Waon therapy on chronic fatigue syndrome: a pilot study. Int ern Med. 2015;54(3):333-8. doi: 10.2169/internalmedicine.54.3042.

Sohar E, Shoenfeld Y, Shapiro Y, Ohry A, Cabili S. Effects of exposure to Finnish sauna. Isr J Med Sci. 1976 Nov;12(11):1275-82.

Soi-ampornkul, Rungtip et al. Potent antioxidant and anti-apoptotic activity of pre-germinated brown rice extract against hydrogen peroxide in neuronal SK-N-SH cells: A model of Alzheimer's disease. Alzheimer's & Dementia: The Journal of the Alzheimer's Association , Volume 8 , Issue 4 , P503.

Spanagel R, Rosenwasser AM, Schumann G, Sarkar DK. Alcohol consumption and the body's biological clock. Alcohol Clin Exp Res. 2005 Aug;29(8):1550-7.

St Hilaire MA, Gronfier C, Zeitzer JM, Klerman EB. A physiologically based mathematical model of melatonin including ocular light suppression and interactions with the circadian pacemaker. J Pineal Res. 2007 Oct;43(3):294-304.

Steck B. Effects of optical radiation on man. Light Resch Techn. 1982;14:130-141.

Steenbergen L, Sellaro R, van Hemert S, Bosch JA, Colzato LS. A randomized controlled trial to test the effect of multispecies probiotics on cognitive reactivity to sad mood. Brain Behav Immun. 2015 Apr 7. pii: S0889-1591(15)00088-4. doi: 10.1016/j.bbi.2015.04.003.

Steenbergen L, Sellaro R, van Hemert S, Bosch JA, Colzato LS. A randomized controlled trial to test the effect of multispecies probiotics on cognitive reactivity to sad mood. Brain Behav Immun. 2015 Aug;48:258-64. doi: 10.1016/j.bbi.2015.04.003.

Stephenson R. Circadian rhythms and sleep-related breathing disorders. Sleep Med. 2007 Sep;8(6):681-7.

Stoebner-Delbarre A, Thezenas S, Kuntz C, Nguyen C, Giordanella JP, Sancho-Garnier H, Guillot B; Le Groupe EPI-CES. Sun exposure and sun protection behavior and attitudes among the French population. Ann Dermatol Venereol. 2005 Aug-Sep;132(8-9 Pt 1):652-7.

Storch EA, Arnold EB, Lewin AB, Nadeau JM, Jones AM, De Nadai AS, Jane Mutch P, Selles RR, Ung D, Murphy TK. The effect of cognitive-behavioral therapy versus treatment as usual for anxiety in children with autism spectrum disorders: a randomized, controlled trial. J Am Acad Child Adolesc Psychiatry. 2013 Feb;52(2):132-142.e2. doi: 10.1016/j.jaac.2012.11.007.

Stubbs B, Vancampfort D, Rosenbaum S, Firth J, Cosco T, Veronese N, Salum GA, Schuch FB. An examination of the anxiolytic effects of exercise for people with anxiety and stress-related disorders: A meta-analysis. Psychiatry Res. 2017 Mar;249:102-108. doi: 10.1016/j.psychres.2016.12.020.

"Study finds Tai chi significantly reduces depression symptoms in Chinese Americans." Massachusetts General Hospital News Release. May 25, 2017.

Ströhle A. Physical activity, exercise, depression and anxiety disorders. J Neural Transm (Vienna). 2009 Jun;116(6):777-84. doi: 10.1007/s00702-008-0092-x.

Sugimoto Y, Nishimura K, Itoh A, Tanahashi T, Nakajima H, Oshiro H, Sun S, Toda T, Yamada J. Serotonergic mechanisms are involved in antidepressant-like effects of bisbenzylisoquinolines liensinine and its analogs isolated from the embryo of Nelumbo nucifera Gaertner seeds in mice. J Pharm Pharmacol. 2015 Aug 5. doi: 10.1111/jphp.12473.

Sullivan A, Nord CE, Evengård B. Effect of supplement with lactic-acid producing bacteria on fatigue and physical activity in patients with chronic fatigue syndrome. Nutr J. 2009 Jan 26;8:4. doi: 10.1186/1475-2891-8-4.

T. Mamiya, T. Asanuma, M. Kise et al. Effects of pre-germinated brown rice on β-amyloid protein-induced learning and memory deficits in mice. Biological and Pharmaceutical Bulletin, vol. 27, no. 7, pp. 1041–1045, 2004.

Taavoni S, Darsareh F, Joolaee S, Haghani H. The effect of aromatherapy massage on the psychological symptoms of postmenopausal Iranian women. Complement Ther Med. 2013 Jun;21(3):158-63. doi: 10.1016/j.ctim.2013.03.007.

Tan DX, Manchester LC, Reiter RJ, Qi WB, Karbownik M, Calvo JR. Significance of melatonin in antioxidative defense system: reactions and products. Biol Signals Recept. 2000 May-Aug;9(3-4):137-59.

Tanabe N, Iso H, Seki N, Suzuki H, Yatsuya H, Toyoshima H, Tamakoshi A; JACC Study Group. Daytime napping and mortality, with a special reference to cardiovascular disease: the JACC study. Int J Epidemiol. 2010 Feb;39(1):233-43. doi: 10.1093/ije/dyp327.

Tang LW, Zheng H, Chen L, Zhou SY, Huang WJ, Li Y, Wu X. Gray matter volumes in patients with chronic fatigue syndrome. Evid Based Complement Alternat Med. 2015;2015:380615. doi: 10.1155/2015/380615.

Tao L, Jiang R, Zhang K, Qian Z, Chen P, Lv Y, Yao Y. Light therapy in non-seasonal depression: An update meta-analysis. Psychiatry Res. 2020 Sep;291:113247. doi: 10.1016/j.psychres.2020.113247.

Taylor AW, Winefield H, Kettler L, Roberts R, Gill TK. A popu-lation study of 5 to 15 year olds: full time maternal employment not associated with high BMI. The importance of screen-based activity, reading for pleasure and sleep duration in children's BMI. Matern Child Health J. 2012 Apr;16(3):587-99. doi: 10.1007/s10995-011-0792-y.

Temviriyanukul P, Sritalahareuthai V, Promyos N, Thangsiri S, Pruesapan K, Srinuanchai W, Nuchuchua O, Siriwan D, On-Nom N, Suttisansanee U. The Effect of Sacred Lotus (Nelumbo nucifera) and Its Mixtures on Phenolic Profiles, Antioxidant Activities, and Inhibitions of the Key Enzymes Relevant to Alzheimer's Disease. Molecules. 2020 Aug 14;25(16):3713. doi: 10.3390/molecules25163713. PMID: 32824050; PMCID: PMC7463813.

Terauchi M, Horiguchi N, Kajiyama A, Akiyoshi M, Owa Y, Kato K, Kubota T. Effects of grape seed proanthocyanidin extract on menopausal symptoms, body composition, and cardiovascular parameters in middle-aged women: a randomized, double-blind, placebo-controlled pilot study. Menopause. 2014 Feb 10.

Teschke R, Lebot V. Proposal for a kava quality standardization code. Food Chem Toxicol. 2011 Oct;49(10):2503-16. doi: 10.1016/j.fct.2011.06.075.

Teschke R, Sarris J, Lebot V. Contaminant hepatotoxins as culprits for kava hepatotoxicity--fact or fiction? Phytother Res. 2013 Mar;27(3):472-4. doi: 10.1002/ptr.4729.

Teschke R, Sarris J, Schweitzer I. Kava hepatotoxicity in traditional and modern use: the presumed Pacific kava paradox hypothesis revisited. Br J Clin Pharmacol. 2012 Feb;73(2):170-4. doi: 10.1111/j.1365-2125.2011.04070.x.

Thabrew H, de Sylva S, Romans SE. Evaluating childhood adversity. Adv Psychosom Med. 2012;32:35-57.

Thakkar RR, Garrison MM, Christakis DA. A systematic review for the effects of television viewing by infants and preschoolers. Pediatrics. 2006 Nov;118(5):2025-31.

Thun, E., Bjorvatn, B., Osland, T., Steen, V., Sivertsen, B., Johansen, T., & ... Pallesen, S. (2012). An actigraphic validation study of seven morningness-eveningness inventories. European Psychologist, 17(3), 222-230. doi:10.1027/1016-9040/a000097

Tildesley NT, Kennedy DO, Perry EK, Ballard CG, Savelev S, Wesnes KA, et al. Salvia lavandulaefolia (Spanish sage) enhances memory in healthy young volunteers. Pharmacol Biochem Behav. 2003;75(3):669–74.

Tildesley NT, Kennedy DO, Perry EK, Ballard CG, Wesnes KA, Scholey AB. Positive modulation of mood and cognitive performance following administration of acute doses of Salvia lavandulaefolia essential oil to healthy young volunteers. Physiol Behav. 2005;83(5):699–709.

Tiwari M. Ayurveda: A Life of Balance. Rochester, VT: Healing Arts, 1995.

Tjora T, Hetland J, Aarø LE, Wold B, Wiium N, Øverland S. The association between smoking and depression from adolescence to adulthood. Addiction. 2014 Jun;109(6):1022-30. doi: 10.1111/add.12522. Epub 2014 Mar 25. PMID: 24552489.

Tobaldini E, Nobili L, Strada S, Casali KR, Braghiroli A, Montano N. Heart rate variability in normal and pathological sleep. Front Physiol. 2013 Oct 16;4:294.

Toledo A, Yli-Uotila E, Kautiainen H, Pirkola S, Partonen T, Snellman E. Tanning dependence and seasonal affective disorder are frequent among sunbathers but are not associated. Psychiatry Res. 2019 Feb;272:387-391. doi: 10.1016/j.psychres.2018.12.090.

Trompetter I, Krick B, Weiss G. Herbal triplet in treatment of nervous agitation in children. Wien Med Wochenschr. 2013 Feb;163(3-4):52-7. doi:10.1007/s10354-012-0165-1.

Tsong T. Deciphering the language of cells. Trends in Biochem Sci. 1989;14: 89-92.

Tubaki BR, Chandrashekar CR, Sudhakar D, Prabha TN, Lavekar GS, Kutty BM. Clinical efficacy of Manasamitra Vataka (an Ayurveda medication) on generalized anxiety disorder with comorbid generalized social phobia: a randomized controlled study. J Altern Complement Med. 2012 Jun;18(6):612-21. doi:10.1089/acm.2010.0778.

Tweed K. Study: Conceiving in Summer Lowers Baby's Future Test Scores. Fox News. 2007 May 9, 2007. (Study done by: Winchester P. 2007. Pediatric Academic Societies annual meeting.)

Uebelhack R, Gruenwald J, Graubaum HJ, Busch R. Efficacy and tolerability of Hypericum extract STW 3-VI in patients with moderate depression: a double-blind, randomized, placebo-controlled clinical trial. Adv Ther. 2004 Jul-Aug;21(4):265-75.

Ulrich RS. Aesthetic and affective response to natural environment. In Altman, I. and Wohlwill, J. F. (eds) Human Behaviour and Environment: Advances in Theory and Research. Volume 6: Behaviour and the Natural Environment. New York: Plenum Press: 1983:85-125.

Ulrich RS. Influences of passive experiences with plants on individual wellbeing and health. In Relf, D. (ed) The Role of Horticulture in Human Well-Being and Social Development: A National Symposium. Portland: Timber Press, Portland. 1992:93 -105.

Ulrich RS. Natural versus urban scenes: some psychophysiological effects. Environment and Behaviour. 1981:523-556.

Ulrich RS. View through window may influence recovery from surgery. Science. 1984;224:420 - 421.

Ulrich RS. Visual landscapes and psychological well being. Landscape Research. 1979;4:17-23.

USDA National Nutrient Database for Standard Reference

Van Cauter E. Slow wave sleep and release of growth hormone. JAMA. 2000 Dec 6;284(21):2717-8.

Vaquero JM, Gallego MC. Sunspot numbers can detect pandemic influenza A: the use of different sunspot numbers. Med Hypotheses. 2007;68(5):1189-90.

Vatansever F, Hamblin MR. Far infrared radiation (FIR): its biological effects and medical applications. Photonics Lasers Med. 2012 Nov 1;4:255-266.

Velusami CC, Agarwal A, Mookambeswaran V. Effect of Nelumbo nucifera Petal Extracts on Lipase, Adipogenesis, Adipolysis, and Central Receptors of Obesity. Evid Based Complement Alternat Med. 2013;2013:145925. doi: 10.1155/2013/145925.

Verhoeven JE, Révész D, Epel ES, Lin J, Wolkowitz OM, Penninx BW. Major depressive disorder and accelerated cellular aging: results from a large psychiatric cohort study. Mol Psychiatry. 2013 Nov 12. doi: 10.1038/mp.2013.151.

Vgontzas AN. The diagnosis and treatment of chronic insomnia in adults. Sleep. 2005 Sep 1;28(9):1047-8.

Villani S. Impact of media on children and adolescents: a 10-year review of the research. J Am Acad Child Adolesc Psychiatry. 2001 Apr;40(4):392-401.

Viner RM, Cole TJ. Television viewing in early childhood predicts adult body mass index. J Pediatr. 2005 Oct;147(4):429-35.

Viola AU, James LM, Schlangen LJ, Dijk DJ. Blue-enriched white light in the workplace improves self-reported alertness, performance and sleep quality. Scand J Work Environ Hlth. 2008 Aug;34(4):297-306.

Virk G, Reeves G, Rosenthal NE, Sher L, Postolache TT. Short exposure to light treatment improves depression scores in patients with seasonal affective disorder: A brief report. Int J Disabil Hum Dev. 2009 Jul;8(3):283-286.

Volz HP, Kieser M. Kava-kava extract WS 1490 versus placebo in anxiety disorders--a randomized placebo-controlled 25-week outpatient trial. Pharmacopsychiatry. 1997 Jan;30(1):1-5. doi: 10.1055/s-2007-979474. PMID: 9065962.

von Schantz M, Archer SN. Clocks, genes and sleep. J R Soc Med. 2003 Oct;96(10):486-9.

Walker M. The Power of Color. New Delhi: B. Jain Publishers. 2002.

Wang T, Xu C, Pan K, Xiong H. Acupuncture and moxibustion for chronic fatigue syndrome in traditional Chinese medicine: a systematic review and meta-analysis. BMC Complement Altern Med. 2017 Mar 23;17(1):163. doi: 10.1186/s12906-017-1647-x.

Wang Y, Liu XJ, Robitaille L, Eintracht S, MacNamara E, Hoffer LJ. Effects of vitamin C and vitamin D administration on mood and distress in acutely hospitalized patients. Am J Clin Nutr. 2013 Sep;98(3):705-11. doi: 10.3945/ajcn.112.056366.

Wang YY, Li XX, Liu JP, Luo H, Ma LX, Alraek T. Traditional Chinese medicine for chronic fatigue syndrome: a systematic review of randomized clinical trials. Complement Ther Med. 2014 Aug;22(4):826-33. doi: 10.1016/j.ctim.2014.06.004.

Wegner M, Helmich I, Machado S, Nardi AE, Arias-Carrion O, Budde H. Effects of exercise on anxiety and depression disorders: review of meta- analyses and neurobiological mechanisms. CNS Neurol Disord Drug Targets. 2014;13(6):1002-14. doi: 10.2174/1871527313666140612102841.

Weller RB, Wang Y, He J, Maddux FW, Usvyat L, Zhang H, Feelisch M, Kotanko P. Does Incident Solar Ultraviolet Radiation Lower Blood Pressure? J Am Heart Assoc. 2020 Mar 3;9(5):e013837. doi: 10.1161/JAHA.119.013837.

Welsh D, Yoo SH, Liu A, Takahashi J, Kay S. Bioluminescence Imaging of Individual Fibroblasts Reveals Persistent, Independently Phased Circadian Rhythms of Clock Gene Expression. Current Biology. 2004;14:2289-2295.

Wichers H., Visser J., Huizing H., Pras N. Occurrence of L-DOPA and dopamine in plants and cell cultures of Mucuna pruriens and effects of 2,4-D and NaCl on these compounds. Plant Cell Tissue Organ Cult. 1993;33:259–264. doi: 10.1007/BF02319010.

Winfree AT. The Timing of Biological Clocks. New York: Scientific American, 1987.

Wood JJ, Fujii C, Renno P, Van Dyke M. Impact of Cognitive Behavioral Therapy on Observed Autism Symptom Severity During School Recess: A Preliminary Randomized, Controlled Trial. J Autism Dev Disord. 2014 Mar 27.

Wu JJ, Cui Y, Yang YS, Kang MS, Jung SC, Park HK, Yeun HY, Jang WJ, Lee S, Kwak YS, Eun SY. Modulatory effects of aromatherapy massage intervention on electroencephalogram, psychological assessments, salivary cortisol and plasma brain-derived neurotrophic factor. Complement Ther Med. 2014 Jun;22(3):456-62. doi: 10.1016/j.ctim.2014.04.001.

Wu Li-li, Zhang Zhenxian, Zhang Ye. Investigation of Lixu Jieyu Prescription In Treating 120 Cases of Chronic Fatigue Syndrome. (Department of TCM in Yue Yang Hospital,Affiliated to Shanghai University of TCM 200437,Shanghai,China). CNKI Jrnl. 2012: 02.

Wyart C, Webster WW, Chen JH, Wilson SR, McClary A, Khan RM, Sobel N. Smelling a single component of male sweat alters levels of cortisol in women. J Neurosci. 2007 Feb 7;27(6):1261-5. doi: 10.1523/JNEUROSCI.4430-06.2007.

Wyart C, Webster WW, Chen JH, Wilson SR, McClary A, Khan RM, Sobel N. Smelling a single component of male sweat alters levels of cortisol in women. J Neurosci. 2007 Feb 7;27(6):1261-5.

Xu YX, Luo HS, Sun D, Wang R, Cai J. Acupuncture in the treatment of chronic fatigue syndrome based on "interaction of brain and kidney" in TCM: a randomized controlled trial. Zhongguo Zhen Jiu. 2019 Feb 12;39(2):123-7. doi:10.13703/j.0255-2930.2019.02.003.

Yamaoka Y. Solid cell nest (SCN) of the human thyroid gland. Acta Pathol Jpn. 1973 Aug;23(3):493-506.

Yan MZ, Chang Q, Zhong Y, Xiao BX, Feng L, Cao FR, Pan RL, Zhang ZS, Liao YH, Liu XM. Lotus Leaf Alkaloid Extract Displays Sedative-Hypnotic and Anxiolytic Effects through GABAA Receptor. J Agric Food Chem. 2015 Oct 28;63(42):9277-85. doi: 10.1021/acs.jafc.5b04141.

Yeager RL, Oleske DA, Sanders RA, Watkins JB 3rd, Eells JT, Henshel DS. Melatonin as a principal component of red light therapy. Med Hypotheses. 2007;69(2):372-6.

Yeung AS, Feng R, Kim DJH, Wayne PM, Yeh GY, Baer L, Lee OE, Denninger JW, Benson H, Fricchione GL, Alpert J, Fava M. A Pilot, Randomized Controlled Study of Tai Chi for Treatment of Depressed Chinese Americans. J Clin Psychiatry. 2017 May;78(5):e522-e528. doi: 10.4088/JCP.16m10772.

Yildiz M, Batmaz S, Songur E, Oral ET. State of the art psychopharmacological treatment options in seasonal affective disorder. Psychiatr Danub. 2016 Mar;28(1):25-9.

You JS, Lee YJ, Kim KS, Kim SH, Chang KJ. Ethanol extract of lotus (Nelumbo nucifera) root exhibits an anti-adipogenic effect in human pre-adipocytes and anti-obesity and anti-oxidant effects in rats fed a high-fat diet. Nutr Res. 2014 Mar;34(3):258-67. doi: 10.1016/j.nutres.2014.01.003.

Yu HL, Zhang PP, Zhang C, Zhang X, Li ZZ, Li WQ, Fu AS. [Effects of rhodiola rosea on oxidative stress and negative emotional states in patients with obstructive sleep apnea]. Lin Chung Er Bi Yan Hou Tou Jing Wai Ke Za Zhi. 2019 Oct;33(10):954-957.

Yuan C, Fondell E, Bhushan A, Ascherio A, Okereke OI, Grodstein F, Willett WC. Long-term intake of vegetables and fruits and subjective cognitive function in US men. Neurology. 2019 Jan 1;92(1):e63-e75. doi: 10.1212/WNL.0000000000006684.

Yuan L, Gu X, Yin Z, Kang W. Antioxidant activities in vitro and hepatoprotective effects of Nelumbo nucifera leaves in vivo. Afr J Tradit Complement Altern Med. 2014 Apr 3;11(3):85-91.

Zaccardi F, Laukkanen T, Willeit P, Kunutsor SK, Kauhanen J, Laukkanen JA. Sauna Bathing and Incident Hypertension: A Prospective Cohort Study. Am J Hypertens. 2017 Jun 13. doi: 10.1093/ajh/hpx102.

Zhai L, Zhang H, Zhang D. Sleep duration and depression among adults: A meta-analysis of prospective studies. Depress Anxiety. 2015 Sep;32(9):664-70. doi: 10.1002/da.22386.

Zhang Z, Cai Z, Yu Y, Wu L, Zhang Y. Effect of Lixujieyu recipe in combination with Five Elements music therapy on chronic fatigue syndrome. J Tradit Chin Med. 2015 Dec;35(6):637-41.

Zhang ZX, Wu LL, Chen M. Effect of lixu jieyu recipe in treating 75 patients with chronic fatigue syndrome. Zhongguo Zhong Xi Yi Jie He Za Zhi. 2009 Jun;29(6):501-5.

Zhao X, Shen J, Chang KJ, Kim SH. Analysis of fatty acids and phytosterols in ethanol extracts of Nelumbo nucifera seeds and rhizomes by GC-MS. J Agric Food Chem. 2013 Jul 17;61(28):6841-7. doi: 10.1021/jf401710h.

Zhao XL, Wang ZM, Ma XJ, Jing WG, Liu A. Chemical constituents from leaves of Nelumbo nucifera. Zhongguo Zhong Yao Za Zhi. 2013 Mar;38(5):703-8.

Zhongguo Zhong Xi Yi Jie He Za Zhi. 2009 Jun;29(6):501-5. Centers for Disease Control and Prevention. Chronic Fatigue Syndrome. Accessed March 7, 2016.

Zhou L, Foster JA. Psychobiotics and the gut-brain axis: in the pursuit of happiness. Neuropsychiatr Dis Treat. 2015 Mar 16;11:715-23. doi: 10.2147/NDT.S61997. eCollection 2015. Foster JA, McVey Neufeld KA. Gut-brain axis: how the microbiome influences anxiety and depression. Trends Neurosci. 2013 May;36(5):305-12. doi: 10.1016/j.tins.2013.01.005.

Zimmerman FJ, Christakis DA. Children's television viewing and cognitive outcomes: a longitudinal analysis of national data. Arch Pediatr Adolesc Med. 2005 Jul;159(7):619-25.

Index

*(Herbs and foods are too numerous to index —
refer to ebook search for complete index ability)*

www.ingramcontent.com/pod-product-compliance
Lightning Source LLC
Chambersburg PA
CBHW031430270326
41930CB00007B/649